PIC' Techniques

PIC MICROCONTROLLER
APPLICATIONS GUIDE

FROM

DAVID BENSON

VERSION 1.0

NOTICE

The material presented in this book is for the education and amusement of students, hobbyists, technicians and engineers. Every effort has been made to assure the accuracy of this information and its suitability for this purpose. Square 1 Electronics and the author assume no responsibility for the suitability of this information for any application nor do we assume any liability resulting from use of this information. No patent liability is assumed for use of the information contained herein.

TRADEMARKS

PIC is a registered trademark of Microchip Technology Inc. in the U.S.A.
Registered trademarks of Microchip Technology, Inc:

PICmicro	MPASM
PIC16/17	MPSIM
PICSTART Plus	MPLAB

Registered trademarks of Microsoft Corporation:

Microsoft Windows	MS-DOS
Microsoft Works	Terminal
HyperTerminal	Notepad

ISBN 0-9654162-3-2

PUBLISHER

Square 1 Electronics
P.O. Box 501
Kelseyville,CA   95451   U.S.A.

Voice   (707)279-8881
FAX   (707)279-8883
EMAIL   sqone@pacific.net
http://www.sq-1.com

PIC'n Techniques

PIC MICROCONTROLLER
APPLICATIONS GUIDE
FROM

SQUARE 1

USING TIMER 1, TIMER 2 AND THE CAPTURE/COMPARE/PWM (CCP) MODULE 36

INTRODUCTION

PIC'n **Techniques** is our second intermediate level book. PIC'n **Up The Pace** is the first. I am assuming you know all the beginner information included in **Easy** PIC'n (our beginner book) either from using the book or from other experience. Some of the circuits used in PIC'n **Up The Pace** are used in this book as well. These circuits are shown in appendices in the back of this book. Complete explanations may be found in PIC'n **Up The Pace**.

The programs included in this book are examples to help you learn. My hope is that you will study the examples in this book and write your own borrowing from what you see here. That way, you will know what's in your code because you created it. If you want to borrow from the code in this book, it is currently available for downloading at the Square 1 website (no charge) or on disk.

Include files are not used in this book because if you use someone else's include file (this includes those provided by Microchip), you won't know precisely what's in it and will spend a lot of time scratching your head because your program isn't working because you didn't pay attention to what the author of the include file had in mind.

If you write the code, you know what's in it and what it does.

Use of macros and most assembler directives is avoided because they confuse people who are learning more often than not. If you end up doing a lot of "PIC'n", you may find them useful.

My objective is to write code that you can understand rather than try to optimize for minimum number of program steps and/or for fastest possible execution. Where programs used previously in this book or borrowed from PIC'n **Up The Pace** are combined for use in a more exotic application, I did not rewrite the code to achieve double duty (shared) use of file registers.

I think you will particularly enjoy the test equipment and data logger projects which combine the techniques you will learn in functional equipment. The real fun, however, is to take all this a step further on your own by using these techniques to design and build PIC-controlled systems for your own applications.

8-PIN MICROCONTROLLERS

The 8-pin microcontrollers being added to the Microchip product line are interesting because they offer a lot of capability (tiny brain) in a small inexpensive package. We will look at the PIC12C508 as an example. It is a 12-bit core base-line part. This will be an overview of features which are unique to the 12C508 as compared to the 16F84 or 16C54 which were covered in **Easy** PIC'n and PIC'n **Up The Pace**.

PIC12C508

PINS AND FUNCTIONS

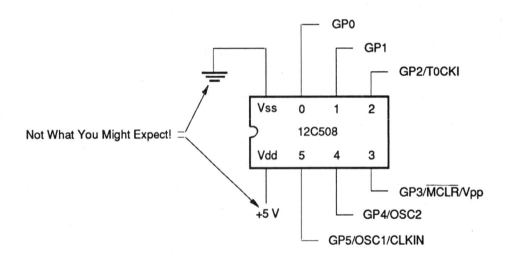

The first thing to observe is that the power and ground pins are NOT in the usual places.

The second thing to observe is that the function of four of the pins is determined/selected by the user/designer (you).

    GP2/T0CKI
    GP3/MCLR/Vpp
    GP4/OSC2
    GP5/OSC1/CLKIN

The "GP" portion of the pin identifier stands for "general purpose" as in "general purpose I/O".

GP0 And GP1 Pins

These pins are always general purpose I/O pins.

GP2/T0CKI Pin

This pin is either a bi-directional I/O pin or the timer 0 (TMR0) clock input (T0CKI) as determined by software via bit 5 (T0CS bit) of the option register. If the T0CS bit is set to "1", the pin is forced to be an input even if the TRIS register GP2 bit is "0".

GP3/$\overline{\text{MCLR}}$/Vpp Pin

This pin may be used as an input port or as $\overline{\text{MCLR}}$ (active low reset to the device with weak internal pullup). When used as an input port, an internal weak pullup can be enabled and wake-up from sleep on pin change can be enabled via software. Pin usage is determined by selection during the device programming cycle.

GP4/OSC2 Pin

This pin is either a bi-directional I/O port (internal RC oscillator mode) or oscillator crystal output as determined by selection during the device programming cycle.

GP5/OSC1/CLKIN Pin

This pin may be a bi-directional I/O port (internal RC oscillator mode) or oscillator crystal input or external clock output as determined by selection during the device programming cycle.

The following table will help to clarify all this.

Pin	Function			Select Function Via
GP0	Bi-directional I/O			Always I/O
GP1	Bi-directional I/O			Always I/O
GP2	Bi-directional I/O or T0CKI			Software
GP3	Input or $\overline{\text{MCLR}}$ (external)			At device program
	Internal RC Clock	External Crystal	External Clock	
GP4	Bi-dir I/O	Clock osc.	No connect	At device program
GP5	Bi-dir I/O	Clock osc.	Ext. clock	At device program

PACKAGES

The PIC12C508 is available in the following packages suitable for the experimenter.

```
-----------------------------------------------------------------
    Part No.      Program Memory    Package         Reprogrammable
-----------------------------------------------------------------
PIC12C508-04/P        EPROM         Plastic DIP     No, OTP
PIC12C508/JW          EPROM         Windowed DIP    Yes, UV erase
```

CLOCK OSCILLATOR

There are four possible clock oscillator configurations:

```
-----------------------------------------------------------------
            Oscillator Type                    Selection Factors
-----------------------------------------------------------------
INTRC    Internal 4 MHz RC oscillator     Built-in, low cost
EXTRC    External RC oscillator           Low cost, range of
                                             possible frequencies
LP       Low frequency crystal (low       Accuracy, higher cost
            power) or external clock
XT       Standard crystal or ceramic      Accuracy, higher cost
            resonator or external clock
```

If the built-in RC oscillator is used, pins GP4 and GP5 are available for use as bidirectional I/O ports. If the built-in RC oscillator is not used, these pins function as OSC1 and OSC2 and operate just as they do on the PIC16F84 when an external oscillator is used.

Use of an external RC oscillator can provide a clock frequency less than 4 MHz. This mode is low cost and is useful where timing is not critical.

CONFIGURATION BITS

There are five configuration bits. Two select clock oscillator type, one is the watchdog timer enable bit, one is the $\overline{MCLR}$ enable bit and one is the code protection bit. The device programmer accesses these bits during the device programming procedure.

A note about the -JW windowed parts - don't turn on the code protection bit! It can't ever be turned off. The windowed part will become an expensive OTP part.

RESET

The reset function $\overline{MCLR}$ may be internal or external. This selection must be identified for the device programmer at the time the chip is programmed. $\overline{MCLR}$ may be external if a reset switch is required to regain control if things run away.

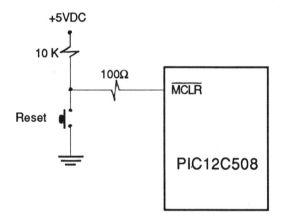

PORT

There are between 2 and 6 port lines available depending on how the user decides to apply the device. Each bidirectional port line may be individually programmed as an input line or output line. This is done using a special instruction (TRIS) which matches a bit pattern with the port lines. A "0" associated with a port line makes it an output, a "1" makes it an input. An example follows.

The PIC12C508 does not have port data direction registers as does the PIC16F84. Use of the TRIS instruction is the way it is done with the PIC12C508.

All unused port lines should be tied to the power supply (CMOS rule - all inputs must go somewhere). On reset, all port lines are inputs.

GPIO REGISTER

The GPIO is an 8-bit I/O register, but only the low order 6 bits are used. Bits 7 and 6 are not implemented and read as "0"s. When a pin is used for a function other than I/O, it will read as "0" in the GPIO.

7	6	5	4	3	2	1	0	
——	——	GP5	GP4	GP3	GP2	GP1	GP0	0x06

Bits7 and 6 are unimplemented, read as "0"
GP3 is an input only pin

TRIS REGISTER

The TRIS register is used to control the direction of the port pins. Executing the TRIS instruction causes the bit pattern in the W register to be loaded into the output driver control register. A "0" in a bit position causes the corresponding pin to become an output. A "1" produces an input.

All GPIO lines are inputs on power-up.

Note that GP2 may be controlled by the option register (used as TOCKI).

Note, also, that GP3 is input only.

If GP5 is used as a clock input, bit 5 must be a "1" in the TRIS register or the chip won't run.

ARCHITECTURE

Program Memory

The PIC12C508 program memory is 12 bits wide and 512 words long.

Program memory may be EPROM or OTP EPROM. Regardless of type, program memory is read-only at run time. PIC12s can only execute code contained in program memory.

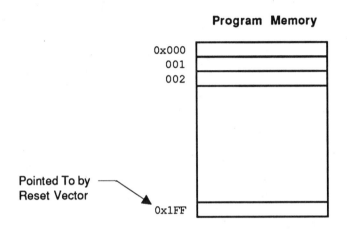

File Registers

The file registers are 8 bits wide with the exception of the program counter which is 9 bits wide. The PIC12C508 has 32 file registers (0x00 - 0x1F).

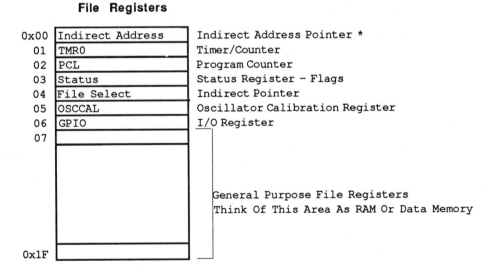

The first seven file registers have specific dedicated purposes). The remaining 25 file registers are there for your use and may be thought of as RAM or data memory for storing data during program execution.

	Hex Address	
f0	0x00	Indirect data addressing register (INDF).
f1	0x01	Real time clock/counter register (TMR0).
f2	0x02	Program counter low (PCL).
f3	0x03	Status word register.
f4	0x04	File select register (FSR).
f5	0x05	Oscillator calibration value (OSCCAL).
f6	0x06	General purpose I/O register (GPIO).
f7 -	0x07 -	General purpose registers (RAM).
f1F	0x1F	

Stack

The 2-level stack is in hardware meaning that it is entirely separate from the file registers (RAM) and cannot overwrite them. Subroutines can be nested 2-deep.

Reset Vector

On reset which occurs on power-up or when the reset switch is employed to pull $\overline{\text{MCLR}}$ low, the PIC12C508 will begin executing instructions at address 0x1FF. After the first instruction is executed, the program counter rolls over to 0x000 and program execution continues at that address.

OSCCAL Calibration Constant

When the internal clock oscillator is used, a calibration constant is used to obtain a frequency as near 4 MHz as possible. The clock oscillator calibration constant must be stored in a register called OSCCAL by the first two program instructions. This constant is a specific value for each part used to calibrate the internal RC clock oscillator. The OSCCAL register is an 8-bit register, but only the high order 4 bits are used.

7	6	5	4	3	2	1	0	
CAL7	CAL6	CAL5	CAL4	—	—	—	—	0x05

8

The 4 calibration bits are loaded into the OSCCAL register during the first two steps of program execution. As part of the manufacturing process, the calibration constant is stored along with a MOVLW instruction at program memory location 0x1FF in the part's EPROM program memory.

```
movlw           CC              ;calibration constant to W register
```

"CC" is used here to represent the calibration constant.

Never overwrite the preprogrammed MOVLW and constant.

When a windowed part is purchased, the calibration constant should be read and recorded before the part is used. Why? Because when the part is erased the first time, the calibration constant will go away and there will be no way to get it back, EVER! To do this, the part must be read using a device programmer. Follow the programmer manufacturer's instructions.

For the PICSTART Plus and MPLAB:

1) Power up PICSTART Plus.
2) Put the device in the PICSTART Plus.
3) Select processor type 12C508.
       Options>Development Mode>Processor.
4) PICSTART Plus>Enable Programmer.
5) Click "Read" button.
6) Close PICSTART Plus Device Programmer window.
7) Window>Calibration Data.

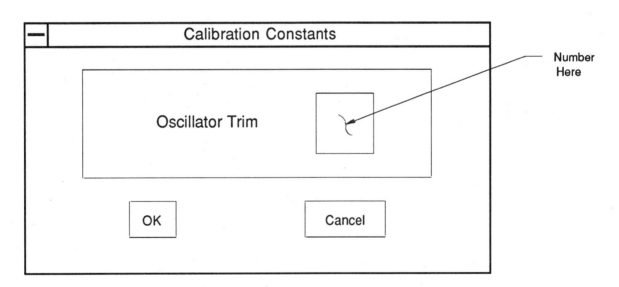

The OSCCAL value ("Oscillator Trim" in dialog box) read from program memory location 0x1FF by MPLAB will be in the form:

$$\_0$$

— Hex "0" (always)
— Hex digit

The result will be two hex digits such as A0 or 90. Record the value where you will be sure to find it and in a way that you will be able to relate it to the part you just read it from. I scribe the number on the metal window "frame" on the part itself to prevent loss or confusion.

Note that an erased part will have an "Oscillator Trim" value "FF".

My intention here is to develop a simple methodology for handling the fact that all new parts (windowed or OTP) have the internal clock calibration constant code in the device at the location pointed to by the reset vector (0x1FF) <u>whether you need it or not</u>.

What happens next depends on whether your application uses an internal or an external clock.

Internal Clock Applications

So what do we do about

```
movlw          CC                    ;calibration constant to W register
```

and location 0x1FF?

- OTP part - it's there.

- New windowed part, never erased - it's there.

- Windowed erased part - you must put it there via a dialog box during the programming procedure.

When programming an erased windowed part with internal RC clock selected during programming procedure setup, the MOVLW instruction and calibration constant will be programmed automatically by MPLAB. Do not include this line of code in your assembly source file.

<u>To Program A Device:</u>

1) Power up the PICSTART Plus.
2) Open your project.
3) Open your source code file.
4) Put the device in the PICSTART Plus.
5) If you are using the internal oscillator in your application and the part is windowed and has been erased:

Window>Calibration Data
Type in the value for the specific part being programmed.
Click "OK".

Otherwise, ignore step 5.
If the part is windowed, erased, and you select internal RC clock during the programming setup procedure, the MOVLW instruction and a calibration constant will be programmed at 0x1FF automatically by MPLAB.
6) PICSTART Plus>Enable Programmer.
Continue with the device programming sequence as usual.

Writing Code:

Start your code at address 0x000.

```
movwf        0x05        ;calibration constant to OSCCAL register
```

Continue with your code at 0x001.

External Clock Applications

Ignore the fact that that the reset vector points to 0x1FF. The instruction located there will fill the W register with garbage, but who cares. Here is what will end up there:

- OTP part - MOVLW CC.

- New windowed part, never erased - MOVLW CC.

- Windowed erased part - XORLW FF.
  The erased part will contain 0xFFF at location 0x1FF. When the PIC12C508 executes this as code, it will be interpreted as XORLW (instruction) FF (data).
  The contents of W will be exclusive OR'ed with the literal value "FF" and the result will be in the W register.

Program execution will start at 0x1FF. The W register will be filled with garbage. The program counter will roll over to 0x000.

Your first line of code should be located at 0x000.

Program the device as usual (forget about the calibration constant). MPLAB does not automatically put calibration constant code at 0x1FF if an external clock is selected during the device programming setup procedure.

OSCCAL Considerations And Rules Restated

- Both windowed and OTP parts come with the MOVLW and calibration constant programmed in EPROM at 0x1FF. Use it if your application utilizes the internal RC clock. If not, work around it.

- Do not overwrite the code and calibration constant at 0x1FF. This includes making sure your main code does not run up into (overwrite) program memory location 0x1FF

- For windowed parts, read and record the calibration constant prior to erasing the part the first time.

Program Counter

The program counter (PC - at 0x02) is 9 bits wide. Bit 8 (9th bit) of the PC is cleared by:

- A CALL instruction.
- Any instruction which writes to the PC.

A GOTO loads all 9 bits of the program counter and will jump to anywhere in the PIC12C508's program memory space.

A CALL loads the lower 8 bits of the program counter. The 9th bit is cleared to 0. All subroutine calls are limited to the first 256 locations of program memory for the PIC12C508.

Any instruction which writes to the program counter changes the low 8 bits and clears the 9th bit, so computed jumps are limited to the first 256 locations of program memory for the PIC12C508.

Option Register

W	W	W	W	W	W	W	W
$\overline{\text{GPWU}}$	$\overline{\text{GPPU}}$	T0CS	T0SE	PSA	PS2	PS1	PS0

7   0

W = Writeable bit
Power on reset 11111111

Bit 7   **$\overline{\text{GPWU}}$**: Enable Wake-up On Pin Change (GP0, GP1, GP2)
                   1 = Disabled
                   0 = Enabled

Bit 6   **$\overline{\text{GPPU}}$**: Enable Weak Pullups (GP0, GP1, GP2)
                   1 = Disabled
                   0 = Enabled

Bit 5   **T0CS**: TMR0 Clock Source Select Bit
                   1 = Transition on T0CKI pin
                   0 = Transition on internal instruction cycle clock,
                       $F_{osc}/4$

Bit 4   **T0SE**: TMR0 Source Edge Select Bit
                   1 = Increment on high to low transition on
                       T0CKI pin
                   0 = Increment on low to high transition on
                       T0CKI pin

Bit 3   **PSA**: Prescaler Assignment Bit
                   1 = Prescaler assigned to WDT
                   0 = Prescaler assigned to TMR0

Bit 2-0   **PS2:PS0**: Prescaler Rate Select Bits

Bits	TMR0 Rate	WDT Rate
000	1:2	1:1
001	1:4	1:2
010	1:8	1:4
011	1:16	1:8
100	1:32	1:16
101	1:64	1:32
110	1:128	1:64
111	1:256	1:128

NOTE: If the T0CS bit is set, GP2 is forced to be an input even
               if TRIS GP2 = 0.

Status Register

R/W	U	R/W	R	R	R/W	R/W	R/W	
GPWUF		PA0	$\overline{TO}$	$\overline{PD}$	Z	DC	C	0x03
7							0	

R = Readable bit
W = Writeable bit
U = Unimplemented bit
Power on reset 00011xxx

Bit 7   **GPWUF:** GPIO Reset Bit
          1 = Reset from wake-up from SLEEP on pin change
          0 = After power up or other reset

Bit 6   Unimplemented

Bit 5   **PAO:** Program Page Preselect Bit
          1 = Page 1 (0x200 0x3FF) - PIC12C509
          0 = Page 0 (0x000 0x1FF) - PIC12C508 and PIC12C509

Bit 4   **$\overline{TO}$:** Time-out Bit
          1 = After power-up, CLRWDT instruction, or SLEEP
                instruction
          0 = WDT time-out occurred

Bit 3   **$\overline{PD}$:** Power-down Bit
          1 = After power-up or by the CLRWDT instruction
          0 = By execution of the SLEEP instruction

Bit 2   **Z:** Zero Bit
          1 = Result of an arithmetic or logic operation
                is zero
          0 = Result of an arithmetic or logic operation
                is not zero

Bit 1   **DC:** Digit Carry/Borrow Bit - See Microchip
                data book

Bit 0   **C:** Carry/Borrow Bit - See Microchip
                data book

TIMING AND COUNTING

The PIC12C508 timer/counter is referred to as the TIMER0 (TMR0) module. It is used the same way as TMR0 in the PIC16C54 as described in **Easy PIC'n.**

PIC12C508 EXAMPLE - INTERNAL CLOCK

Following is an example for the PIC12C508 designed to illustrate the differences with respect to the 16F84. We will use the internal RC oscillator and internal reset as these features will be new to you. We will assume that you have a brand new windowed part.

- Internal RC clock oscillator mode - 4 MHz.
- Internal reset.
- 5 output port lines with LEDs (GP0, 1, 2, 4, 5).
- 1 input port line with pullup resistor (GP3).

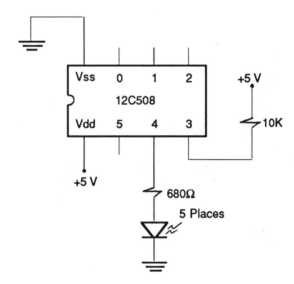

Remember to read and record the OSCCAL value first!

If the part has never been erased, the OSCCAL constant is preprogrammed at 0x1FF. If the part is erased (blank), enter the calibration constant.

> Window>Calibration Data
> Type in the value for the specific part being programmed.

The oscillator and $\overline{\text{MCLR}}$ modes will be selected at the time the part is programmed.

The first two program steps must:

- Store the OSCCAL constant at 0x05 (0x000).
- Clear the T0CS bit in the option register so pin GP2 can be an output port.

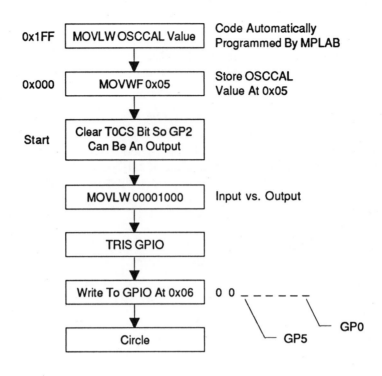

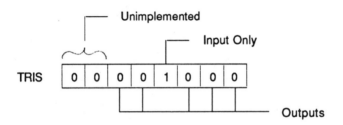

```
;=======8pin.ASM============================4/16/98==
        list    p=12c508
        radix   hex
;-----------------------------------------------------
;       cpu equates (memory map)
oscal   equ     05
gpio    equ     06
;-----------------------------------------------------
        org     0x000
;
        movwf   oscal          ;store oscal value
start   movlw   b'11011111'    ;clear tocs bit to '0' so
                               ;    gp2 can be an output
        option
        movlw   b'00001000'    ;port line direction
        tris    gpio           ;copy w tristate, gpio outputs
        movlw   b'00100010'    ;bits 5,1 on - bits 4,2,0 off
        movwf   gpio           ;load gpio with contents of W
```

16

```
circle   goto    circle       ;done
;
         end
;---------------------------------------------------------
;at blast time, select:
;        oscillator internal RC
;        watchdog timer off
;        code protect off
;        master clear internal
;=========================================================
```

PIC12C508 EXAMPLE - EXTERNAL CLOCK

Following is an example for the PIC12C508. We will use an external oscillator (crystal oscillator in a can) and internal reset.

- External clock oscillator mode (XT).
- Internal reset.
- 3 output port lines with LEDs (GP0, 1, 2).
- 1 input port line with pullup resistor (GP3).

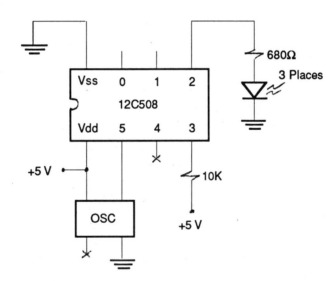

If the part is windowed, new, and has never been erased, remember to read and record the OSC-CAL value first, just in case you need it some day.

Code starts at program memory location 0x000.

The oscillator and $\overline{MCLR}$ modes will be selected at the time the part is programmed.

Program the device as usual (forget about the calibration constant with the exception of not overwriting it).

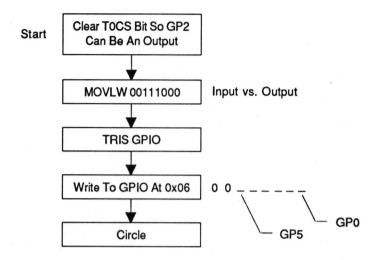

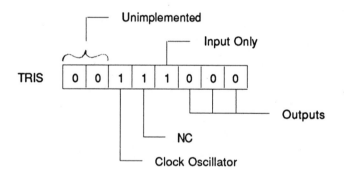

```
;=======8pin2.ASM============================4/16/98==
        list    p=12c508
        radix   hex
;----------------------------------------------------
;       cpu equates (memory map)
oscal   equ     05
gpio    equ     06
;----------------------------------------------------
        org     0x000
;
start   movlw   b'11011111' ;clear tocs bit to '0' so
                            ;   gp2 can be an output
        option
        movlw   b'00111000' ;port line direction
        tris    gpio        ;copy w tristate, gpio outputs
        movlw   b'00000101' ;bits 2,0 on - bit 1 off
        movwf   gpio        ;load gpio with contents of W
circle  goto    circle      ;done
;
        end
```

18

```
;-------------------------------------------------------
;at blast time, select:
;        oscillator external crystal (XT)
;        watchdog timer off
;        code protect off
;        master clear internal
;=======================================================
```

TEST EQUIPMENT FOR
TIMING AND COUNTING EXPERIMENTS

TEST EQUIPMENT FOR DETECTING A SHORT SINGLE PULSE AND MEASURING IT'S WIDTH

Since I don't have a storage oscilloscope, I built a PIC-based pulse detector which measures the width of a single pulse. This device can be used to test the output of an example circuit when a short pulse (microseconds range) is produced. To develop this, I used two '84 on a board circuits, one to generate a pulse of known length and the other to detect it and measure (verify) the pulse width. The '84 on a board circuit for experimenting is presented in PIC'n Up The Pace and Appendix C.

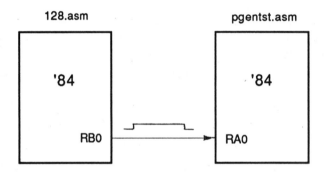

For initial test purposes, the sending '84 generates a 128 microsecond pulse and the receiving '84 counts up in microseconds while the pulse is high and displays the result via LEDs at port B. Simple! Then the detection/measuring device can be used to look for a pulse generated by a PIC16C63 using the techniques we will develop later in this book.

The pulse generator (sender) looks like this:

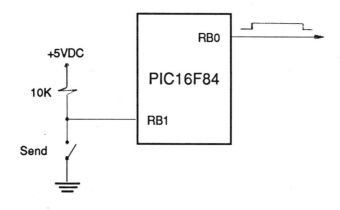

The program used to generate the 128 microsecond test pulse is:

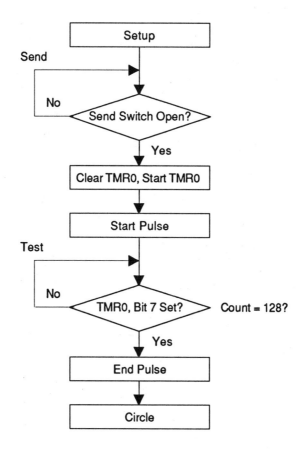

```
;=======128.ASM======================================9/26/98==
;timer/counter demo
;       single time interval
;       internal clock
;       128 microsecond pulse out
;-----------------------------------------------------------------
        list    p=16f84
        radix   hex
;-----------------------------------------------------------------
;       cpu equates (memory map)
tmr0    equ     0x01
portb   equ     0x06
intcon  equ     0x0b
;-----------------------------------------------------------------
        org     0x000
;
start   movlw   b'00000010' ;port B in/out
        tris    portb
        bcf     portb,0     ;low
        bcf     portb,2     ;low
        bcf     portb,3     ;low
        bcf     portb,4     ;low
        bcf     portb,5     ;low
        bcf     portb,6     ;low
        bcf     portb,7     ;low
        bcf     intcon,2    ;clear TMR0 interrupt flag
        bcf     intcon,7    ;disable global interrupts
        bcf     intcon,5    ;disable TMR0 interrupts
        clrf    tmr0        ;clear TMR0
        clrwdt              ;clr WDT prep prescale assign
        movlw   b'11011111' ;set up timer/counter
        option
send    btfss   portb,1     ;switch open?
        goto    send        ;not yet
        clrf    tmr0        ;start timer/c, clr prescaler
        bsf     portb,0     ;start pulse
test    btfss   tmr0,7      ;look for count=128
        goto test           ;not yet
        bcf     portb,0     ;end pulse
circle  goto    circle      ;done
;
        end
;-----------------------------------------------------------------
;at blast time, select:
;       memory unprotected
;       watchdog timer disabled (default is enabled)
;       standard crystal (using 4 MHz osc for test) XT
;       power-up timer on
;=================================================================
```

The pulse detection/measuring device (receiver) looks like this:

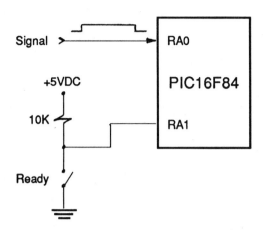

The object is to count pulses from a source of known frequency (internal instruction clock, 1 MHz) while the incoming pulse to be measured is high. The count will be the pulse width in microseconds.

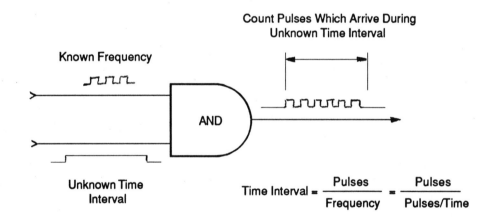

The flow chart for the program is:

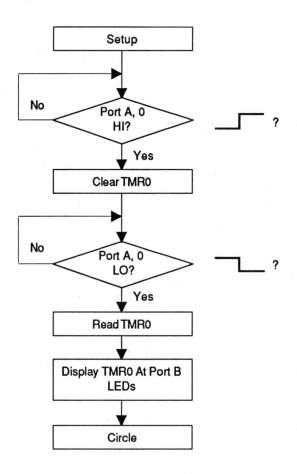

The code follows:

```
;======PGENTST.ASM===============================9/25/98==
        list    p=16f84
        radix   hex
;------------------------------------------------------------
;       cpu equates (memory map)
tmr0    equ     0x01
porta   equ     0x05
portb   equ     0x06
;------------------------------------------------------------
        org     0x000
;
start   movlw   0xff            ;port A inputs
        tris    porta
        movlw   0x00            ;port B outputs
        tris    portb
        clrf    portb           ;LEDs off
;
        clrf    tmr0            ;clear TMR0 before assign wdt
        clrwdt                  ;clr WDT prep prescale assign
        movlw   b'11011111'     ;set up timer/counter
        option
;
ready   btfss   porta,1         ;ready?
        goto    ready           ;not yet
p_hi    btfss   porta,0         ;monitor signal
        goto    p_hi
        clrf    tmr0            ;clear TMR0
p_lo    btfsc   porta,0         ;monitor signal
        goto    p_lo
        movf    tmr0,w          ;read timer 0
        movwf   portb           ;display TMR0 contents
circle  goto    circle          ;done
;
        end
;------------------------------------------------------------
;at blast time, select:
;       memory unprotected
;       watchdog timer disabled (default is enabled)
;       standard crystal (using 4 MHz osc for test) XT
;       power-up timer on
;============================================================
```

Code for generating pulses of four different width follows. The code will be used in conjunction with an '84 on a board to test circuits presented later in the book.

PULSE GENERATOR - 32 microseconds

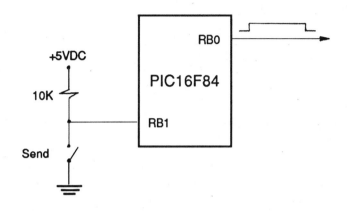

```
;======32.ASM=====================================10/2/98==
;timer/counter demo
;       single time interval
;       internal clock
;       32 microsecond pulse out
;------------------------------------------------------------
        list    p=16f84
        radix   hex
;------------------------------------------------------------
;       cpu equates (memory map)
tmr0    equ     0x01
portb   equ     0x06
intcon  equ     0x0b
;------------------------------------------------------------
        org     0x000
;
start   movlw   b'00000010' ;port B in/out
        tris    portb
        bcf     portb,0     ;low
        bcf     portb,2     ;low
        bcf     portb,3     ;low
        bcf     portb,4     ;low
        bcf     portb,5     ;low
        bcf     portb,6     ;low
        bcf     portb,7     ;low
        bcf     intcon,2    ;clear TMR0 interrupt flag
        bcf     intcon,7    ;disable global interrupts
        bcf     intcon,5    ;disable TMR0 interrupts
        clrf    tmr0        ;clear TMR0
        clrwdt              ;clr WDT prep prescale assign
        movlw   b'11011111' ;set up timer/counter
        option
send    btfss   portb,1     ;switch open?
        goto    send        ;not yet
        clrf    tmr0        ;start timer/c, clr prescaler
```

```
        bsf     portb,0    ;start pulse
test    btfss   tmr0,5     ;look for count=32
        goto test          ;not yet
        bcf     portb,0    ;end pulse
circle  goto    circle     ;done
;
        end
;-------------------------------------------------------------
;at blast time, select:
;       memory unprotected
;       watchdog timer disabled (default is enabled)
;       standard crystal (using 4 MHz osc for test) XT
;       power-up timer on
;=============================================================
```

PULSE GENERATOR - 128 microseconds

See 128.asm presented previously.

PULSE GENERATOR - 2000 microseconds

We will use a PIC16F84 to generate a single pulse of known length, 2000 microseconds in this case. Timer 0 in the '84 is an 8-bit counter and won't hold 2000. We will use the prescaler to divide the internal clock signal by 8 and let TMR0 count to 250 (250x8=2000). Since TMR0 counts up, it will be loaded with 6 and will roll over when the count reaches 255 plus 1 generating an interrupt.

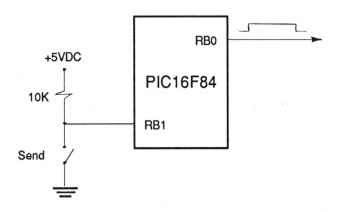

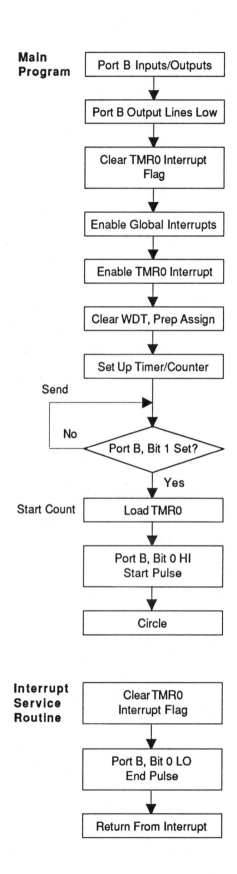

Main Program

Port B Inputs/Outputs

Port B Output Lines Low

Clear TMR0 Interrupt Flag

Enable Global Interrupts

Enable TMR0 Interrupt

Clear WDT, Prep Assign

Set Up Timer/Counter

Send

No

Port B, Bit 1 Set?

Yes

Start Count — Load TMR0

Port B, Bit 0 HI Start Pulse

Circle

Interrupt Service Routine

Clear TMR0 Interrupt Flag

Port B, Bit 0 LO End Pulse

Return From Interrupt

28

```
;=======2000.ASM====================================9/2/98==
;timer/counter demo
;       single time interval
;       internal clock divided by 8
;       2000 microsecond pulse out
;-------------------------------------------------------------
        list    p=16f84
        radix   hex
;-------------------------------------------------------------
;       cpu equates (memory map)
tmr0    equ     0x01
portb   equ     0x06
intcon  equ     0x0b
;-------------------------------------------------------------
        org     0x000
        goto    start           ;skip over location pointed
                                ;   to by interrupt vector
        org     0x004
        goto    iserv
;
start   movlw   b'00000010' ;port B in/out
        tris    portb
        bcf     portb,0     ;low
        bcf     portb,2     ;low
        bcf     portb,3     ;low
        bcf     portb,4     ;low
        bcf     portb,5     ;low
        bcf     portb,6     ;low
        bcf     portb,7     ;low
        bcf     intcon,2    ;clear TMR0 interrupt flag
        bsf     intcon,7    ;enable global interrupts
        bsf     intcon,5    ;enable TMR0 interrupts
        clrwdt              ;clr WDT prep prescale assign
        movlw   b'11010010' ;set up timer/counter
        option
send    btfss   portb,1     ;switch open?
        goto    send        ;not yet
        movlw   0x05        ;inc 250 times to rollover
        movwf   tmr0        ;start timer/c, clr prescaler
        bsf     portb,0     ;start pulse
circle  goto    circle      ;wait for interrupt
;
iserv   bcf     intcon,2    ;clear TMR0 interrupt flag
        bcf     portb,0     ;end pulse
        retfie              ;done
;
        end
;-------------------------------------------------------------
;at blast time, select:
;       memory unprotected
;       watchdog timer disabled (default is enabled)
;       standard crystal (using 4 MHz osc for test) XT
;       power-up timer on
;=============================================================
```

As with the previous example, power up with the send switch closed. Open the switch to send the pulse.

PULSE GENERATOR - 65280 microseconds

Finally, we will need a program to output a pulse 65280 microseconds wide. This program uses timer 0 and a file register counter called "count" to count the number of times timer 0 rolls over. The sequence starts with timer 0 clear and the count register loaded with 0xFF. When the number of pulses fed into timer 0 reaches 65,280, timer 0 rolls over for the 255th time and the count register contains zero. To look at this another way, the program decrements the count register each time timer 0 overflows. When the contents of count reaches zero, the game is over and the number of pulses received by timer 0 is 65,280.

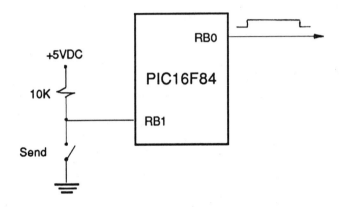

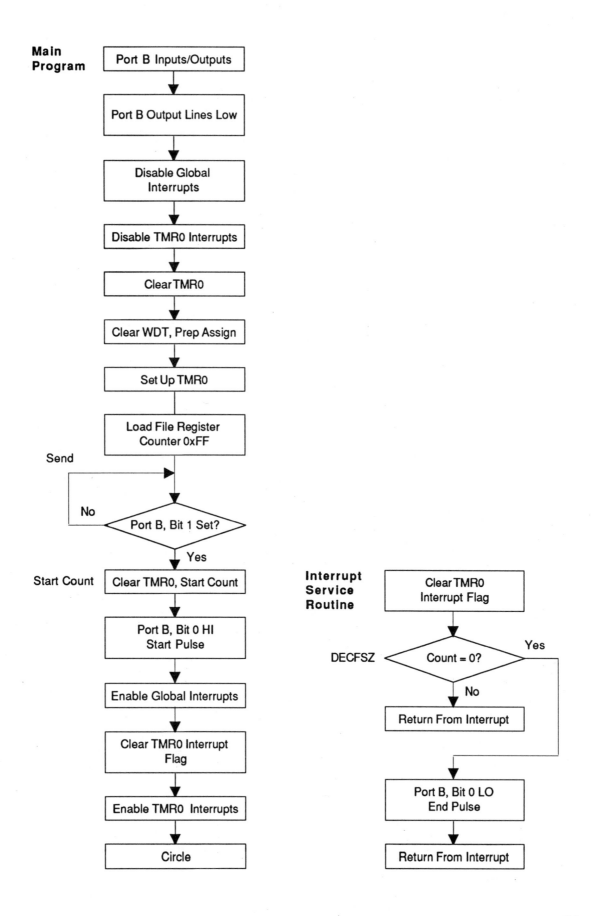

Main Program

Port B Inputs/Outputs

Port B Output Lines Low

Disable Global Interrupts

Disable TMR0 Interrupts

Clear TMR0

Clear WDT, Prep Assign

Set Up TMR0

Load File Register Counter 0xFF

Send

Port B, Bit 1 Set?

No

Yes

Start Count — Clear TMR0, Start Count

Port B, Bit 0 HI Start Pulse

Enable Global Interrupts

Clear TMR0 Interrupt Flag

Enable TMR0 Interrupts

Circle

Interrupt Service Routine

Clear TMR0 Interrupt Flag

DECFSZ — Count = 0?

Yes

No

Return From Interrupt

Port B, Bit 0 LO End Pulse

Return From Interrupt

```
;======65280.ASM=============================10/2/98==
;timer/counter demo
;        single time interval
;        internal clock
;        65280 microsecond pulse out
;-----------------------------------------------------------
         list    p=16f84
         radix   hex
;-----------------------------------------------------------
;        cpu equates (memory map)
tmr0     equ     0x01
status   equ     0x03
portb    equ     0x06
intcon   equ     0x0b
count    equ     0x0c
;-----------------------------------------------------------
;        bit equates
z        equ     2
;-----------------------------------------------------------
         org     0x000
         goto    start           ;skip over location pointed
                                 ;  to by interrupt vector
         org     0x004
         goto    iserv
;
start    movlw   b'00000010' ;port B in/out
         tris    portb
         bcf     portb,0         ;low
         bcf     portb,2         ;low
         bcf     portb,3         ;low
         bcf     portb,4         ;low
         bcf     portb,5         ;low
         bcf     portb,6         ;low
         bcf     portb,7         ;low
         bcf     intcon,7        ;disable global interrupts
         bcf     intcon,5        ;disable TMR0 interrupts
         clrf    tmr0            ;prep assign
         clrwdt                  ;clr WDT prep prescale assign
         movlw   b'11011111' ;set up timer/counter
         option
         movlw   0xff
         movwf   count           ;load counter
send     btfss   portb,1         ;switch open?
         goto    send            ;not yet
         clrf    tmr0            ;start timer/c, clr prescaler
         bsf     portb,0         ;start pulse
         bsf     intcon,7        ;enable global interrupts
         bcf     intcon,2        ;clear TMR0 interrupt flag
         bsf     intcon,5        ;enable TMR0 interrupts
circle   goto    circle          ;wait for interrupt
;
iserv    bcf     intcon,2        ;clear TMR0 interrupt flag
         decfsz  count,f         ;dec count, = zero?
```

```
        retfie              ;no
        bcf       portb,0   ;yes, end pulse
round   goto      round     ;done, circle
;

        end
;-----------------------------------------------------------
;at blast time, select:
;       memory unprotected
;       watchdog timer disabled (default is enabled)
;       standard crystal (using 4 MHz osc for test) XT
;       power-up timer on
;===========================================================
```

TEST EQUIPMENT FOR GENERATING A FREQUENCY OUTPUT

An '84 on a board can be used easily to generate a 100 KHz square wave for test purposes. A simple software delay loop does the job.

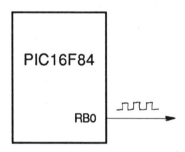

The flow chart and code follow:

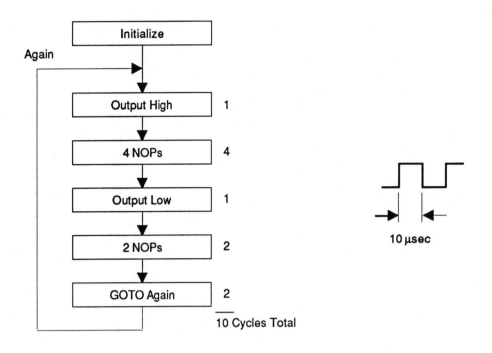

```
;=======FREQOUT.ASM====================================9/10/98==
;timer/counter demo
;       100 KHz out
;       internal clock
;--------------------------------------------------------------
        list    p=16f84
        radix   hex
;--------------------------------------------------------------
;       cpu equates (memory map)
portb   equ     0x06
;--------------------------------------------------------------
        org     0x000
;
start   movlw   b'00000000' ;port B outputs
        tris    portb
        movfw   portb          ;all low
again   bsf     portb,0        ;bit 0 high
        nop
        nop
        nop
        nop
        bcf     portb,0        ;output low
        nop
        nop
        goto    again
;
        end
;--------------------------------------------------------------
;at blast time, select:
;       memory unprotected
;       watchdog timer disabled (default is enabled)
```

```
;          standard crystal (using 4 MHz osc for test) XT
;          power-up timer on
;================================================================
```

USING TIMER 1, TIMER 2
AND
THE CAPTURE/COMPARE/PWM MODULE

PIC16C63 TEST CIRCUIT

Timer 1 (TMR1), timer 2 (TMR2), and capture/compare/PWM (CCP) modules are found in many PIC16 parts. A test circuit based on the PIC16C63 is shown here as an example you may use for experiments. I elected to use a 16-pin DIP socket as a connector for port B so that the keypad board described in "PIC'n Up The Pace" (see Appendix E) can be connected via a 16-conductor ribbon cable with DIP plugs. This scheme requires putting the LEDs for port B on a separate small board with a 16-pin DIP socket used as a connector. The LED board is connected for all experiments except those utilizing the keypad.

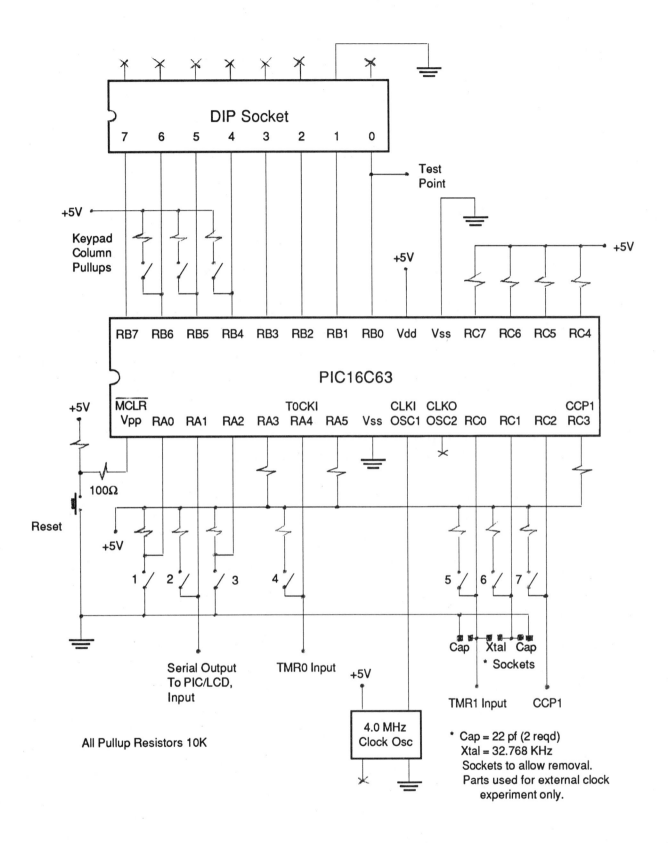

DIP Socket

7 6 5 4 3 2 1 0

Test Point

+5V

Keypad Column Pullups

+5V

+5V

RB7 RB6 RB5 RB4 RB3 RB2 RB1 RB0 Vdd Vss RC7 RC6 RC5 RC4

PIC16C63

MCLR
Vpp RA0 RA1 RA2 RA3 RA4 RA5 Vss OSC1 OSC2 RC0 RC1 RC2 RC3

+5V

TOCKI

CLKI CLKO

CCP1

100Ω

Reset

+5V

1   2   3   4   5   6   7

Cap Xtal Cap

* Sockets

Serial Output
To PIC/LCD,
Input

TMR0 Input

+5V

TMR1 Input   CCP1

4.0 MHz
Clock Osc

* Cap = 22 pf (2 reqd)
  Xtal = 32.768 KHz
  Sockets to allow removal.
  Parts used for external clock
  experiment only.

All Pullup Resistors 10K

LED BOARD

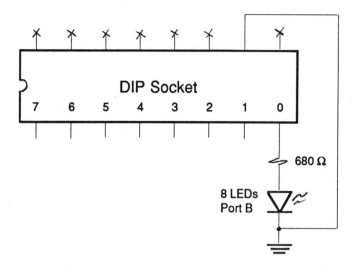

The '63 on a board has the following I/O:

- Eight port B pins brought out to a 16-pin DIP socket for use with LED board or keypad board.
- Three DIP switches with pullup resistors on port B for use with the keypad.
- Connections for TMR0 (input), TMR1 (input), and the CCP1 module (input/output).
- Two DIP switches with pullup resistors for use as inputs (RA0, RA2).
- Sockets for a 32.768 KHz crystal and two 22 pF capacitors for use with TMR1.
- Serial output pin for use with a PIC/LCD circuit (RA1)(see PIC'n Up The Pace and Appendix D for details).
- Pullup resistors on the unused pins.

On my breadboard, I used the following DIP switch and terminal block assignments/layout. To help avoid confusion, a list of switch settings will be shown for each experiment so you won't have to think so hard about which switches should be open and which ones should be closed.

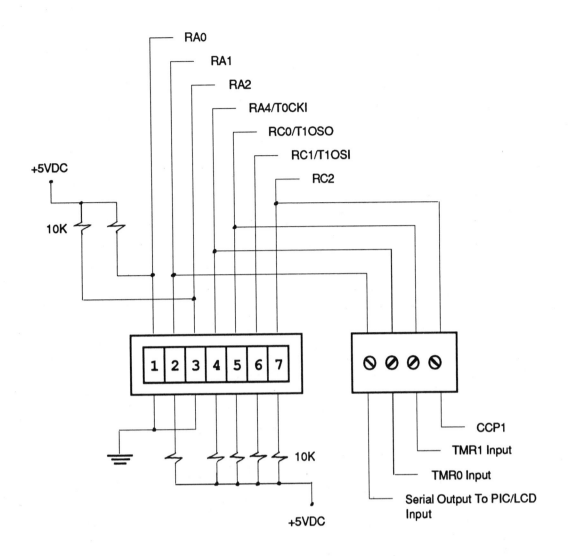

Pull Up Lines When Not Being Used.
Example: Not Using Any Lines.

DIP Switches

1	2	3	4	5	6	7
O	C	O	C	C	C	C

I leave the LED board connected to the '63 board for all experiments except those involving the keypad. This way, I know the port B lines are not left floating. The 3 port B DIP switches are open except when the keypad is connected.

The simple program shown may be used to see if your PIC16C63 circuit comes alive. The LEDs at port B bits 7, 6, 5, 4 should be off and the remaining four should be on.

DIP Switches

```
1   2   3   4   5   6   7

O   C   O   C   C   C   C
```

```
;=======TST63.ASM=============================4/30/98==
        list    p=16c63
        radix   hex
;-------------------------------------------------------
;       cpu equates (memory map)
portb   equ     06
;-------------------------------------------------------
        org     0x000
;
start   movlw   0x00            ;load w with 0x00
        tris    portb           ;copy w tristate, port B
                                ;   outputs
        movlw   0x0f            ;load w with 0x0F
        movwf   portb           ;load port B with contents
                                ;   of w
circle  goto    circle          ;done
;
        end
;-------------------------------------------------------
;at blast time, select:
;       memory unprotected
;       watchdog timer disabled (default is enabled)
;       standard crystal (using 4 MHz osc for test) XT
;       power-up timer on
;       brown-out detect on
;=======================================================
```

BEFORE WE TAKE OFF

There are some details we need to be aware of.

The register addresses used in the examples are for the PIC16C63. If you plan to use a different device, check the Microchip data book to be sure the addresses are correct for the device you intend to use.

The PIC16C63 peripheral control register descriptions are in Appendix B called "Control Registers" in the back of the book so you can find them easily for reference.

TMR1, TMR2 and the CCP modules are "peripherals". The list of modules considered "peripherals is device (part number) dependent. Note that timer 0 (TMR0) is not called a peripheral and that the register bits that control it are not in the peripheral control registers (they are in the status register).

There is a peripheral interrupt enable (PIE) register and a peripheral interrupt (flag) register (PIR). Note that there is a peripheral interrupt enable bit in the interrupt control (INTCON) register which must be set to allow interrupts from any of the peripherals. Remember also that the global interrupt enable bit in the INTCON register must be set to allow peripheral interrupts.

Remember that an "interrupt" flag may be polled to determine its status instead of using it to trigger an interrupt.

The INTCON register in the PIC16C63 is not the same as for the PIC16F84. The difference is bit 6 which is the peripheral interrupt enable bit in the '63 where as in the '84 it is the EE write complete interrupt.

The PIC16C63 has two CCP modules designated CCP1 and CCP2. We will use only CCP1 (and will ignore the existence of CCP2) to simplify the learning process.

Finally, the output of the timing and counting examples will, in general, be slightly inaccurate because of things like a program loop looking for a bit to change state catching it a cycle or two after it actually occurs or because of program steps taking a few extra instruction cycles. In most cases, the error will be very small and inconsequential. If these errors are significant in your particular application, you can analyze the code and compensate by changing the value(s) loaded into the timer to correct the results. Or you can simply change the values used to correct the output and forget about analysis (assuming your measuring equipment is more accurate than a crystal-controlled PIC16).

TIMER 2 (TMR2): 8-BIT TIMER

TMR2 has the following features:

- 8-bit timer.
- Source of pulses is the internal instruction clock (timing applications only).
- Prescaler divides the incoming pulse train by 1, 4, or 16.
- Postscaler divides the comparator output by 1, 2, 3 16
- 8-bit period register (PR2).
- Comparator to look for TMR2/PR2 match.
- TMR2 may be cleared, written to, or read at any time.
- The period register may be written to or read.
- TMR2 may be used as a general purpose timer.
- TMR2 may be used with the CCP module for PWM.
- TMR2 may be used with the SSP module for baud rate generation.

TMR2 Description

A simplified block diagram of TMR2 follows:

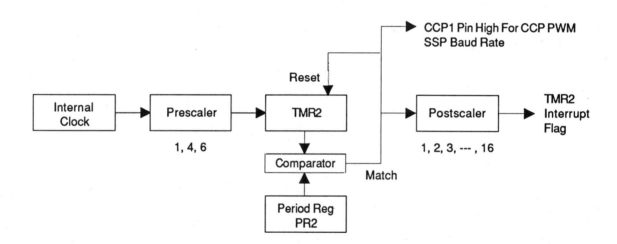

TMR2 is incremented by the internal instruction clock ($f_{osc}/4$) (prescaled) from 0x00 until it's contents match the period register. On the next increment, it is reset to 0x00. For each match of TMR2 and it's period register, a pulse is output to a postscaler. The postscaler output sets the TMR2 interrupt flag in the PIR1 register. The output of the TMR2 module may be:

- Read TMR2.
- TMR2 interrupt flag.

The match output from the comparator (directly) is used to reset TMR2 in PWM applications (see PWM section), and is used in SSP serial applications (baud rate).

The interrupt generated by TMR2 is called both the TMR2 interrupt and the TMR2 match interrupt in the Microchip literature. The term match interrupt implies that an interrupt occurs at every match, which may not be true depending on the postscaler ratio. We will refer to this interrupt as the TMR2 interrupt.

TMR2 can be turned on or off via a control bit in the TMR2 control register T2CON.

TMR2 is cleared by any device reset (POR, BOR, $\overline{\text{MCLR}}$, WDT).

The prescaler and postscaler are cleared by:

- Write to TMR2.
- Write to T2CON, the TMR2 control register.
- Any device reset (POR, BOR, $\overline{\text{MCLR}}$, WDT).

PR2 is filled with 1's on reset (full count).

A write to the T2CON register does not clear TMR2.

How To Choose/Select Mode Of Operation

T2CON register:

```
                                    Bit(s)
                                    -------
     Prescaler select                 1,0
     Postscaler select              6,5,4,3
     TMR2 on/off                       2
```

Interrupts

Enable using PIE1 register:

```
                                     Bit
                                     ---
     TMR2 interrupt enable            1
```

Enable using INTCON register:

```
                                     Bit
                                     ---
     Peripheral interrupt enable      6
     Global interrupt enable          7
```

Flag - PIR1 register:

```
                                     Bit
                                     ---
     TMR2 interrupt flag              1
```

TMR2 Application - Free Running Mode (via TMR2 interrupt)

The first example is similar to the TMR0 free running mode with internal clock example in **Easy** PIC'n.

Use internal clock, prescaler 1:16, postscaler 1:16, period 255.
Time interval 65 milliseconds.
Output to port B, bit 0.

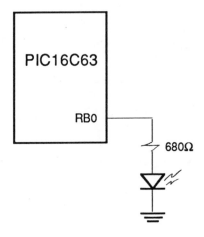

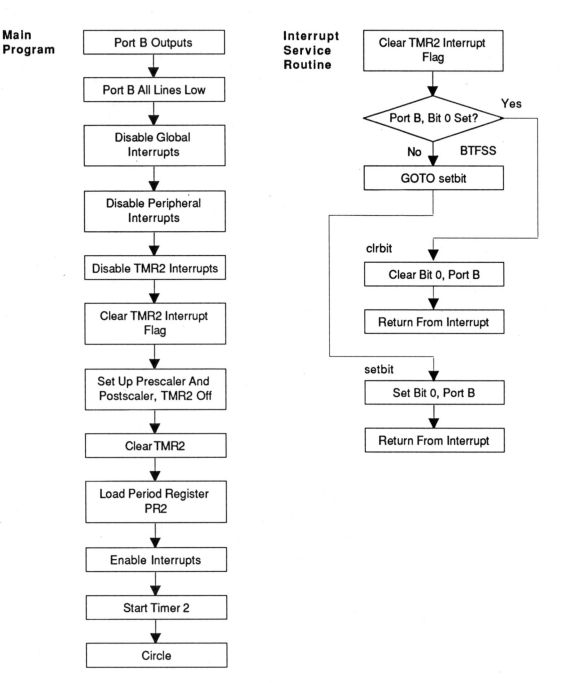

Main Program

- Port B Outputs
- Port B All Lines Low
- Disable Global Interrupts
- Disable Peripheral Interrupts
- Disable TMR2 Interrupts
- Clear TMR2 Interrupt Flag
- Set Up Prescaler And Postscaler, TMR2 Off
- Clear TMR2
- Load Period Register PR2
- Enable Interrupts
- Start Timer 2
- Circle

Interrupt Service Routine

- Clear TMR2 Interrupt Flag
- Port B, Bit 0 Set? — Yes / No BTFSS
- GOTO setbit

clrbit
- Clear Bit 0, Port B
- Return From Interrupt

setbit
- Set Bit 0, Port B
- Return From Interrupt

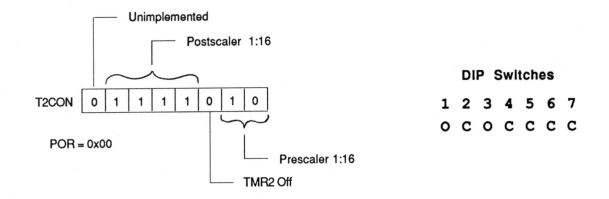

Unimplemented

Postscaler 1:16

T2CON | 0 | 1 | 1 | 1 | 1 | 0 | 1 | 0 |

POR = 0x00

Prescaler 1:16

TMR2 Off

DIP Switches

1	2	3	4	5	6	7
O	C	O	C	C	C	C

```
;=======TMR2.ASM=================================8/30/98==
        list    p=16c63
        radix   hex
;----------------------------------------------------------
;timer 2 demo
;       free running, time interval 65 milliseconds
;       internal clock, prescaler 1:16, postscaler 1:16,
;          period 255
;----------------------------------------------------------
;       cpu equates (memory map)
status  equ     0x03
portb   equ     0x06
intcon  equ     0x0b
pir1    equ     0x0c
tmr2    equ     0x11
t2con   equ     0x12
trisb   equ     0x86
pie1    equ     0x8c
pr2     equ     0x92
;----------------------------------------------------------
;       bit equates
rp0     equ     5
;----------------------------------------------------------
        org     0x000
        goto    start       ;skip over location pointed to by
                            ;   interrupt vector
        org     0x004
        goto    iserv
;
start   bsf     status,rp0  ;switch to bank 1
        movlw   b'00000000' ;port B outputs
        movwf   trisb
        bcf     status,rp0  ;switch back to bank 0
        movwf   portb       ;port B lines low
        bcf     intcon,7    ;disable global interrupts
        bcf     intcon,6    ;disable peripheral interrupts
        bsf     status,rp0  ;bank 1
        bcf     pie1,1      ;disable tmr2 interrupt
```

```
        bcf     status,rp0   ;bank 0
        bcf     pir1,1       ;clear tmr2 interrupt flag
        movlw   b'01111010'  ;prescaler and postscaler setup,
        movwf   t2con        ;   tmr2 off
        clrf    tmr2         ;clear timer 2
        bsf     status,rp0   ;bank 1
        movlw   b'11111111'  ;period=255
        movwf   pr2
        bcf     status,rp0   ;bank 0
        bsf     intcon,7     ;enable global interrupts
        bsf     intcon,6     ;enable peripheral interrupts
        bsf     status,rp0   ;bank 1
        bsf     pie1,1       ;enable tmr2 interrupt
        bcf     status,rp0   ;bank 0
        bsf     t2con,2      ;timer 2 on
circle  goto    circle       ;done
;
iserv   bcf     pir1,1       ;clear TMR2 interrupt flag,
                             ;   enable further interrupts
        btfss   portb,0      ;port B, bit 0 status?
        goto    setbit       ;bit is clear
clrbit  bcf     portb,0      ;clear port B, bit 0
        retfie               ;return from interrupt
setbit  bsf     portb,0      ;set port B, bit 0
        retfie               ;return from interrupt
;
        end
;-------------------------------------------------------------
;at blast time, select:
;       memory unprotected
;       watchdog timer disabled (default is enabled)
;       standard crystal (using 4 MHz osc for test) XT
;       power-up timer on
;       brown-out detect on
;=============================================================
```

Run the program and look at the port B, bit 0 LED.

Example:

> With a 4 MHz clock oscillator, the internal instruction clock will have
>   a frequency of 1 MHz and each cycle will be 1 microsecond in
>   duration (ie. period = 1 microsecond).
> 1 microsecond multiplied by 16 = 16 microseconds between pulses out of
>   the prescaler.
> Count to 255 in TMR2 = 4080 microseconds between pulses out of TMR2.
> Multiply by 16 in postscaler = 65,280 microseconds = 65 millisecond
>   output interval.
>
> 1 µsec x 16 x 255 x 16 = 65,280 µsec = 65 msec

65 msec

This is the time between each HI/LO or LO/HI transition at the port
    line. The time to execute the interrupt service routine adds to
    this slightly.

When thinking in terms of frequency, the prescaler divides the frequency. When thinking in terms of period, the prescaler multiplies the period.

TMR2 Application - Free Running (via period register)

This time, we will use the period register and poll (watch) the TMR2 interrupt flag (won't use interrupts). The prescaler will divide the internal instruction clock by 16 giving 16 microseconds per pulse into TMR2. The period register PR2 will be loaded with decimal 10. The postscaler will divide by 10.

16 μsec x 10 x 10 = 1600 μsec = 1.6 msec time interval

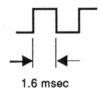

1.6 msec

The prescaler output will increment TMR2 until it's contents match the contents of PR2 (match occurs) sending a pulse to the postscaler and resetting TMR2.

Use internal clock, prescaler 1:16, postscaler 1:10, period 10.
Time interval 1.6 milliseconds.
Output to port B, bit 0.

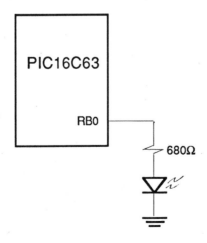

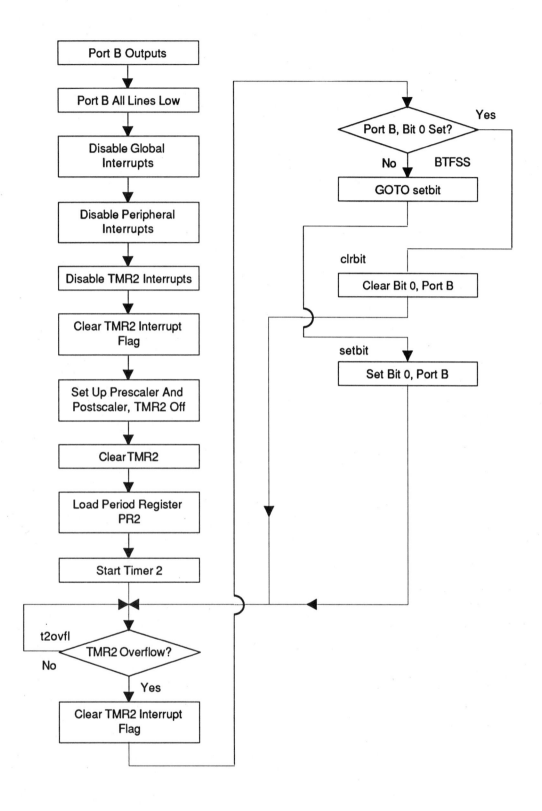

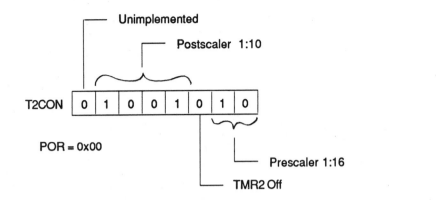

T2CON | 0 | 1 | 0 | 0 | 1 | 0 | 1 | 0 |

Unimplemented

Postscaler 1:10

POR = 0x00

Prescaler 1:16

TMR2 Off

DIP Switches

1	2	3	4	5	6	7
O	C	O	C	C	C	C

```
;=======TSTTMR2.ASM=========================8/30/98==
;timer 2 demo
;       free running
;       internal clock divided by 16 (prescaler)
;       period value = 10
;       postscaler 1:10
;----------------------------------------------------
        list    p=16c63
        radix   hex
;----------------------------------------------------
;       cpu equates (memory map)
tmr0    equ     0x01
status  equ     0x03
portb   equ     0x06
intcon  equ     0x0b
pir1    equ     0x0c
tmr2    equ     0x11
t2con   equ     0x12
trisb   equ     0x86
pie1    equ     0x8c
pr2     equ     0x92
;----------------------------------------------------
;       bit equates
rp0     equ     5
;----------------------------------------------------
        org     0x000
;
start   bsf     status,rp0  ;switch to bank 1
        movlw   b'00000000' ;port B outputs
        movwf   trisb
        bcf     status,rp0  ;switch back to bank 0
        movlw   b'00000000' ;all outputs low
        movwf   portb
        bcf     intcon,7    ;disable global interrupts
        bcf     intcon,6    ;disable     peripheral interrupts
        bsf     status,rp0  ;to bank 1
        bcf     pie1,1      ;disable tmr2 interrupt
        bcf     status,rp0  ;to bank 0
        bcf     pir1,1      ;clear tmr2 interrupt flag
```

```
        movlw    b'01001010'  ;prescaler = 1:16,
                              ;  postscaler = 1:10
        movwf    t2con        ;tmr2 off
        clrf     tmr2         ;clear tmr2
        bsf      status,rp0   ;bank 1
        movlw    d'10'        ;decimal 10
        movwf    pr2          ;load period register
        bcf      status,rp0   ;bank 0
        bsf      t2con,2      ;tmr2 on
t2ovfl  btfss    pir1,1       ;watch tmr2 interrupt flag
        goto     t2ovfl       ;not yet
        bcf      pir1,1       ;flag set, so clear flag
        btfss    portb,0      ;port B, bit 0 status?
        goto     setbit       ;bit is clear
clrbit  bcf      portb,0      ;clear port B, bit 0
        goto     t2ovfl       ;repeat
setbit  bsf      portb,0      ;set port B, bit 0
        goto     t2ovfl       ;repeat
;
        end
;------------------------------------------------------
;at blast time, select:
;       memory unprotected
;       watchdog timer disabled (default is enabled)
;       standard crystal (using 4 MHz osc for test) XT
;       power-up timer on
;       brown-out detect on
;======================================================
```

Run the program and look at port B with an oscilloscope. The pulse width should be 1.6 milliseconds pulse a hair for software overhead.

You have a design choice of polling the TMR2 interrupt flag or waiting for an interrupt and servicing it. Either way, the interrupt flag must be cleared in software each time it pops up.

TMR1: 16-BIT TIMER/COUNTER AND CAPTURE/COMPARE MODULE

TMR1/CCP Simplified

Timer 1 (TMR1) is a 16-bit timer/counter. The resolution it provides is quite useful. A capture/compare module may be used in conjunction with timer 1 to do some neat tricks. We will try a few of them.

First, timer 1 may be used in the typical way be reading it's contents or looking at the overflow flag.

TMR1 - Timer/Counter

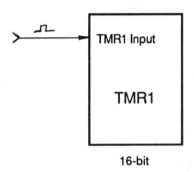

16-bit

The contents of timer 1 may be <u>captured</u> (grabbed) for use triggered by a signal edge from circuitry external to the PIC16.

TMR1 - Capture

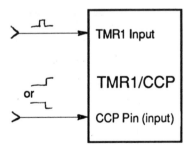

Pulses coming into timer 1 increment the counter. When a capture command signal edge arrives, the counter contents are captured and an interrupt flag is set. The captured value is available to be read.

The contents of timer 1 may be continuously <u>compared</u> to the contents of a compare register which has been loaded previously with some value. When the contents of timer 1 are incremented to a value equal to the contents of the compare register, an output occurs which may be a level change on the capture/compare module's output pin, an interrupt , or both.

TMR1 - Compare

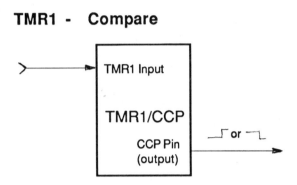

Using the CCP module makes it possible to read timer 1 and store its contents for later use when a signal edge (external) is detected while the PIC16 is busy doing other things (<u>capture</u>). Using the CCP module also makes it possible to drive a pin high or low when the contents of timer 1 are incremented to a predetermined value totally independent from other tasks the PIC16 may be performing at the moment (<u>compare</u>).

The source of pulses feeding timer 1 may be the internal clock for timing applications. This allows fine resolution (1 microsecond for 4 MHz clock oscillator). Alternatively, the source of pulses might be an external clock or it could be a circuit which has a pulse output for an application based on counting pulses.

TMR1 Description

TMR1 used in conjunction with the CCP module has the following features:

- 16-bit timer/ counter consisting of two 8-bit registers.
- Source of pulses either internal instruction clock or external via PIC16 pin.
- Prescaler divides the incoming pulse train by 1, 2, 4, or 8.
- TMR1 may be cleared or read at any time.
- An edge input via a pin can be used to trigger a read of TMR1 (capture) coupled with setting an interrupt flag so the PIC16 knows the number read is available.
- TMR1 can be incremented via event or clock pulses until it's contents matches a number previously loaded into a comparator register (compare) triggering an output via a pin, or setting an interrupt flag, or both.
- A single time interval or frequency output may be generated using a compare function.

TMR1 increments from 0x0000 to 0xFFFF and rolls over to 0x0000.

TMR1 may be cleared, read, and turned on or off.

A simplified block diagram of TMR1 (without the CCP module) follows:

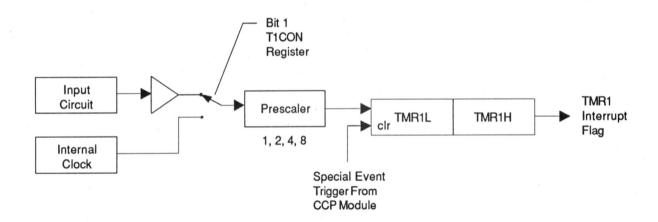

First, note that the source of pulses input to TMR1 may be the internal instruction clock ($f_{osc}/4$) for timing applications or an external source for either timing or counting applications. The selection of source is determined by a bit in the T1CON register. Second, notice that a prescaler is used to divide the incoming pulse train by 1, 2, 4, or 8 as determined by two bits in the T1CON register. TMR1 may be turned on or off using a bit in the T1CON register. TMR1 itself consists of a register pair (8 bits each). On TMR1 overflow, a flag bit is set in the PIR1 register and an interrupt occurs if enabled by a bit in the PIE1 register.

External inputs to TMR1 may be one of two types. The most common is via the T1CKI pin.

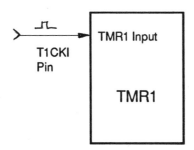

When pulses are fed to pin T1CKI from an external source, TMR1 increments on every rising edge (exception noted later) on the T1CKI pin (divided by the prescaler). This mode of operation is selected by setting the TMR1CS bit in the T1CON register. When external pulses are fed into TMR1 via the T1CKI pin (port C, bit 0), the pin must be configured as an input.

We will use only what is called the synchronous mode for our examples and this is selected by clearing the $\overline{T1SYNC}$ bit in the T1CON register.

You won't need to concern yourself with this now, but there are some external clock input timing specs (synchronous counter mode) to be aware of.

<u>Prescaler 1:1.</u>

```
The external input at the T1CKI pin must be high for at least 2 Tosc and
low for at least 2 Tosc where Tosc is the period of the external clock
oscillator.
```

<u>Prescaler other than 1:1</u>

```
The external input at the T1CKI pin must be high or low for at least
4 Tosc  divided by the prescaler value   Also, the minimum pulse width
requirements called out in the "Electrical Specifications" in the
Microchip data book must not be violated.
```

The other circuit possibility is a crystal clock oscillator created by connecting a crystal between pins T1OSI and T1OSO. The oscillator may operate up to 200 KHz. The primary application is real-time using a 32.768 KHz crystal (details later).

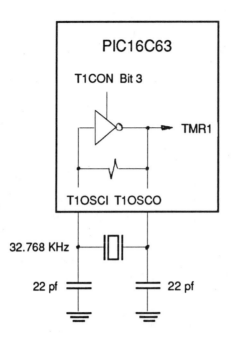

CCP1 Module - Capture Mode

The CCP1 module uses the CCP1 pin as it's input.

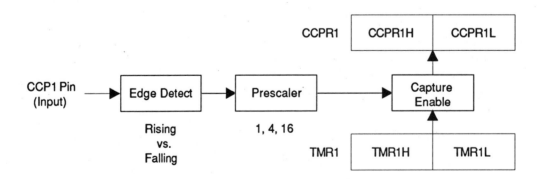

The 16-bit contents of TMR1 is captured when one of the following events occurs on pin CCP1:

- Every falling edge (exception noted later).
- Every rising edge (exception noted later).
- Every 4th rising edge.
- Every 16th rising edge.

When the selected event occurs, the contents of TMR1 are captured in a capture register and the CCP1 interrupt flag is set (flag must be cleared in software). The number captured is available for whatever use the programmer intends.

CCP1 Module - Compare Mode

The CCP1 module uses the CCP1 pin as an output.

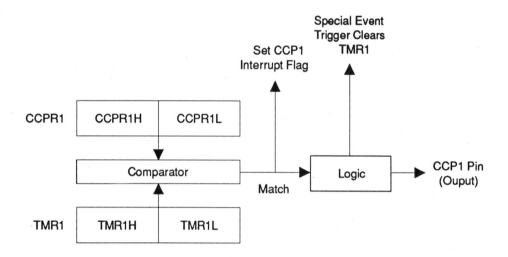

When the CCP1 compare mode is selected:

- TMR1 may free-run or count external pulses. TMR1 is incremented.
- When a match occurs, the CCP1 pin is:

    - Driven high.
    - Driven low.
    - Remains unchanged.

    - And the CCP1 interrupt flag is set.

- A special event trigger may be used to reset TMR1 when a match occurs.
  Note that the special event trigger does not set the TMR1 interrupt flag.

CCP1 Module - PWM Mode

See the PWM section.

CCP1 Pin

The CCP1 pin must be initialized as an input or output as part of the program. The pin is forced low when a bit pattern calling for the compare mode is loaded into the CCP1CON register.

If the CCP1 pin is configured as an output, a write to the port can cause a capture condition. Therefore, the CCP1 interrupt enable bit should be cleared to disable interrupts prior to writing to the port and the CCP1 interrupt flag should be cleared following writing to the port.

CCPR1L And CCPR1H Register Pair

The CCPR1L and CCPR1H register pair is used as the capture register in the capture mode and as the compare register in the compare mode. We will refer to this register pair as the capture register or as the compare register depending on the application.

How To Choose/Select Mode Of Operation

T1CON register:

```
                                                   Bit(s)
                                                   ------
     Clock source internal/external                  1
     Oscillator enable control on/off (input circuit) 3
     T1SYNC                                           2
        If external source, sync for our applications
     Prescaler select                                5,4
     TMR1 on/off                                      0
```

CCP1CON register:

```
                                                   Bit(s)
                                                   ------
     CCP1 mode select                              3,2,1,0
                                                   ------
        Module off                                  0000
        Capture, every falling edge                 0100
                 every rising edge                  0101
                 every 4th rising edge              0110
                 every 16th rising edge             0111
        Compare, set output pin on match and        1000
                    set CCP1 interrupt flag
                 clear output pin on match and      1001
                    set CCP1 interrupt flag
                 software interrupt on match and    1010
                    set CCP1 interrupt flag
                 trigger special event on match,    1011
                    set CCP1 interrupt flag and
                    clear TMR1
        PWM (see PWM section)                        11xx
```

Interrupts

Enable using PIE1 register:

	Bit
TMR1 overflow interrupt enable	0
CCP1 interrupt enable	2

Enable using INTCON register:

	Bit
Peripheral interrupt enable	6
Global interrupt enable	7

Flags - PIR1 register:

	Bit
TMR1 overflow interrupt flag	0
CCP1 interrupt flag	2

Reading And Writing TMR1

If TMR1 can be stopped, reading and writing is simply a mater of reading or writing the high and low registers (individually). Reading or writing TMR1 while it is running is another matter.

Writing To TMR1 While It Is Running

First, clear the TMR1L register to ensure that a rollover into the TMR1H register will not occur soon. Load TMR1H. Then load TMR1L. All interrupts must be disabled while the write operation takes place and re-enabled afterwards.

```
clrf     tmr1l      ;clear low byte - prevent rollover into high
                    ;   byte
movlw    ......     ;define value to be loaded into high byte
movwf    tmr1h,f    ;load high byte
movlw    ......     ;define value to be loaded into low byte
movwf    tmr1l,f    ;load low byte
```

Reading TMR1 While It Is Running

Reading the 16-bit TMR1 involves reading two 8-bit values. The danger is that a TMR1 overflow may occur between reads. If an overflow occurs, it must be detected in software. Detection of an overflow must cause TMR1 to be read a second time to obtain valid data. All interrupts must be disabled while the read operation takes place and re-enabled afterwards.

```
;subroutine - read timer 1 on-the-fly
        movf    tmr1h,w     ;read high byte
        movwf   t1_hi       ;store
        movf    tmr1l,w     ;read low byte
        movwf   t1_lo       ;store
        movf    tmr1h,w     ;read high byte again
        subwf   t1_hi,w     ;subtract first read from second read
        btfsc   status,z    ;is result 0?
        return              ;read valid
        movf    tmr1h,w     ;rollover occurred, read high byte again
        movwf   t1_hi       ;store
        movf    tmr1l,w     ;read low byte
        movwf   t1_lo       ;store
        return
```

Long Time Intervals

Long time intervals may be generated by counting rollovers of timer 1.

Controlling The CCP1 Pin In Compare Mode

When using the compare mode, the CCP1 pin must be made an output via the TRISC register. Turning on the CCP1 module in the compare mode (by writing to the CCP1CON register) forces the CCP1 pin low (no matter what). The version of MPSIM built in to MPLAB that I am currently using does not do this, but the hardware does, which is what counts in the end.

This means that if you want to generate a single time interval output via the CCP1 pin so as to take advantage of the "auto off" feature, you will need to use a trick to force the pin high at the beginning of the time interval. The trick is to load the compare register with the value 0x0001 and put the CCP1 module in the compare mode programmed to force the CCP1 pin high on match which will occur right away (TMR1 counts to 1). Then load the compare register with the value corresponding to the desired time interval and flip the bit in CCP1CON which will tell the CCP1 pin to go low on the next match.

This technique will be used in the example programs.

More Than One Way To Do Timing Stuff

As usual, there is more than one way to do things. Here are some concepts to stimulate your thinking about timing applications and the compare mode.

TMR1 can be turned on to start a time interval which ends automatically via the CCP1 module operating in the compare mode. This is fine if TMR1 is being used for only the one application at the moment. The trick for controlling the CCP1 pin described earlier must be used.

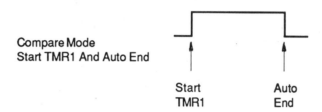

Compare Mode
Start TMR1 And Auto End

Start   Auto
TMR1   End

If TMR1 is being shared by more than one function at (the same time), TMR1 may be operated in the free running mode. Generating a time interval begins with reading TMR1, adding the required time interval to the contents of TMR1 just obtained, and storing the result in the compare register. When TMR1 is incremented to that number, an output is automatically generated.

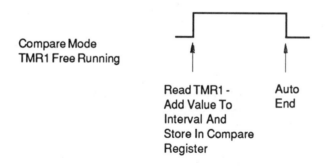

Compare Mode
TMR1 Free Running

Read TMR1 -   Auto
Add Value To   End
Interval And
Store In Compare
Register

The same technique can be used to generate a periodic output.

Compare Mode
TMR1 Free Running
Add To Compare Register To
Create Periodic Waveform
 • Use Interrupt Service Routine
 • Must Toggle Rise/Fall Bit

The experiments which follow include examples to illustrate these concepts.

TIMING AND COUNTING EXPERIMENTS

Free Running Output (via TMR1 interrupt)

To begin your hands-on familiarization with timer 1, we will start with an example using the same techniques used previously with timer 0 and timer 2. We will set up TMR1 to free run and use an interrupt service routine to toggle an output pin.

Use internal instruction clock, prescale 1:8, count 0xFFFF = 65,536.
Output port B, bit 0.
Time interval 8 microseconds x 65,536 = 524 milliseconds.

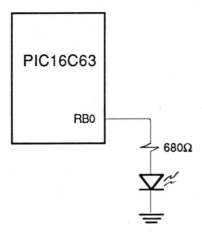

The code is written in a logical sequence for ease of understanding, especially at the flow chart level. You can eliminate some bank switching by combining some of the bank 1 steps if you want to streamline the code.

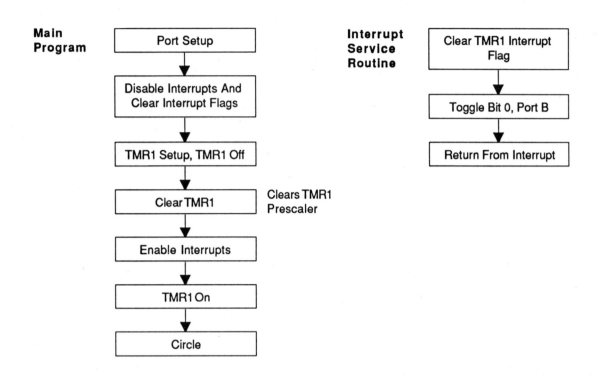

Main Program

Port Setup
↓
Disable Interrupts And Clear Interrupt Flags
↓
TMR1 Setup, TMR1 Off
↓
Clear TMR1   Clears TMR1 Prescaler
↓
Enable Interrupts
↓
TMR1 On
↓
Circle

Interrupt Service Routine

Clear TMR1 Interrupt Flag
↓
Toggle Bit 0, Port B
↓
Return From Interrupt

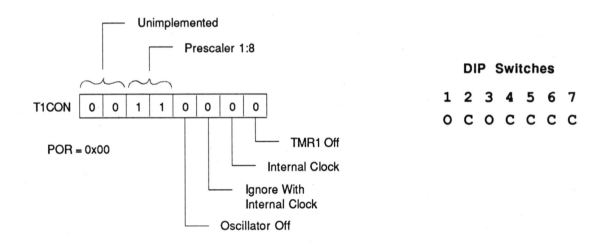

Unimplemented

Prescaler 1:8

T1CON | 0 | 0 | 1 | 1 | 0 | 0 | 0 | 0 |

POR = 0x00

TMR1 Off
Internal Clock
Ignore With Internal Clock
Oscillator Off

DIP Switches

1	2	3	4	5	6	7
O	C	O	C	C	C	C

```
;=======TMR1.ASM================================8/28/98==
        list    p=16c63
        radix   hex
;-------------------------------------------------------------
;timer 1 demo
;       free running, time interval 524 milliseconds
;       internal clock, prescaler 1:8, count to 65,536
;-------------------------------------------------------------
;       cpu equates (memory map)
status  equ     0x03
portb   equ     0x06
```

```
intcon    equ       0x0b
pir1      equ       0x0c
tmr1l     equ       0x0e
tmr1h     equ       0x0f
t1con     equ       0x10
trisb     equ       0x86
pie1      equ       0x8c
;------------------------------------------------------------
;         bit equates
rp0       equ       5
;------------------------------------------------------------
          org       0x000
          goto      start         ;skip over location pointed to by
                                  ;   interrupt vector
          org       0x004
          goto      iserv
;
start     bsf       status,rp0    ;switch to bank 1
          movlw     b'00000000'   ;port B outputs
          movwf     trisb
          bcf       status,rp0    ;switch back to bank 0
          movwf     portb         ;port B lines low
          bcf       intcon,7      ;disable global interrupts
          bcf       intcon,6      ;disable peripheral interrupts
          bsf       status,rp0    ;bank 1
          bcf       pie1,0        ;disable tmr1 interrupt
          bcf       status,rp0    ;bank 0
          bcf       pir1,0        ;clear tmr1 interrupt flag
          movlw     b'00110000'   ;prescaler and tmr1 setup,
          movwf     t1con         ;   tmr1 off
          clrf      tmr1h         ;clear timer 1 high
          clrf      tmr1l         ;clear timer 1 low, clear prescaler
          bsf       intcon,7      ;enable global interrupts
          bsf       intcon,6      ;enable peripheral interrupts
          bsf       status,rp0    ;bank 1
          bsf       pie1,0        ;enable tmr1 interrupt
          bcf       status,rp0    ;bank 0
          bsf       t1con,0       ;timer 1 on
circle    goto      circle        ;done
;
iserv     bcf       pir1,0        ;clear TMR1 interrupt flag,
                                  ;   enable further interrupts
          btfss     portb,0       ;port B, bit 0 status?
          goto      setbit        ;bit is clear
clrbit    bcf       portb,0       ;clear port B, bit 0
          nop                     ;equalize paths
          retfie                  ;return from interrupt
setbit    bsf       portb,0       ;set port B, bit 0
          retfie                  ;return from interrupt
;
          end
;------------------------------------------------------------
;at blast time, select:
;         memory unprotected
```

64

```
;       watchdog timer disabled (default is enabled)
;       standard crystal (using 4 MHz osc for test) XT
;       power-up timer on
;       brown-out detect on
;==============================================================
```

PULSER CIRCUIT

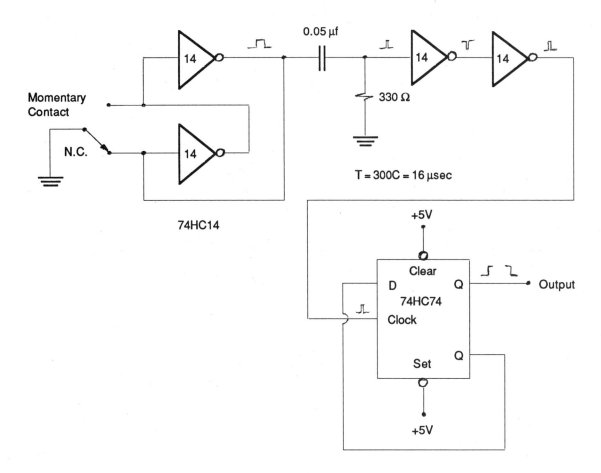

Event Counting (via TMR1)

• Count Events, Read TMR1 Contents On-The-Fly

For this example, the contents of timer 1 will be displayed continuously using a program loop. A pulser is used to inject pulses into TMR1.

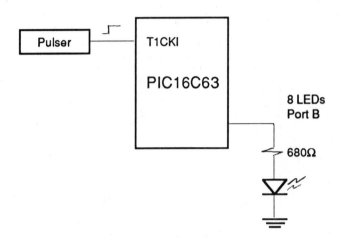

Timer 1 is supposed to increment on every rising edge. Timer 1 has a "weird" in that what constitutes the first rising edge is determined by the initial logic level of the T1CKI pin when timer 1 is turned on. If it is high initially (on reset with this experimental setup), the count indeed will begin on the first rising edge (increment on every rising edge).

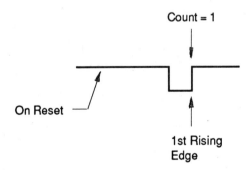

If the level at T1CKI is low on reset, the first rising edge won't cause TMR1 to increment (i.e. not every rising edge will be counted).

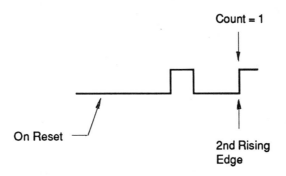

This can prove to be a "gotcha" if you are not aware of it.

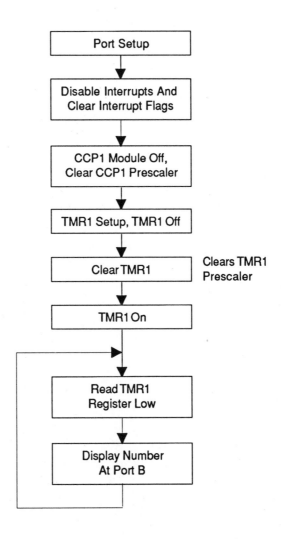

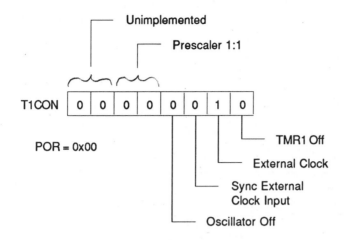

DIP Switches

1	2	3	4	5	6	7
O	C	O	C	O	C	C

```
;=======READ.ASM==================================8/10/98==
        list    p=16c63
        radix   hex
;------------------------------------------------------------
;timer 1 - read event count on-the-fly demo
;------------------------------------------------------------
;       cpu equates (memory map)
status  equ     0x03
portb   equ     0x06
intcon  equ     0x0b
pir1    equ     0x0c
tmr1l   equ     0x0e
tmr1h   equ     0x0f
t1con   equ     0x10
ccp1con equ     0x17
trisb   equ     0x86
trisc   equ     0x87
pie1    equ     0x8c
;------------------------------------------------------------
;       bit equates
rp0     equ     5
;------------------------------------------------------------
        org     0x000
;
start   bsf     status,rp0  ;switch to bank 1
        movlw   b'00000000' ;port B outputs
        movwf   trisb
        bsf     trisc,0     ;port C, bit 0 timer 1 input
        bcf     status,rp0  ;switch back to bank 0
        movlw   b'00000000' ;port B lines low
        movwf   portb
        bcf     intcon,7    ;disable global interrupts
        bcf     intcon,6    ;disable peripheral interrupts
        bsf     status,rp0  ;bank 1
        bcf     pie1,0      ;disable tmr1 interrupt
        bcf     pie1,2      ;disable ccp1 interrupt
        bcf     status,rp0  ;bank 0
```

```
          clrf      ccp1con           ;ccp1 module off, clear ccp1 prescaler
          movlw     b'00000010' ;tmr1 prescaler and tmr1 setup,
          movwf     t1con            ;    tmr1 off
          clrf      tmr1h            ;clear timer 1 high
          clrf      tmr1l            ;clear timer 1 low, clear prescaler
          bsf       t1con,0          ;timer 1 on
read      movf      tmr1l,w          ;read timer 1 low
          movwf     portb            ;display count at port B
          goto      read
;
          end
;-----------------------------------------------------------
;at blast time, select:
;       memory unprotected
;       watchdog timer disabled (default is enabled)
;       standard crystal (using 4 MHz osc for test) XT
;       power-up timer on
;       brown-out detect on
;===========================================================
```

• Capture TMR1 Count When An External Event Occurs

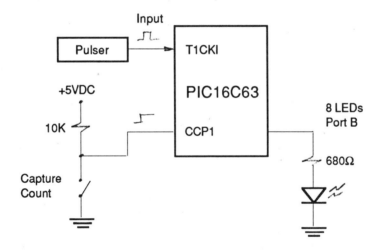

For this experiment, we will use a pulser to inject pulses into timer 1 via the T1CKI pin. The objective is to increment TMR1 (via the prescaler) on every rising edge. The input at T1CKI pin must be high on reset or the result will be one count short. The count will be displayed in binary via the port B LEDs.

A pullup resistor and switch are used to generate a capture on a rising edge via the CCP1 pin which is configured as an input. Power-up the circuit with the switch closed (LEDs will be off) and then open the switch (rising edge) when you want to capture the contents of timer 1.

Inject a few pulses at the T1CKI pin. Capture the count using the switch on the CCP1 pin and see if the displayed count equals the number of rising edges you injected.

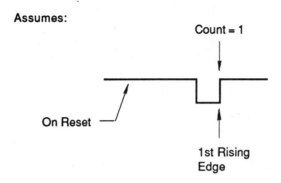

Assumes:

Count = 1

On Reset

1st Rising Edge

Main Program

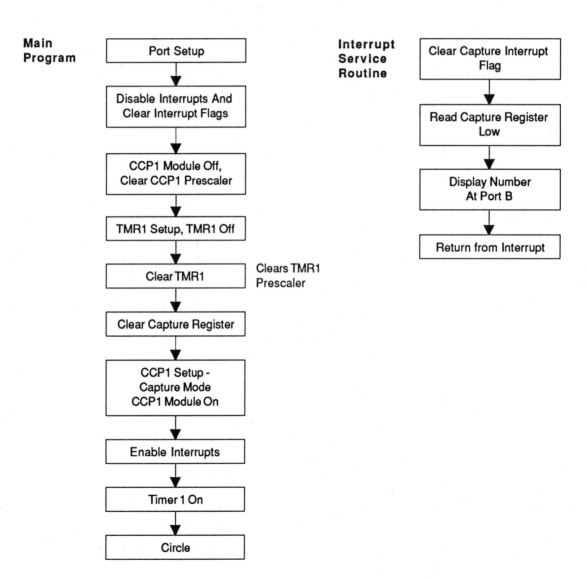

Port Setup

↓

Disable Interrupts And Clear Interrupt Flags

↓

CCP1 Module Off, Clear CCP1 Prescaler

↓

TMR1 Setup, TMR1 Off

↓

Clear TMR1 — Clears TMR1 Prescaler

↓

Clear Capture Register

↓

CCP1 Setup - Capture Mode CCP1 Module On

↓

Enable Interrupts

↓

Timer 1 On

↓

Circle

Interrupt Service Routine

Clear Capture Interrupt Flag

↓

Read Capture Register Low

↓

Display Number At Port B

↓

Return from Interrupt

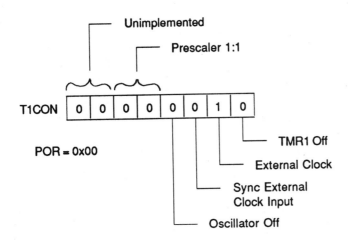

Unimplemented

Prescaler 1:1

T1CON | 0 | 0 | 0 | 0 | 0 | 0 | 1 | 0 |

POR = 0x00

TMR1 Off

External Clock

Sync External
Clock Input

Oscillator Off

DIP Switches

1 2 3 4 5 6 7

O C O C O C C

Closed On Reset
Open To Capture

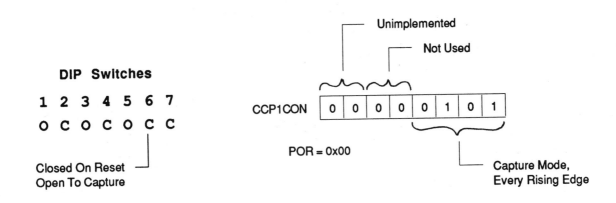

Unimplemented

Not Used

CCP1CON | 0 | 0 | 0 | 0 | 0 | 1 | 0 | 1 |

POR = 0x00

Capture Mode,
Every Rising Edge

```
;======CAPT.ASM================================8/7/98==
        list    p=16c63
        radix   hex
;------------------------------------------------------
;timer 1 and ccp1 module - capture mode demo
;------------------------------------------------------
;       cpu equates (memory map)
status  equ     0x03
portb   equ     0x06
intcon  equ     0x0b
pir1    equ     0x0c
tmr1l   equ     0x0e
tmr1h   equ     0x0f
t1con   equ     0x10
ccpr1l  equ     0x15
ccpr1h  equ     0x16
ccp1con equ     0x17
trisb   equ     0x86
trisc   equ     0x87
pie1    equ     0x8c
;------------------------------------------------------
;       bit equates
rp0     equ     5
ccp1    equ     2               ;ccp1 bit 2, port C
```

```
;------------------------------------------------------------
        org     0x000
        goto    start       ;skip over location pointed to by
                            ;   interrupt vector
        org     0x004
        goto    iserv
;
start   bsf     status,rp0  ;switch to bank 1
        movlw   b'00000000' ;port B outputs
        movwf   trisb
        bsf     trisc,0     ;port C, bit 0 timer 1 input
        bsf     trisc,ccp1  ;ccp1 pin input
        bcf     status,rp0  ;switch back to bank 0
        movlw   b'00000000' ;port B lines low
        movwf   portb
        bcf     intcon,7    ;disable global interrupts
        bcf     intcon,6    ;disable peripheral interrupts
        bsf     status,rp0  ;bank 1
        bcf     pie1,0      ;disable tmr1 interrupt
        bcf     pie1,2      ;disable ccp1 interrupt
        bcf     status,rp0  ;bank 0
        bcf     pir1,2      ;clear ccp1 interrupt flag
        clrf    ccp1con         ;ccp1 module off, clear ccp1 prescaler
        movlw   b'00000010' ;tmr1 prescaler and tmr1 setup,
        movwf   t1con       ;   tmr1 off
        clrf    tmr1h       ;clear timer 1 high
        clrf    tmr1l       ;clear timer 1 low, clear prescaler
        clrf    ccpr1h      ;clear capture register high
        clrf    ccpr1l      ;clear capture register low
        movlw   b'00000101' ;ccp1 prescaler mode,
        movwf   ccp1con     ;   ccp1 capture mode, ccp1 on
        bsf     intcon,7    ;enable global interrupts
        bsf     intcon,6    ;enable peripheral interrupts
        bsf     status,rp0  ;bank 1
        bsf     pie1,2      ;enable ccp1 interrupt
        bcf     status,rp0  ;bank 0
        bsf     t1con,0     ;timer 1 on
circle  goto    circle      ;done
;
iserv   bcf     pir1,2      ;clear ccp1 interrupt flag,
                            ;   enable further interrupts
        movf    ccpr1l,w    ;read capture register low
        movwf   portb       ;display captured count at port B
        retfie              ;return from interrupt
;
        end
;------------------------------------------------------------
;at blast time, select:
;       memory unprotected
;       watchdog timer disabled (default is enabled)
;       standard crystal (using 4 MHz osc for test) XT
;       power-up timer on
;       brown-out detect on
;============================================================
```

72

• Count Events Up To Predetermined Number And Generate An Output (compare)

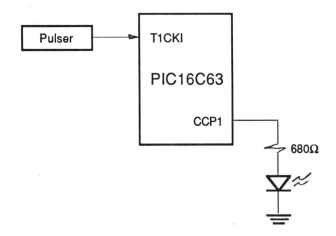

For the compare mode experiment, we will load the compare register (low byte) with a small number such as binary 8. The CCP1 pin must be configured as an output. We will input 8 rising edges via the T1CKI pin and that should trigger an output at the CCP1 pin (goes high), lighting the LED connected to it via a current limiting resistor. Remember that the T1CKI input pin must be high on reset. Try some other numbers to get a feel for how this works.

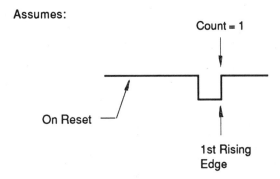

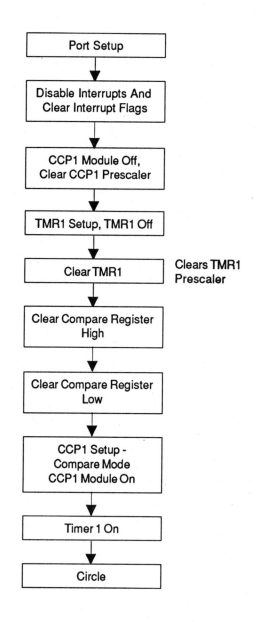

Port Setup

Disable Interrupts And
Clear Interrupt Flags

CCP1 Module Off,
Clear CCP1 Prescaler

TMR1 Setup, TMR1 Off

Clear TMR1 — Clears TMR1 Prescaler

Clear Compare Register
High

Clear Compare Register
Low

CCP1 Setup -
Compare Mode
CCP1 Module On

Timer 1 On

Circle

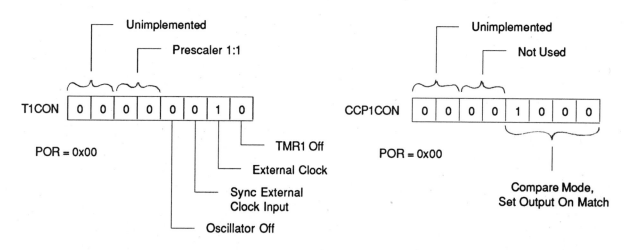

Unimplemented

Prescaler 1:1

T1CON | 0 | 0 | 0 | 0 | 0 | 0 | 1 | 0

POR = 0x00

TMR1 Off

External Clock

Sync External
Clock Input

Oscillator Off

Unimplemented

Not Used

CCP1CON | 0 | 0 | 0 | 0 | 1 | 0 | 0 | 0

POR = 0x00

Compare Mode,
Set Output On Match

DIP Switches

1 2 3 4 5 6 7

O C O C O C O

```
;======CMPR.ASM============================8/28/98==
        list    p=16c63
        radix   hex
;-------------------------------------------------------------
;timer 1 and ccp1 module - compare mode demo
;-------------------------------------------------------------
;       cpu equates (memory map)
status  equ     0x03
portc   equ     0x07
intcon  equ     0x0b
pir1    equ     0x0c
tmr1l   equ     0x0e
tmr1h   equ     0x0f
t1con   equ     0x10
ccpr1l  equ     0x15
ccpr1h  equ     0x16
ccp1con equ     0x17
trisc   equ     0x87
pie1    equ     0x8c
;-------------------------------------------------------------
;       bit equates
rp0     equ     5
ccp1    equ     2               ;ccp1 bit 2, port C
;-------------------------------------------------------------
        org     0x000
;
start   bsf     status,rp0      ;switch to bank 1
        bsf     trisc,0         ;port C, bit 0 timer 1 input
        bcf     trisc,ccp1      ;ccp1 pin output
        bcf     status,rp0      ;switch back to bank 0
        bcf     portc,ccp1      ;ccp1 pin low
        bcf     intcon,7        ;disable global interrupts
        bcf     intcon,6        ;disable peripheral interrupts
        bsf     status,rp0      ;bank 1
        bcf     pie1,0          ;disable timer 1 interrupts
        bcf     pie1,2          ;disable ccp1 interrupts
        bcf     status,rp0      ;bank 0
        clrf    ccp1con         ;ccp1 module off
        movlw   b'00000010'     ;tmr1 prescaler and tmr1 setup,
        movwf   t1con           ;   tmr1 off
        clrf    tmr1h           ;clear timer 1 high
        clrf    tmr1l           ;clear timer 1 low
        clrf    ccpr1h          ;clear compare register high
        movlw   d'8'            ;load compare register low with dec 8
        movwf   ccpr1l
        movlw   b'00001000'     ;ccp1 compare mode, ccp1 pin high
```

```
                            ;    on match, ccp module on,
                            ;    ccp1 pin low
        movwf   ccp1con
        bsf     t1con,0     ;timer 1 on
circle  goto    circle      ;done
;
        end
;----------------------------------------------------------
;at blast time, select:
;       memory unprotected
;       watchdog timer disabled (default is enabled)
;       standard crystal (using 4 MHz osc for test) XT
;       power-up timer on
;       brown-out detect on
;==========================================================
```

Single Time Interval Output (via TMR1 and CCP, compare mode)

• Start TMR1, Auto End

Single Long Pulse - 500 milliseconds

The clock input for TMR1 may be the internal instruction clock, an external clock connected to the T1CKI pin, or an external crystal (details on external crystal later). We will use the internal clock for this example. The output is via the CCP1 pin and an LED.

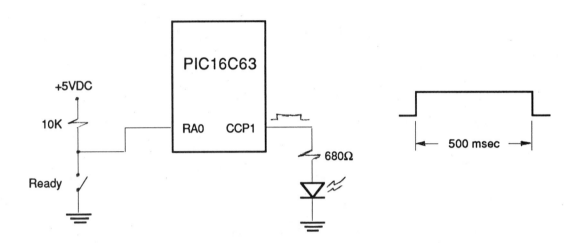

Generating a single time interval represented by a positive-going pulse output on the CCP1 pin requires some gymnastics. First, the CCP1 pin must be assigned as an output using the TRISC register. Second, when the CCP1 module is turned on (by writing the compare mode bit pattern to the CCP1CON register), the CCP1 pin is forced low (no matter what). To accomplish our objective, which is to indicate the start of the time interval with a rising edge, we will:

1) Load timer 1 with the value 0x0001.
2) Enable interrupts.
3) Load the CCP1CON register with the bit pattern 1000 (bits3,2,1,0) which puts the
    CCP1 module in the compare mode, calls for CCP1 pin high on match, turns on
    the CCP1 module, and causes the CCP1 pin to be low initially.
4) Start timer 1.

The arrival of the first pulse at the input of timer 1 will result in a match causing a CCP1 interrupt. The interrupt service routine will:

1) Clear the CCP1 interrupt flag.
2) Flip a bit in the CCP1CON register making it so the CCP1 pin will go low on
    the next match.
3) Load the compare registers.
4) Return from interrupt.

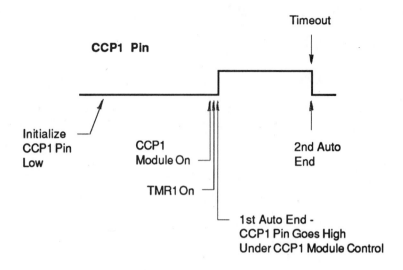

Timeout

CCP1 Pin

Initialize
CCP1 Pin
Low

CCP1
Module On

TMR1 On

1st Auto End -
CCP1 Pin Goes High
Under CCP1 Module Control

2nd Auto
End

Turning on the CCP1 module forces the CCP1 pin low (previously initialized low). Timer 1 starts counting and a match occurs as soon as the first clock pulse is received resulting in a CCP1 interrupt and forcing the CCP1 pin high. Timer 1 continues to be incremented. Bit 0 in the CCP1CON register is set by the interrupt service routine so that when the next match occurs, the CCP1 pin will be forced low. The interrupt service routine loads the compare registers with the desired value and then returns control to the main program. Timer 1 increments until a match occurs and the output pin (CCP1) goes low.

Notice that 3 internal clock cycles are used by the single pulse compare gymnastics. You can shave the value used for the second compare to compensate.

```
BCF    t1con,o              1 cycle
First pulse into TMR1        1 cycle
CCP1 pin goes high          1 cycle
Total                       3 cycles
```

Timer 1 is incremented until it's contents match the value stored in the compare register. This is how the duration of the time interval is controlled.

The desired time interval for this example is 500 milliseconds.
Use internal instruction clock, prescale 1:8.
8 microseconds x 62,500 = 500 milliseconds.

The hexadecimal number which represents decimal 62,500 is:

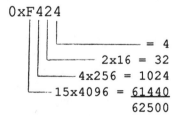

```
0xF424
              = 4
       2x16 = 32
      4x256 = 1024
    15x4096 = 61440
              62500
```

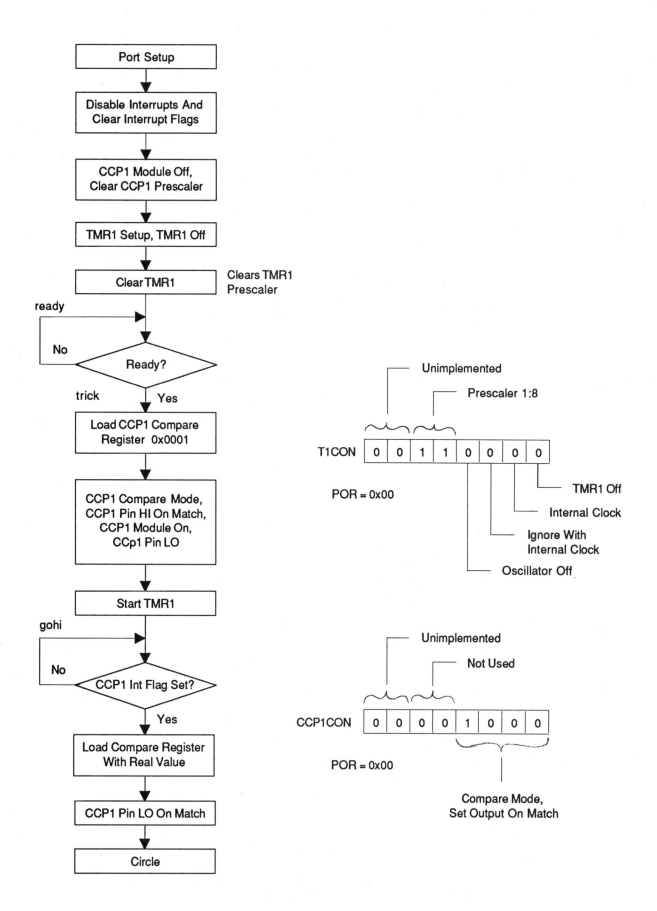

Port Setup

Disable Interrupts And
Clear Interrupt Flags

CCP1 Module Off,
Clear CCP1 Prescaler

TMR1 Setup, TMR1 Off

Clear TMR1 — Clears TMR1 Prescaler

ready

No

Ready?

trick   Yes

Load CCP1 Compare
Register 0x0001

CCP1 Compare Mode,
CCP1 Pin HI On Match,
CCP1 Module On,
CCp1 Pin LO

Start TMR1

gohi

No

CCP1 Int Flag Set?

Yes

Load Compare Register
With Real Value

CCP1 Pin LO On Match

Circle

Unimplemented

Prescaler 1:8

T1CON | 0 | 0 | 1 | 1 | 0 | 0 | 0 | 0 |

POR = 0x00

TMR1 Off

Internal Clock

Ignore With
Internal Clock

Oscillator Off

Unimplemented

Not Used

CCP1CON | 0 | 0 | 0 | 0 | 1 | 0 | 0 | 0 |

POR = 0x00

Compare Mode,
Set Output On Match

DIP Switches

```
1 2 3 4 5 6 7

C C O C C C O
|
└─ Closed On Reset
   Open When Ready
```

```
;======SNGL.ASM=====================================8/31/98==
        list    p=16c63
        radix   hex
;------------------------------------------------------------
;timer 1 and ccp1 module - single time interval demo
;------------------------------------------------------------
;       cpu equates (memory map)
status  equ     0x03
porta   equ     0x05
portc   equ     0x07
intcon  equ     0x0b
pir1    equ     0x0c
tmr1l   equ     0x0e
tmr1h   equ     0x0f
t1con   equ     0x10
ccpr1l  equ     0x15
ccpr1h  equ     0x16
ccp1con equ     0x17
trisa   equ     0x85
trisc   equ     0x87
pie1    equ     0x8c
;------------------------------------------------------------
;       bit equates
rp0     equ     5
ccp1    equ     2               ;ccp1 bit 2, port C
;------------------------------------------------------------
        org     0x000
;
start   bsf     status,rp0   ;switch to bank 1
        bcf     trisc,ccp1   ;ccp1 pin output
        bcf     status,rp0   ;switch back to bank 0
        bcf     portc,ccp1   ;ccp1 pin low
        bcf     intcon,7     ;disable global interrupts
        bcf     intcon,6     ;disable peripheral interrupts
        bsf     status,rp0   ;bank 1
        bcf     pie1,0       ;disable timer 1 interrupts
        bcf     pie1,2       ;disable ccp1 interrupts
        bcf     status,rp0   ;bank 0
        bcf     pir1,2       ;clear ccp1 interrupt flag
        clrf    ccp1con           ;ccp1 module off
        movlw   b'00110000'  ;tmr1 prescaler and tmr1 setup,
        movwf   t1con        ;    tmr1 off
        clrf    tmr1h        ;clear timer 1 high
```

```
        clrf    tmr1l           ;clear timer 1 low
ready   btfss   porta,0         ;ready?
        goto    ready           ;not yet
trick   clrf    ccpr1h          ;clear compare register high
        movlw   0x01            ;load compare register low
        movwf   ccpr1l
        movlw   b'00001000'     ;ccp1 compare mode, ccp1 pin high
        movwf   ccp1con         ;   on match, ccp1 module on,
                                ;   ccp1 pin low
        bsf     t1con,0         ;timer 1 on
gohi    btfss   pir1,2          ;ccp1 interrupt flag set?
        goto    gohi            ;not yet
        movlw   0xf4            ;load compare register high
        movwf   ccpr1h
        movlw   0x24            ;load compare register low
        movwf   ccpr1l
        bsf     ccp1con,0       ;ccp1 pin low on match
circle  goto    circle          ;done
;
        end
;--------------------------------------------------------------
;at blast time, select:
;       memory unprotected
;       watchdog timer disabled (default is enabled)
;       standard crystal (using 4 MHz osc for test) XT
;       power-up timer on
;       brown-out detect on
;==============================================================
```

Single Short Pulse - 128 microseconds

Let's go back to testing the '63. This time, we will use a 128 microsecond time interval and test the output using the '84 on a board running pgentst.asm.

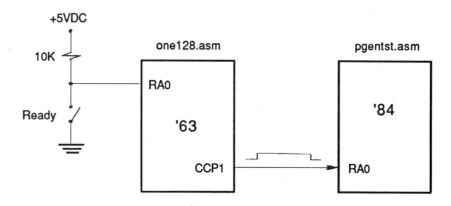

I found that the measurement result was always a little bit low. First, the 128 microsecond pulse generated may not be exactly 128 microseconds long because the program loop which tests TMR0, bit 7 may not be testing the bit at the very instant it is set. At the receiving end, the loops looking at the input may not detect the leading and trailing edges of the pulse at exactly the right time. For the 128 microsecond example, my readings were a mix of 123 and 126 microseconds. This error may or may not be significant, depending on the application. The longer the pulse, the less significant the error (few microseconds) becomes.

```
;=======ONE128.ASM==================================9/28/98==
        list    p=16c63
        radix   hex
;--------------------------------------------------------------
;timer 1 and ccp1 module - single time interval demo
;--------------------------------------------------------------
;       cpu equates (memory map)
status  equ     0x03
porta   equ     0x05
portc   equ     0x07
intcon  equ     0x0b
pir1    equ     0x0c
tmr1l   equ     0x0e
tmr1h   equ     0x0f
t1con   equ     0x10
ccpr1l  equ     0x15
ccpr1h  equ     0x16
ccp1con equ     0x17
trisa   equ     0x85
trisc   equ     0x87
pie1    equ     0x8c
;--------------------------------------------------------------
;       bit equates
rp0     equ     5
ccp1    equ     2               ;ccp1 bit 2, port C
;--------------------------------------------------------------
        org     0x000
;
start   bsf     status,rp0   ;switch to bank 1
        bsf     trisa,0      ;port A, bit 0 input
        bcf     trisc,ccp1   ;ccp1 pin output
        bcf     status,rp0   ;switch back to bank 0
        bcf     portc,ccp1   ;ccp1 pin low
        bcf     intcon,7     ;disable global interrupts
        bcf     intcon,6     ;disable peripheral interrupts
        bsf     status,rp0   ;bank 1
        bcf     pie1,0       ;disable timer 1 interrupts
        bcf     pie1,2       ;disable ccp1 interrupts
        bcf     status,rp0   ;bank 0
        bcf     pir1,2       ;clear ccp1 interrupt flag
        clrf    ccp1con      ;ccp1 module off
        movlw   b'00000000'  ;tmr1 prescaler and tmr1 setup,
        movwf   t1con        ;   tmr1 off
        clrf    tmr1h        ;clear timer 1 high
        clrf    tmr1l        ;clear timer 1 low
```

```
ready    btfss   porta,0     ;ready?
         goto ready          ;not yet
trick    clrf    ccpr1h      ;clear compare register high
         movlw   0x01        ;load compare register low
         movwf   ccpr1l
         movlw   b'00001000' ;ccp1 compare mode, ccp1 pin high
         movwf   ccp1con     ;   on match, ccp1 module on,
                             ;   ccp1 pin low
         bsf     t1con,0     ;timer 1 on
gohi     btfss   pir1,2      ;ccp1 interrupt flag set?
         goto    gohi        ;not yet
         movlw   0x00        ;load compare register high
         movwf   ccpr1h
         movlw   0x40        ;load compare register low
         movwf   ccpr1l
         bsf     ccp1con,0   ;ccp1 pin low on match
circle   goto    circle      ;done
;
         end
;-----------------------------------------------------------
;at blast time, select:
;       memory unprotected
;       watchdog timer disabled (default is enabled)
;       standard crystal (using 4 MHz osc for test) XT
;       power-up timer on
;       brown-out detect on
;===========================================================
```

Free Running Output (via TMR1 and CCP, compare mode)

• Clear TMR1 Each Cycle

Generating a free running output works in much the same way as creating the single interval in the example shown earlier. Here, the state of the output pin (CCP1) is changed every time the timer value matches the compare register value. Notice that the bit in the CCP1CON register which determines whether the CCP1 pin goes high or low on timeout must also be toggled.

Use internal instruction clock, prescale 1:8.
8 microseconds x 62,500 = 500 milliseconds.

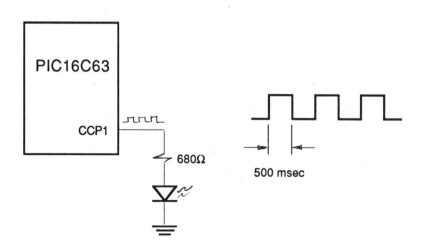

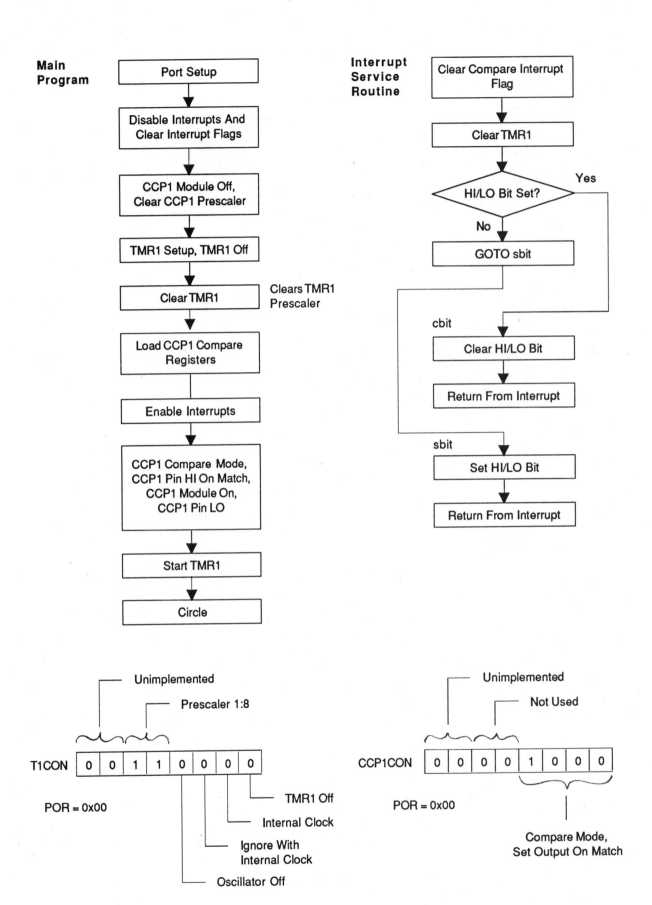

Main Program

Port Setup

↓

Disable Interrupts And Clear Interrupt Flags

↓

CCP1 Module Off, Clear CCP1 Prescaler

↓

TMR1 Setup, TMR1 Off

↓

Clear TMR1 — Clears TMR1 Prescaler

↓

Load CCP1 Compare Registers

↓

Enable Interrupts

↓

CCP1 Compare Mode, CCP1 Pin HI On Match, CCP1 Module On, CCP1 Pin LO

↓

Start TMR1

↓

Circle

Interrupt Service Routine

Clear Compare Interrupt Flag

↓

Clear TMR1

↓

HI/LO Bit Set? — Yes →

No ↓

GOTO sbit

cbit

Clear HI/LO Bit

↓

Return From Interrupt

sbit

Set HI/LO Bit

↓

Return From Interrupt

T1CON: | 0 | 0 | 1 | 1 | 0 | 0 | 0 | 0 |

Unimplemented
Prescaler 1:8
TMR1 Off
Internal Clock
Ignore With Internal Clock
Oscillator Off

POR = 0x00

CCP1CON: | 0 | 0 | 0 | 0 | 1 | 0 | 0 | 0 |

Unimplemented
Not Used
Compare Mode, Set Output On Match

POR = 0x00

DIP Switches

```
1 2 3 4 5 6 7

C C O C C C O
│
└── Closed On Reset
    Open When Ready
```

```
;======FREE.ASM===================================8/28/98==
        list    p=16c63
        radix   hex
;---------------------------------------------------------
;timer 1 and ccp1 module - free running compare mode demo
;---------------------------------------------------------
;       cpu equates (memory map)
status  equ     0x03
portc   equ     0x07
intcon  equ     0x0b
pir1    equ     0x0c
tmr1l   equ     0x0e
tmr1h   equ     0x0f
t1con   equ     0x10
ccpr1l  equ     0x15
ccpr1h  equ     0x16
ccp1con equ     0x17
trisc   equ     0x87
pie1    equ     0x8c
;---------------------------------------------------------
;       bit equates
rp0     equ     5
ccp1    equ     2               ;ccp1 bit 2, port C
;---------------------------------------------------------
        org     0x000
        goto    start           ;skip over location pointed to by
                                ;   interrupt vector
        org     0x004
        goto    iserv
;
start   bsf     status,rp0      ;switch to bank 1
        bcf     trisc,ccp1      ;ccp1 pin output
        bcf     status,rp0      ;switch back to bank 0
        bcf     portc,ccp1      ;ccp1 pin low
        bcf     intcon,7        ;disable global interrupts
        bcf     intcon,6        ;disable peripheral interrupts
        bsf     status,rp0      ;bank 1
        bcf     pie1,0          ;disable timer 1 interrupts
        bcf     pie1,2          ;disable ccp1 interrupts
        bcf     status,rp0      ;bank 0
        bcf     pir1,2          ;clear ccp1 interrupt flag
        clrf    ccp1con         ;ccp1 module off
        movlw   b'00110000'     ;tmr1 prescaler and tmr1 setup,
```

```
        movwf    t1con        ;    tmr1 off
        clrf     tmr1h        ;clear timer 1 high
        clrf     tmr1l        ;clear timer 1 low
        movlw    0xf4         ;load compare register high
        movwf    ccpr1h
        movlw    0x24         ;load compare register low
        movwf    ccpr1l
        bsf      intcon,7     ;enable global interrupts
        bsf      intcon,6     ;enable peripheral interrupts
        bsf      status,rp0   ;bank 1
        bsf      pie1,2       ;enable ccp1 compare interrupt
        bcf      status,rp0   ;bank 0
        movlw    b'00001000'  ;ccp1 compare mode, ccp1 pin high
        movwf    ccp1con      ;    on match, ccp1 module on,
                              ;    ccp1 pin low
        bsf      t1con,0      ;timer 1 on
circle  goto     circle       ;done
;
iserv   bcf      pir1,2       ;clear ccp1 interrupt flag,
                              ;    enable further interrupts
        clrf     tmr1h        ;clear timer 1 high
        clrf     tmr1l        ;clear timer 1 low
        btfss    ccp1con,0    ;control bit status?
        goto     sbit         ;bit is clear
cbit    bcf      ccp1con,0    ;clear control bit
        retfie                ;return from interrupt
sbit    bsf      ccp1con,0    ;set control bit
        retfie                ;return from interrupt
;
        end
;------------------------------------------------------------
;at blast time, select:
;       memory unprotected
;       watchdog timer disabled (default is enabled)
;       standard crystal (using 4 MHz osc for test) XT
;       power-up timer on
;       brown-out detect on
;============================================================
```

Free Running Output (via TMR1 and CCP, compare mode)

• Free Running TMR1, Add Interval Value To Compare Register Each Cycle

This example is useful in situations where timer 1 is used for more than one application simultaneously. The free running output is initiated by reading TMR1 while it is running, adding the time interval value to the TMR1 reading, and storing the result in the compare register. From then on, the interval value is added to the compare register contents each time a CCP1 interrupt occurs. We will use the subroutine for reading timer 1 while it is running and double precision addition.

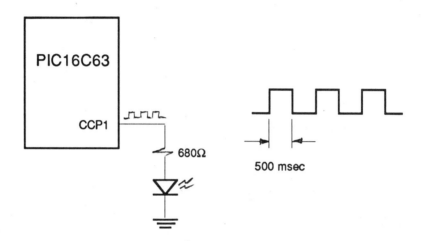

Since you are getting used to this stuff by now, the flow charts will be less detailed.

Main Program

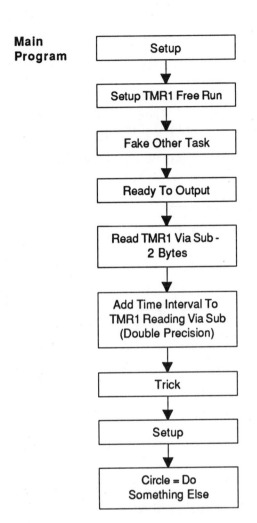

Setup

↓

Setup TMR1 Free Run

↓

Fake Other Task

↓

Ready To Output

↓

Read TMR1 Via Sub - 2 Bytes

↓

Add Time Interval To TMR1 Reading Via Sub (Double Precision)

↓

Trick

↓

Setup

↓

Circle = Do Something Else

Interrupt Service Routine

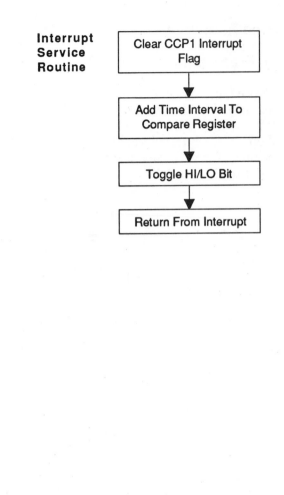

Clear CCP1 Interrupt Flag

↓

Add Time Interval To Compare Register

↓

Toggle HI/LO Bit

↓

Return From Interrupt

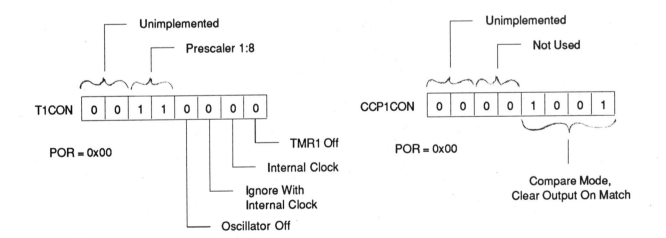

Unimplemented

Prescaler 1:8

T1CON | 0 | 0 | 1 | 1 | 0 | 0 | 0 | 0 |

POR = 0x00

TMR1 Off

Internal Clock

Ignore With Internal Clock

Oscillator Off

Unimplemented

Not Used

CCP1CON | 0 | 0 | 0 | 0 | 1 | 0 | 0 | 1 |

POR = 0x00

Compare Mode, Clear Output On Match

DIP Switches

1 2 3 4 5 6 7

O C O C C C O

```
;=======FREEADD.ASM================================9/1/98==
        list    p=16c63
        radix   hex
;------------------------------------------------------------
;timer 1 and ccp1 module - free running compare mode demo
;    read timer 1 on-the-fly
;------------------------------------------------------------
;       cpu equates (memory map)
status  equ     0x03
portc   equ     0x07
intcon  equ     0x0b
pir1    equ     0x0c
tmr1l   equ     0x0e
tmr1h   equ     0x0f
t1con   equ     0x10
ccpr1l  equ     0x15
ccpr1h  equ     0x16
ccp1con equ     0x17
trisc   equ     0x87
pie1    equ     0x8c
t1_hi   equ     0x20
t1_lo   equ     0x21
lsb2    equ     0x22
msb2    equ     0x23
int_hi  equ     0x24
int_lo  equ     0x25
;------------------------------------------------------------
;       bit equates
c       equ     0
z       equ     2
rp0     equ     5
ccp1    equ     2               ;ccp1 bit 2, port C
;------------------------------------------------------------
        org     0x000
        goto    start           ;skip over location pointed to by
                                ;    interrupt vector
        org     0x004
        goto    iserv
;
start   bsf     status,rp0      ;switch to bank 1
        bcf     trisc,ccp1      ;ccp1 pin output
        bcf     status,rp0      ;switch back to bank 0
        bcf     portc,ccp1      ;ccp1 pin low
        bcf     intcon,7        ;disable global interrupts
        bcf     intcon,6        ;disable peripheral interrupts
        bsf     status,rp0      ;bank 1
```

```
        bcf     pie1,0          ;disable timer 1 interrupts
        bcf     pie1,2          ;disable ccp1 interrupts
        bcf     status,rp0      ;bank 0
        bcf     pir1,2          ;clear ccp1 interrupt flag
        clrf    ccp1con         ;ccp1 module off
        movlw   b'00110000'     ;tmr1 prescaler and tmr1 setup,
        movwf   t1con           ;   tmr1 off
        clrf    tmr1h           ;clear timer 1 high
        clrf    tmr1l           ;clear timer 1 low
        bsf     t1con,0         ;timer 1 on
        nop                     ;fake do something else
        nop
        nop                     ;ready to output
        call    read            ;read timer 1 on-the-fly
        movlw   0xf4            ;add interval to timer 1 reading
        movwf   msb2            ;load interval high
        movlw   0x24            ;load interval low
        movwf   lsb2
dblplus movf    t1_lo,w         ;fetch timer 1 reading low
        addwf   lsb2,f          ;add low bytes, result in lsb2
        btfsc   status,c        ;carry set?
        incf    msb2,f          ;yes, add 1 to msb result
        movf    t1_hi,w         ;fetch timer 1 reading high
        addwf   msb2,f          ;add high bytes, result in msb2
trick   clrf    ccpr1h          ;clear compare register high
        movlw   0x01            ;load compare register low
        movwf   ccpr1l
        movlw   b'00001000'     ;ccp1 compare mode, ccp1 pin high
        movwf   ccp1con         ;   on match, ccp1 module on,
                                ;   ccp1 pin low
gohi    btfss   pir1,2          ;ccp1 interrupt flag set?
        goto    gohi            ;not yet
        movf    msb2,w          ;load compare register high
        movwf   ccpr1h
        movf    lsb2,w          ;load compare register low
        movwf   ccpr1l
        bsf     ccp1con,0       ;ccp1 pin low on match
        bsf     intcon,7        ;enable global interrupts
        bsf     intcon,6        ;enable peripheral interrupts
        bsf     status,rp0      ;bank 1
        bsf     pie1,2          ;enable ccp1 compare interrupt
        bcf     status,rp0      ;bank 0
circle  goto    circle          ;done
;-----------------------------------------------------------
;note that interrupts must be disabled when using the
;   read subroutine
read    movf    tmr1h,w         ;read high byte
        movwf   t1_hi           ;store
        movf    tmr1l,w         ;read low byte
        movwf   t1_lo           ;store
        movf    tmr1h,w         ;read high byte again
        subwf   t1_hi,w         ;subtract first read from second read
        btfsc   status,z        ;is result 0?
        return                  ;read valid
```

```
        movf    tmr1h,w    ;rollover occured, read high byte again
        movwf   t1_hi      ;store
        movf    tmr1l,w    ;read low byte
        movwf   t1_lo      ;store
        return
;-------------------------------------------------------------
iserv   bcf     pir1,2     ;clear ccp1 interrupt flag,
                           ;   enable further interrupts
        movlw   0xf4       ;load interval high
        movwf   int_hi
        movlw   0x24       ;load interval low
        movwf   int_lo
dbladd  movf    int_lo,w   ;fetch interval low
        addwf   lsb2,f     ;add low bytes, result in lsb2
        btfsc   status,c   ;carry set?
        incf    msb2,f     ;yes, add 1 to msb result
        movf    int_hi,w   ;fetch interval high
        addwf   msb2,f     ;add high bytes, result in msb2
        movf    msb2,w     ;load compare register high
        movwf   ccpr1h
        movf    lsb2,w     ;load compare register low
        movwf   ccpr1l
        btfss   ccp1con,0  ;control bit status?
        goto    sbit       ;bit is clear
cbit    bcf     ccp1con,0  ;clear control bit
        nop                ;delay 1 cycle to equalize paths
        retfie             ;return from interrupt
sbit    bsf     ccp1con,0  ;set control bit
        retfie             ;return from interrupt
;-------------------------------------------------------------
        end
;-------------------------------------------------------------
;at blast time, select:
;       memory unprotected
;       watchdog timer disabled (default is enabled)
;       standard crystal (using 4 MHz osc for test) XT
;       power-up timer on
;       brown-out detect on
;=============================================================
```

Time Measurement (period/interval/time between events)

• Via TMR1 Read

An unknown time interval may be measured by using the time interval signal to gate a second signal of known frequency.

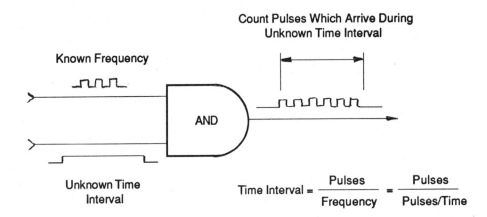

The signal of known frequency will appear at the output of the AND gate only while both signals are high. The pulses appearing at the output of the AND gate are then counted. The number of pulses divided by the frequency (multiplied by the period) of the reference signal is the time interval.

A time interval generated by some circuit external to a PIC16C63 may be measured using timer 1. The time interval might be the time between two pulses or the time a single pulse is high. For this experiment, we will use a PIC16F84 to generate a single pulse of known length and use timer 1 in a PIC16C63 to measure the time it is high.

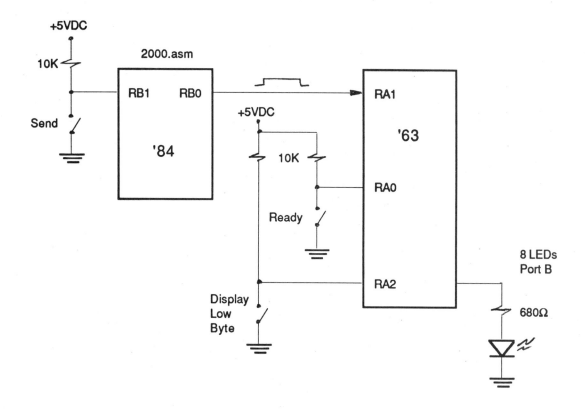

The selection of numbers used here is arbitrary. We will use a time interval of 2000 microseconds generated by a PIC16F84. The circuit and software are in the chapter Test Equipment For Timing And Counting Experiments.

The internal clock of the PIC16C63 will be used as the signal of known frequency (1 MHz, period 1 microsecond). The internal clock pulses will be fed into timer 1 (prescaler 1:1) during the time the port line connected to the '84 is high. A "ready" switch will be used so that measurement does not begin until everything is stable. The program displays the timer 1 high byte at the port B LEDs as soon as the measurement is complete. The timer 1 low byte may subsequently be displayed by opening the "display low byte" switch.

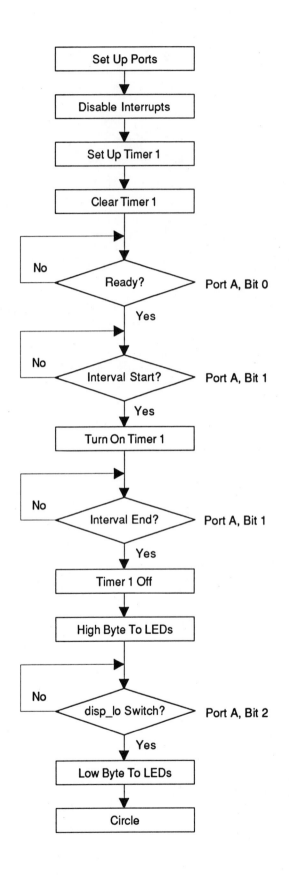

```
                Unimplemented
                    Prescaler 1:1                         DIP Switches

                                                     1 2 3 4 5 6 7
     T1CON  0  0  0  0  0  0  0  0                    C O C C C C C

     POR = 0x00                                                    Closed On Reset
                                             TMR1 Off              Open To Display Low Byte

                                    Internal Clock

                              Ignore With
                              Internal Clock              Closed On Reset
                                                          Open When Ready
                        Oscillator Off
```

```
;=======PERIOD.ASM=====================================9/3/98==
        list    p=16c63
        radix   hex
;--------------------------------------------------------------
;period measurement demo
;       internal clock, prescaler 1:1
;--------------------------------------------------------------
;       cpu equates (memory map)
status  equ     0x03
porta   equ     0x05
portb   equ     0x06
intcon  equ     0x0b
pir1    equ     0x0c
tmr1l   equ     0x0e
tmr1h   equ     0x0f
t1con   equ     0x10
trisa   equ     0x85
trisb   equ     0x86
pie1    equ     0x8c
;--------------------------------------------------------------
;       bit equates
rp0     equ     5
;--------------------------------------------------------------
        org     0x000
;
start   bsf     status,rp0  ;switch to bank 1
        movlw   b'00000000' ;port B outputs
        movwf   trisb
        movlw   b'00011111' ;port A inputs
        movwf   trisa
        bcf     status,rp0  ;switch back to bank 0
        movlw   b'00000000' ;port B lines low
        movwf   portb
        bcf     intcon,7    ;disable global interrupts
        bcf     intcon,6    ;disable peripheral interrupts
        bsf     status,rp0  ;bank 1
        bcf     pie1,0      ;disable tmr1 interrupt
        bcf     status,rp0  ;bank 0
```

```
            bcf       pir1,0        ;clear tmr1 interrupt flag
            movlw     b'00000000'   ;prescaler and tmr1 setup,
            movwf     t1con         ;   tmr1 off
            clrf      tmr1h         ;clear timer 1 high
            clrf      tmr1l         ;clear timer 1 low, clear prescaler
ready       btfss     porta,0       ;ready?
            goto      ready
istart      btfss     porta,1       ;watch for rising edge
            goto      istart
            bsf       t1con,0       ;timer 1 on
iend        btfsc     porta,1       ;watch for falling edge
            goto      iend
            bcf       t1con,0       ;timer 1 off
            movf      tmr1h,w       ;get timer 1 high
            movwf     portb         ;display via port B LEDs
disp_lo     btfss     porta,2       ;watch display low byte switch
            goto      disp_lo
            movf      tmr1l,w       ;get timer 1 low
            movwf     portb         ;display via port B LEDs
circle      goto      circle        ;done
;
            end
;------------------------------------------------------------
;at blast time, select:
;      memory unprotected
;      watchdog timer disabled (default is enabled)
;      standard crystal (using 4 MHz osc for test) XT
;      power-up timer on
;      brown-out detect on
;============================================================
```

Procedure:

1) In preparation for power-up:
    A) "Ready" switch on '63 closed.
    B) "Display low byte" switch on '63 closed
    C) "Send" switch on '84 closed.
2) Power-up both '84 and '63.
3) Open the "ready" switch on the '63.
4) Open the "send" switch on '84.
5) The high byte will be displayed on the '63 LEDs.
6) Open the "display low byte" switch on the '63.
7) The low byte will be displayed on the '63 LEDs.

Decoding result:

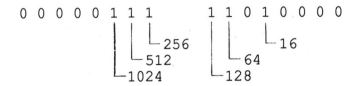

```
      Total: 2000
```

• TMR1 And CCP, Capture Mode

A time interval may be measured using another technique. Timer 1 may be in the free run mode. The time interval signal is fed into the CCP1 pin and used to capture the time values from timer 1 at the start and end of the time interval.

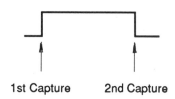

1st Capture   2nd Capture

The first capture is on a rising edge and the second is on a falling edge.

Timer 1 is merrily doing it's thing when the captures occur.

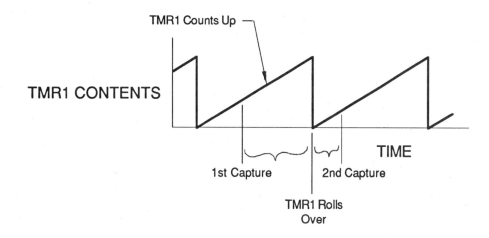

Timer 1 will be part of the way to a full count when the first capture occurs. We are really interested in obtaining the time remaining to rollover. This can be obtained by complementing the captured value. Complementing a value means changing all the 1s to 0s and visa versa. The result is the complement of the value and is equal to the difference between the value and 0xFFFF for a 16-bit number. There is an instruction COMF which does this.

The complement of the first capture value is added to second capture value. The second value captured represents the time from rollover to the second capture. The result is the number of pulses corresponding to the time interval between the two captures.

Two flags are used, one to indicate that the first capture has occurred and the other to indicate that the task has been completed.

The objectives for the interrupt service routine are:

- Read timer 1 on-the-fly - 1st capture and 2nd capture.
- Determine whether or not timer 1 overflowed between captures.
- Clear the timer 1 overflow flag after the first capture.
- When a CCP1 interrupt occurs, determine which edge (rising or falling, first or second) caused the interrupt.
- When the first edge is detected, set the 1st capture flag and store the count value.
- When the second edge is detected, set the 2nd capture flag, store the count value and do the math = calculate the time interval.

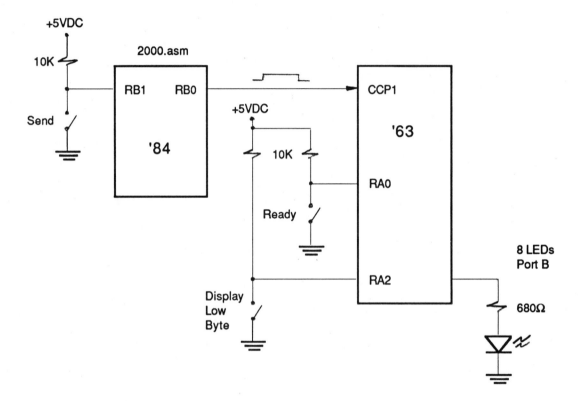

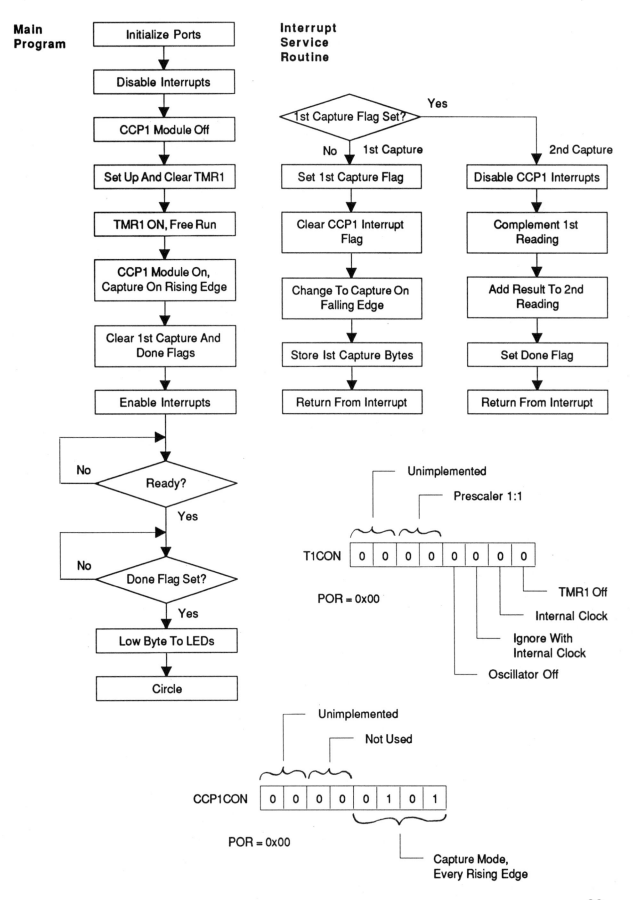

Main Program

Initialize Ports

Disable Interrupts

CCP1 Module Off

Set Up And Clear TMR1

TMR1 ON, Free Run

CCP1 Module On, Capture On Rising Edge

Clear 1st Capture And Done Flags

Enable Interrupts

Ready? — No

Yes

Done Flag Set? — No

Yes

Low Byte To LEDs

Circle

Interrupt Service Routine

1st Capture Flag Set?

No — 1st Capture

Yes — 2nd Capture

1st Capture:
Set 1st Capture Flag

Clear CCP1 Interrupt Flag

Change To Capture On Falling Edge

Store Ist Capture Bytes

Return From Interrupt

2nd Capture:
Disable CCP1 Interrupts

Complement 1st Reading

Add Result To 2nd Reading

Set Done Flag

Return From Interrupt

T1CON | 0 | 0 | 0 | 0 | 0 | 0 | 0 | 0 |

Unimplemented

Prescaler 1:1

POR = 0x00

TMR1 Off
Internal Clock
Ignore With Internal Clock
Oscillator Off

CCP1CON | 0 | 0 | 0 | 0 | 0 | 1 | 0 | 1 |

Unimplemented

Not Used

POR = 0x00

Capture Mode, Every Rising Edge

DIP Switches

```
1 2 3 4 5 6 7

C C C C C C C
```

Closed On Reset
Open To Display Low Byte

Closed On Reset
Open When Ready

```
;======PDCCP.ASM================================9/8/98==
        list    p=16c63
        radix   hex
;-----------------------------------------------------------
;timer 1 and ccp1 module - period measurement demo
;   timer 1 free running
;   capture at start and end of period pulse
;-----------------------------------------------------------
;       cpu equates (memory map)
status  equ     0x03
porta   equ     0x05
portb   equ     0x06
portc   equ     0x07
intcon  equ     0x0b
pir1    equ     0x0c
tmr1l   equ     0x0e
tmr1h   equ     0x0f
t1con   equ     0x10
ccpr1l  equ     0x15
ccpr1h  equ     0x16
ccp1con equ     0x17
trisa   equ     0x85
trisb   equ     0x86
trisc   equ     0x87
pie1    equ     0x8c
one_hi  equ     0x20
one_lo  equ     0x21
lsb2    equ     0x22
msb2    equ     0x23
flags   equ     0x24            ;1st capture flag bit 0
                                ;   done flag bit 1
;-----------------------------------------------------------
;       bit equates
c       equ     0
z       equ     2
rp0     equ     5
ccp1    equ     2               ;ccp1 bit 2, port C
;-----------------------------------------------------------
        org     0x000
        goto    start           ;skip over location pointed to by
```

```
                          ;    interrupt vector
        org     0x004
        goto    iserv
;
start   bsf     status,rp0      ;switch to bank 1
        movlw   b'00000000'     ;port B outputs
        movwf   trisb
        movlw   b'00011111'     ;port A inputs
        movwf   trisa
        bsf     trisc,ccp1      ;ccp1 pin input
        bcf     status,rp0      ;switch back to bank 0
        movlw   b'00000000'     ;port B lines low
        movwf   portb
        bcf     intcon,7        ;disable global interrupts
        bcf     intcon,6        ;disable peripheral interrupts
        bsf     status,rp0      ;bank 1
        bcf     pie1,0          ;disable timer 1 interrupts
        bcf     pie1,2          ;disable ccp1 interrupts
        bcf     status,rp0      ;bank 0
        bcf     pir1,2          ;clear ccp1 interrupt flag
        clrf    ccp1con         ;ccp1 module off
        movlw   b'00000000'     ;tmr1 prescaler and tmr1 setup,
        movwf   t1con           ;   tmr1 off
        clrf    tmr1h           ;clear timer 1 high
        clrf    tmr1l           ;clear timer 1 low
        bsf     t1con,0         ;timer 1 on, free running
        movlw   b'00000101'     ;capture on rising edge, ccp1
        movwf   ccp1con         ;   module on
        clrf    flags           ;clear 1st capture and done flags
        bsf     intcon,7        ;enable global interrupts
        bsf     intcon,6        ;enable peripheral interrupts
        bsf     status,rp0      ;bank 1
        bsf     pie1,2          ;enable ccp1 interrupts
        bcf     status,rp0      ;bank 0
ready   btfss   porta,0         ;ready?
        goto    ready
done    btfss   flags,1         ;done?
        goto    done
        movf    msb2,w          ;get period high
        movwf   portb           ;display via port B LEDs
disp_lo btfss   porta,2         ;watch display low byte switch
        goto    disp_lo
        movf    lsb2,w          ;get period low
        movwf   portb           ;display via port B LEDs
circle  goto    circle          ;done
;--------------------------------------------------------------
iserv   btfsc   flags,0         ;1st capture flag set?
        goto    cap2            ;yes, goto 2nd capture
        bsf     flags,0         ;no, set 1st capture flag
        bcf     pir1,2          ;clear ccp1 interrupt flag,
                                ;   enable second interrupt
        bcf     ccp1con,0       ;second capture on falling edge
        movf    ccpr1h,w        ;get 1st capture high
        movwf   one_hi          ;store
```

```
        movf    ccpr11,w    ;get 1st capture low
        movwf   one_lo      ;store
        retfie
cap2    bsf     status,rp0  ;bank 1
        bcf     pie1,2      ;disable ccp1 interrupts
        bcf     status,rp0  ;bank 0
        comf    one_hi,f    ;complement 1st capture high
        comf    one_lo,f    ;complement 1st capture low
        movf    ccpr1h,w    ;get 2nd capture high
        movwf   msb2        ;store
        movf    ccpr11,w    ;get 2nd capture low
        movwf   lsb2        ;store
dblplus movf    one_lo,w    ;fetch complement of 1st low
        addwf   lsb2,f      ;add low bytes, result in lsb2
        btfsc   status,c    ;carry set?
        incf    msb2,f      ;yes, add 1 to msb result
        movf    one_hi,w    ;fetch complement of 1st high
        addwf   msb2,f      ;add high bytes, result in msb2
        bsf     flags,1     ;set "done" flag
        retfie
;-----------------------------------------------------------
        end
;-----------------------------------------------------------
;at blast time, select:
;       memory unprotected
;       watchdog timer disabled (default is enabled)
;       standard crystal (using 4 MHz osc for test) XT
;       power-up timer on
;       brown-out detect on
;===========================================================
```

Procedure:

1) In preparation for power-up:
    A) "Ready" switch on '63 closed.
    B) "Display low byte" switch on '63 closed
    C) "Send" switch on '84 closed.
2) Power-up both '84 and '63.
3) Open the "ready" switch on the '63.
4) Open the "send" switch on '84.
5) The high byte will be displayed on the '63 LEDs.
6) Open the "display low byte" switch on the '63.
7) The low byte will be displayed on the '63 LEDs.

The result will be the same as for the previous example.

Frequency Measurement (via TMR1 and CCP, gate via TMR0)

Measuring frequency is the flip side of measuring a time interval. Frequency may be measured by using the known time interval signal to gate a second signal of unknown frequency.

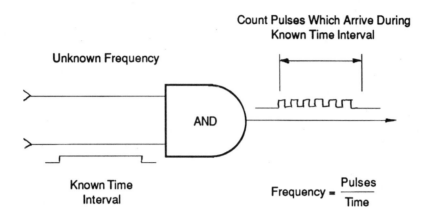

The signal of unknown frequency will appear at the output of the AND gate only while both signals are high. The pulses appearing at the output of the AND gate are then counted. The number of pulses divided by the time interval is the frequency.

The frequency of a signal generated by some circuit external to a PIC16C63 may be measured using timer 1. For this experiment, we will use a PIC16F84 to generate a signal of "unknown" frequency and use timer 1 in a PIC16C63 to measure that frequency.

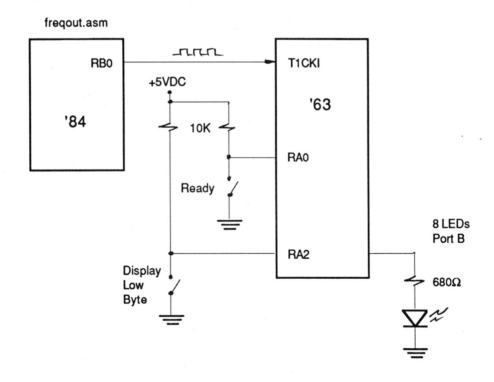

Again the selection of numbers used here is arbitrary. We will use a frequency of 100 KHz generated by a PIC16F84. This is done using a very simple program involving software time delays (freqout.asm).

In the PIC16C63, we will use timer 0 to generate a sample time of 0.1 second which should result in 10,000 pulses being counted by timer 1. Using a timer 1 prescaler value of 1:1 will result in maximum resolution.

Since timer 0 is an 8-bit counter, it will roll over every 256 counts. We will need a file register counter to count TMR0 rollovers.

$$\frac{100,000}{256} = 390.625 \text{ TMR0 rollovers}$$

$$390.625 - 256 = 134.625 \qquad .625 \times 256 = 160$$

The file register counter will count up to 255 and roll over on the next count. We will have the program watch for this to happen and then look for the file register counter to reach 134 as it counts up the second time. Next, the program will look to see when the count in TMR0 reaches 160. It will do this by watching bit 7 to be set (128), followed by watching for bit 5 to be set (32). The sum of 128 and 32 is 160.

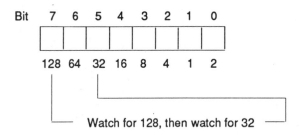

There are, of course, other ways to do this. This method does not require use of interrupts and uses a minimum of program steps once the final count in TMR0 is reached (source of error).

To review, the program will:

- Clear TMR1.
- Start TMR1, count signal pulses coming from the '84.
- Do timing via 256 TMR0 rollovers, 134 more TMR0 rollovers, 160 TMR0 counts.
- Stop TMR1.
- Read TMR1.
- Display TMR1 high byte.
- Display TMR1 low byte when "display low byte" switch is opened.

The frequency is the number of pulses counted by timer 1 during the 0.1 second sample period times 10.

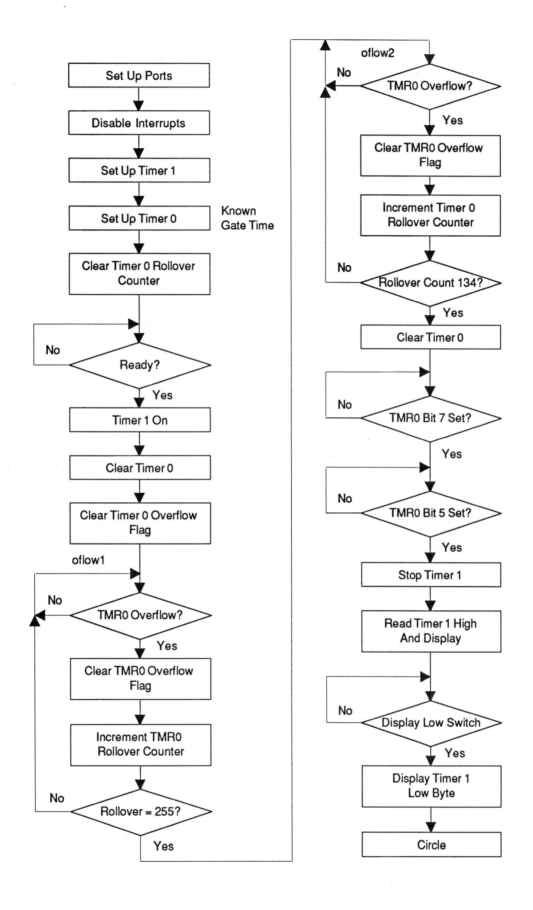

Set Up Ports

Disable Interrupts

Set Up Timer 1

Set Up Timer 0 — Known Gate Time

Clear Timer 0 Rollover Counter

Ready? — No / Yes

Timer 1 On

Clear Timer 0

Clear Timer 0 Overflow Flag

oflow1

TMR0 Overflow? — No / Yes

Clear TMR0 Overflow Flag

Increment TMR0 Rollover Counter

Rollover = 255? — No / Yes

oflow2

TMR0 Overflow? — No / Yes

Clear TMR0 Overflow Flag

Increment Timer 0 Rollover Counter

Rollover Count 134? — No / Yes

Clear Timer 0

TMR0 Bit 7 Set? — No / Yes

TMR0 Bit 5 Set? — No / Yes

Stop Timer 1

Read Timer 1 High And Display

Display Low Switch — No / Yes

Display Timer 1 Low Byte

Circle

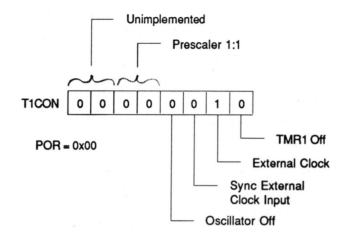

Unimplemented

Prescaler 1:1

T1CON | 0 | 0 | 0 | 0 | 0 | 0 | 1 | 0 |

POR = 0x00

TMR1 Off

External Clock

Sync External
Clock Input

Oscillator Off

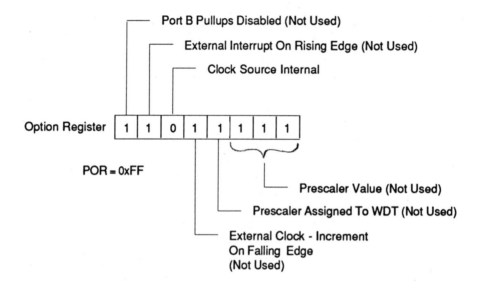

Port B Pullups Disabled (Not Used)

External Interrupt On Rising Edge (Not Used)

Clock Source Internal

Option Register | 1 | 1 | 0 | 1 | 1 | 1 | 1 | 1 |

POR = 0xFF

Prescaler Value (Not Used)

Prescaler Assigned To WDT (Not Used)

External Clock - Increment
On Falling Edge
(Not Used)

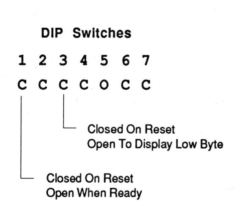

DIP Switches

1 2 3 4 5 6 7

C C C C O C C

Closed On Reset
Open To Display Low Byte

Closed On Reset
Open When Ready

106

```
;=======FREQ.ASM====================================9/10/98==
          list    p=16c63
          radix   hex
;-----------------------------------------------------------
;frequency measurement demo
;         gate via tmr0, internal clock, prescaler 1:1
;-----------------------------------------------------------
;         cpu equates (memory map)
tmr0      equ     0x01
status    equ     0x03
porta     equ     0x05
portb     equ     0x06
intcon    equ     0x0b
tmr1l     equ     0x0e
tmr1h     equ     0x0f
t1con     equ     0x10
opt       equ     0x81
trisa     equ     0x85
trisb     equ     0x86
trisc     equ     0x87
pie1      equ     0x8c
count     equ     0x20
;-----------------------------------------------------------
;         bit equates
z         equ     2
rp0       equ     5
;-----------------------------------------------------------
          org     0x000
;
start     bsf     status,rp0  ;switch to bank 1
          movlw   b'00000000' ;port B outputs
          movwf   trisb
          movlw   b'00011111' ;port A inputs
          movwf   trisa
          bsf     trisc,0         ;port C, bit 0 input, tmr1 input
          bcf     status,rp0  ;switch back to bank 0
          movlw   b'00000000' ;port B lines low
          movwf   portb
          bcf     intcon,7    ;disable global interrupts
          bcf     intcon,6    ;disable peripheral interrupts
          bcf     intcon,5    ;disable timer 0 interrupts
          bsf     status,rp0  ;bank 1
          bcf     pie1,0      ;disable tmr1 interrupt
          bcf     status,rp0  ;bank 0
          movlw   b'00000010' ;prescaler and tmr1 setup,
          movwf   t1con       ;    tmr1 off
          clrf    tmr1h       ;clear timer 1 high
          clrf    tmr1l       ;clear timer 1 low, clear prescaler
          clrf    tmr0        ;clear timer 0
          clrwdt              ;clr WDT, prep prescaler assign
          bsf     status,rp0  ;bank 1
          movlw   b'11011111' ;set up timer 0
          movwf   opt
```

```
          bcf       status,rp0    ;bank 0
          clrf      count         ;clear tmr0 rollover counter
ready     btfss     porta,0       ;ready?
          goto      ready
          bsf       t1con,0       ;turn on timer 1
          clrf      tmr0          ;clear timer 0
          bcf       intcon,2      ;clear timer 0 interrupt flag
oflow1    btfss     intcon,2      ;timer 0 overflow?
          goto      oflow1        ;not yet
          bcf       intcon,2      ;clear timer 0 interrupt flag
          incf      count,f       ;inc timer 0 overflow counter
          movf      count,w       ;compare
          sublw     0xff          ;decimal 255
          btfss     status,z      ;test z flag, skip next instruction
                                  ;   if flag is set
          goto      oflow1        ;again
oflow2    btfss     intcon,2      ;timer 0 overflow?
          goto      oflow2        ;not yet
          bcf       intcon,2      ;clear tmr0 interrupt flag
          incf      count,f       ;inc timer 0 overflow counter
          movf      count,w       ;compare
          sublw     0x86          ;decimal 134
          btfss     status,z      ;test z flag, skip next instruction
                                  ;   if flag is set
          goto      oflow2        ;again
          clrf      tmr0          ;clear timer 0
t128      btfss     tmr0,7        ;look for timer 1=128
          goto      t128
t32       btfss     tmr0,5        ;look for timer 1=32 (128+32=160)
          goto      t32
          bcf       t1con,0       ;stop timer 1
          movf      tmr1h,w       ;get timer 1 high
          movwf     portb         ;display via port B LEDs
disp_lo   btfss     porta,2       ;watch display low byte switch
          goto      disp_lo
          movf      tmr1l,w       ;get timer 1 low
          movwf     portb         ;display via port B LEDs
circle    goto      circle        ;done
;
          end
;----------------------------------------------------------------
;at blast time, select:
;      memory unprotected
;      watchdog timer disabled (default is enabled)
;      standard crystal (using 4 MHz osc for test) XT
;      power-up timer on
;      brown-out detect on
;================================================================
```

Procedure:

1) In preparation for power-up:
    A) "Ready" switch on '63 closed.
    B) "Display low byte" switch on '63 closed
2) Power-up both '84 and '63.
3) Open the "ready" switch on the '63.
4) The high byte will be displayed on the '63 LEDs.
5) Open the "display low byte" switch on the '63.
6) The low byte will be displayed on the '63 LEDs.

External 32,768 Hz Watch Crystal-Based Clock For TMR1

The input of timer 1 can be connected to a crystal oscillator circuit which is on-chip. A crystal and two capacitors are connected externally. The principal application of this is real-timekeeping. Watch crystals are readily available which have a frequency is 32,768 Hz.

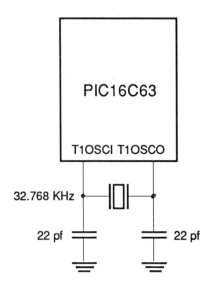

When the timer 1 oscillator is enabled (T1CON bit 3 set), the T1OSO and T1OSI pins become inputs. The corresponding bits in the TRISC register are ignored.

As it turns out, 32,768 is a power of 2, which is very convenient. Timer 1 is a 16-bit counter. the number 32,768 is represented by 15 bits. We can handle this by setting bit 15 (16th bit) in timer 1 after each rollover so that inputting 32,768 pulses will cause a rollover.

To get this working in a simplistic way, we will write a program to blink an LED at the rate of one blink per second (precisely).

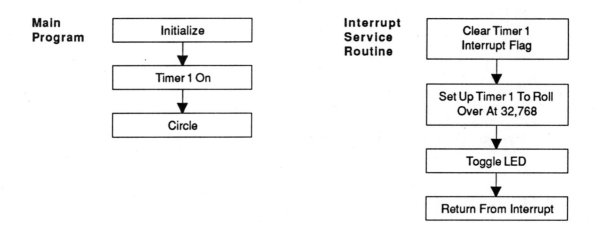

```
;=======SECONDS.ASM================================9/11/98==
        list    p=16c63
        radix   hex
;----------------------------------------------------------------
;seconds demo
;       external oscillator, 32768 Hz, timer 1, prescaler 1:1
;----------------------------------------------------------------
;       cpu equates (memory map)
status  equ     0x03
portb   equ     0x06
intcon  equ     0x0b
pir1    equ     0x0c
tmr1l   equ     0x0e
tmr1h   equ     0x0f
t1con   equ     0x10
trisb   equ     0x86
pie1    equ     0x8c
;----------------------------------------------------------------
;       bit equates
rp0     equ     5
;----------------------------------------------------------------
        org     0x000
        goto    start           ;skip over location pointed to by
                                ;   interrupt vector
        org     0x004
        goto    iserv
;
start   bsf     status,rp0      ;switch to bank 1
        movlw   b'00000000'     ;port B outputs
        movwf   trisb
        bcf     status,rp0      ;switch back to bank 0
        movlw   b'00000000'     ;port B lines low
        movwf   portb
        bcf     intcon,7        ;disable global interrupts
        bcf     intcon,6        ;disable peripheral interrupts
        bsf     status,rp0      ;bank 1
        bcf     pie1,0          ;disable tmr1 interrupts
```

```
          bcf       status,rp0    ;bank 0
          bcf       pir1,0        ;clear timer 1 interrupt flag
          movlw     b'00001010'   ;prescaler and tmr1 setup,
          movwf     t1con         ;   tmr1 off
          clrf      tmr1h         ;clear timer 1 high
          clrf      tmr1l         ;clear timer 1 low, clear prescaler
          bsf       intcon,7      ;enable global interrupts
          bsf       intcon,6      ;enable peripheral interrupts
          bsf       status,rp0    ;bank 1
          bsf       pie1,0        ;enable tmr1 interrupts
          bcf       status,rp0    ;bank 0
          bsf       t1con,0       ;timer 1 on
circle    goto      circle
;------------------------------------------------------------
iserv     bcf       pir1,0        ;clear timer 1 interrupt flag
          bsf       tmr1h,7       ;set up timer 1 to roll over at
                                  ;   32,768 counts
          btfss     portb,0       ;port B, bit 0 status?
          goto      setbit        ;bit is clear
clrbit    bcf       portb,0       ;clear port B, bit 0
          retfie                  ;return from interrupt
setbit    bsf       portb,0       ;set port B, bit 0
          retfie                  ;return from interrupt
;------------------------------------------------------------
          end
;------------------------------------------------------------
;at blast time, select:
;         memory unprotected
;         watchdog timer disabled (default is enabled)
;         standard crystal (using 4 MHz osc for test) XT
;         power-up timer on
;         brown-out detect on
;============================================================
```

When the oscillator is operating properly, a 32.768 KHz sine wave with an amplitude of approximately 3.5 volts will be present at the T1OSO pin (pin 11, PIC16C63). If the example program does not run, check pin 11 with an oscilloscope to be sure that the oscillator is functioning properly. The values for the capacitors called out in Microchip's data books are not consistent (15 pF and 33 pF). 22 pF caps worked for me.

The user must provide a software delay to ensure proper oscillator startup. This has not been done in this example and so you will notice that the time from power-up to first blink is more than one second. This is something to keep in mind when you design your own applications.

To illustrate real-timekeeping, we can create a very simple clock. This is not meant for your office or living room. It will serve as a simple example and may be used as a basis for control or data logging applications.

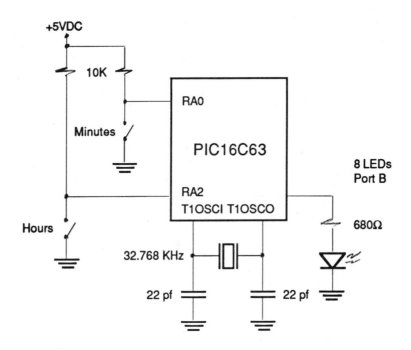

A timer 1 interrupt is generated at precisely 1 second intervals. Software will be used to develop minutes and hours as illustrated by the following flow chart. The default display is seconds in binary via the port B LEDs. Opening the minutes switch will cause minutes to be displayed as long as the switch is open. Similarly, opening the hours switch will result in hours being displayed until the switch is closed. The clock runs for 24 hours from the time the PIC16 is reset and rolls over meaning all counters are cleared and counting starts over.

Again, note that the most significant bit of timer 1 is set after each rollover so that 32,768 oscillator pulses will cause an overflow.

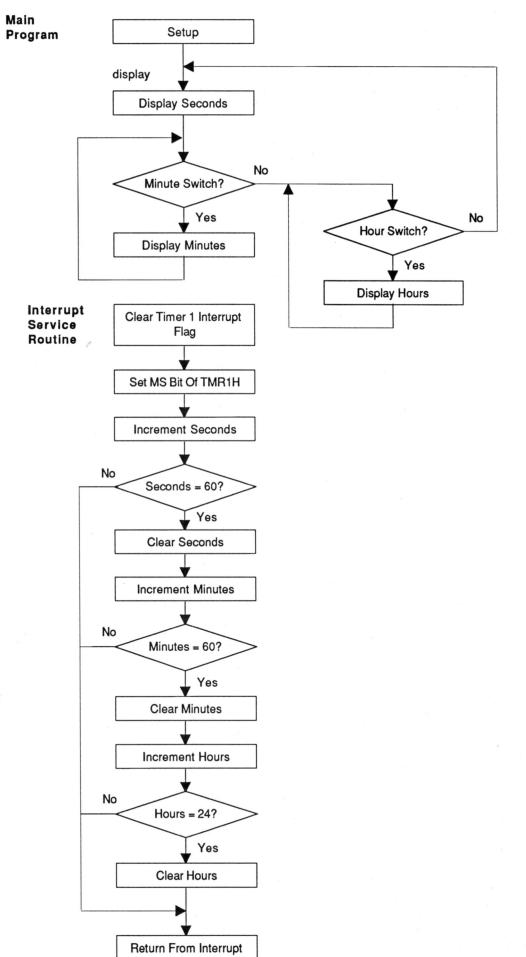

Main Program

Setup

display

Display Seconds

Minute Switch? — No

Yes

Display Minutes

Hour Switch? — No

Yes

Display Hours

Interrupt Service Routine

Clear Timer 1 Interrupt Flag

Set MS Bit Of TMR1H

Increment Seconds

Seconds = 60? — No

Yes

Clear Seconds

Increment Minutes

Minutes = 60? — No

Yes

Clear Minutes

Increment Hours

Hours = 24? — No

Yes

Clear Hours

Return From Interrupt

113

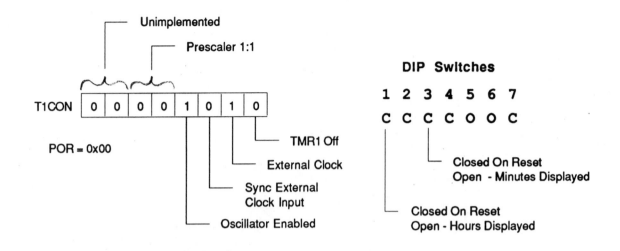

```
;=======TIME.ASM====================================9/11/98==
        list    p=16c63
        radix   hex
;-------------------------------------------------------------
;seconds, minutes, hours demo
;       external oscillator, 32768 Hz, timer 1, prescaler 1:1
;-------------------------------------------------------------
;       cpu equates (memory map)
status  equ     0x03
porta   equ     0x05
portb   equ     0x06
intcon  equ     0x0b
pir1    equ     0x0c
tmr1l   equ     0x0e
tmr1h   equ     0x0f
t1con   equ     0x10
trisa   equ     0x85
trisb   equ     0x86
pie1    equ     0x8c
sec     equ     0x20
min     equ     0x21
hr      equ     0x22
;-------------------------------------------------------------
;       bit equates
z       equ     2
rp0     equ     5
;-------------------------------------------------------------
        org     0x000
        goto    start       ;skip over location pointed to by
                            ;   interrupt vector
        org     0x004
        goto    iserv
;
start   bsf     status,rp0  ;switch to bank 1
        movlw   b'00000000' ;port B outputs
        movwf   trisb
        movlw   b'00011111' ;port A inputs
```

```
        movwf   trisa
        bcf     status,rp0  ;switch back to bank 0
        movlw   b'00000000' ;port B lines low
        movwf   portb
        bcf     intcon,7    ;disable global interrupts
        bcf     intcon,6    ;disable peripheral interrupts
        bsf     status,rp0  ;bank 1
        bcf     pie1,0      ;disable tmr1 interrupts
        bcf     status,rp0  ;bank 0
        bcf     pir1,0      ;clear timer 1 interrupt flag
        movlw   b'00001010' ;prescaler and tmr1 setup,
        movwf   t1con       ;    tmr1 off
        clrf    tmr1h       ;clear timer 1 high
        clrf    tmr1l       ;clear timer 1 low, clear prescaler
        clrf    sec
        clrf    min
        clrf    hr
        bsf     intcon,7    ;enable global interrupts
        bsf     intcon,6    ;enable peripheral interrupts
        bsf     status,rp0  ;bank 1
        bsf     pie1,0      ;enable tmr1 interrupts
        bcf     status,rp0  ;bank 0
        bsf     t1con,0     ;timer 1 on
display movf    sec,w       ;get seconds
        movwf   portb       ;display seconds
minutes btfss   porta,0     ;display minutes?
        goto    hours       ;no
        movf    min,w       ;get minutes
        movwf   portb       ;display minutes
        goto    minutes
hours   btfss   porta,2     ;display hours?
        goto    display     ;no
        movf    hr,w        ;get hours
        movwf   portb       ;display hours
        goto    hours
;--------------------------------------------------------------
iserv   bcf     pir1,0      ;clear timer 1 interrupt flag
        bsf     tmr1h,7     ;set up timer 1 to roll over at
                            ;   32,768 counts
        incf    sec,f
        movf    sec,w       ;compare
        sublw   d'60'       ;seconds = 60?
        btfss   status,z    ;test z flag, skip next instruction
                            ;   if flag is set
        retfie
        clrf    sec         ;clear seconds
        incf    min,f       ;increment minutes
        movf    min,w       ;compare
        sublw   d'60'       ;minutes = 60?
        btfss   status,z    ;test z flag, skip next instruction
                            ;   if flag is set
        retfie
        clrf    min         ;clear minutes
        incf    hr,f        ;increment hours
```

```
        movf    hr,w        ;compare
        sublw   d'24'       ;hours = 24?
        btfsc   status,z    ;test z flag, skip next instruction
                            ;   if flag is clear
        clrf    hr          ;clear hours
        retfie
;---------------------------------------------------------------
        end
;---------------------------------------------------------------
;at blast time, select:
;       memory unprotected
;       watchdog timer disabled (default is enabled)
;       standard crystal (using 4 MHz osc for test) XT
;       power-up timer on
;       brown-out detect on
;===============================================================
```

PULSE WIDTH MODULATION (PWM) USING TMR2 AND THE CCP MODULE

The fundamentals of PWM are explained in PIC'n Up The Pace along with techniques for do-it-yourself PWM using software. Here we will talk about doing PWM using hardware peripherals built into many of the PIC16 variants.

A PWM output may be generated on the CCP1 pin by using TMR2, PR2 and CCP1 module. We will use 8 bits to represent the duty cycle for now to keep things simple.

A simplified block diagram shows the basic concept:

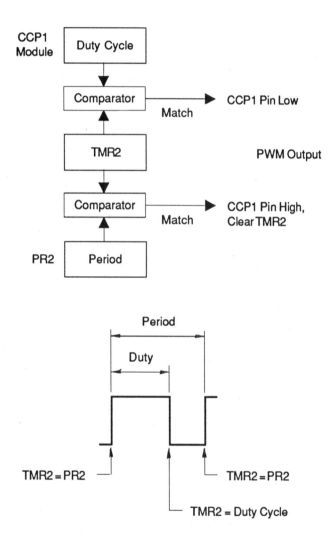

TMR2 increments. A comparator looks for a match between TMR2 and the duty cycle register. When a match occurs, the CCP1 pin is driven low. A second comparator looks for a match between TMR2 and the period number in the PR2 register. When a match occurs, the CCP1 pin is driven high and TMR2 is cleared to start the next period. This process repeats over and over giving a PWM output. The duty cycle may be changed on-the-fly to change the analog voltage output on the CCP1 pin by loading a different duty cycle number in the duty cycle register which is CCPR1L.

Notice that the TMR2 postscaler is not involved in PWM applications.

Generating a PWM output via the CCP1 pin (8-bit duty cycle) requires:

- Make CCP1 an output pin.
- Disable the appropriate interrupts.
- Load the period register.
- Clear two bits of the CCP1CON register not used in the 8-bit mode.
- Load the (initial) duty cycle.
- Set up timer 2.
- Select PWM mode for CCP1 module.
- Start timer 2.

A short program will serve to demonstrate how all this works. The object is to generate a PWM output on the CCP1 pin. Timer 2 is fed by the internal instruction clock and the prescaler choices are 1:1, 1:4, and 1:16. I arbitrarily chose to use 1:4 as the prescaler value and 0xFF (for decimal 256 counts) as the period register value.

$$\text{period} = (1 \times 10^{-6} \text{ seconds})(4)(256) = 1024 \text{ microseconds}$$

The duty cycle for our demonstration is 50 percent, so 0x7F is loaded into CCPR1L which serves as the duty cycle register (8 bits).

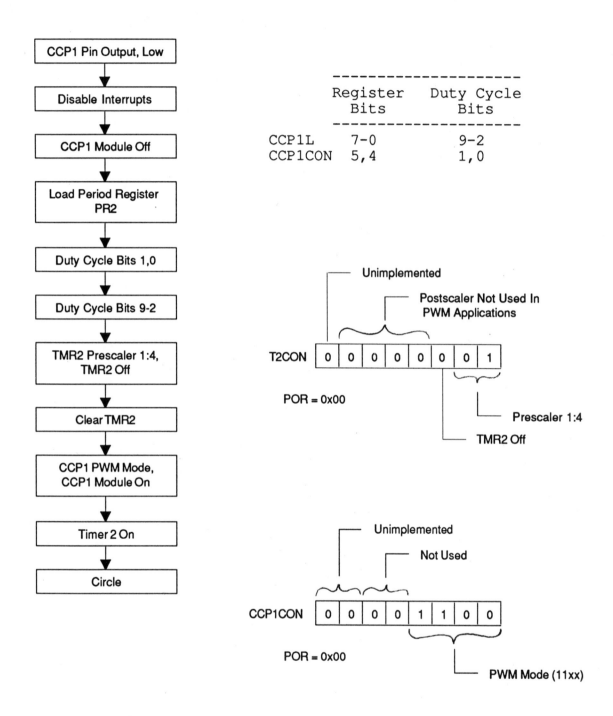

	Register Bits	Duty Cycle Bits
CCP1L	7-0	9-2
CCP1CON	5,4	1,0

Flowchart:
- CCP1 Pin Output, Low
- Disable Interrupts
- CCP1 Module Off
- Load Period Register PR2
- Duty Cycle Bits 1,0
- Duty Cycle Bits 9-2
- TMR2 Prescaler 1:4, TMR2 Off
- Clear TMR2
- CCP1 PWM Mode, CCP1 Module On
- Timer 2 On
- Circle

T2CON: 0 0 0 0 0 0 0 1
- Unimplemented
- Postscaler Not Used In PWM Applications
- Prescaler 1:4
- TMR2 Off
POR = 0x00

CCP1CON: 0 0 0 0 1 1 0 0
- Unimplemented
- Not Used
- PWM Mode (11xx)
POR = 0x00

DIP Switches

```
1 2 3 4 5 6 7

C C O C C C O
```

```
;======HDWPWMX.ASM===============================11/9/98==
        list    p=16c63
        radix   hex
;--------------------------------------------------------
;       cpu equates (memory map)
status  equ     0x03
portc   equ     0x07
intcon  equ     0x0b
tmr2    equ     0x11
t2con   equ     0x12
ccpr1l  equ     0x15
ccp1con equ     0x17
trisc   equ     0x87
pie1    equ     0x8c
pr2     equ     0x92
;--------------------------------------------------------
;       bit equates
rp0     equ     5
ccp1    equ     2               ;ccp1 bit 2, port C
;--------------------------------------------------------
        org     0x000
;
start   bsf     status,rp0      ;switch to bank 1
        bcf     trisc,ccp1      ;ccp1 pin output
        bcf     status,rp0      ;switch back to bank 0
        bcf     portc,ccp1      ;ccp1 pin low
        bcf     intcon,7        ;disable global interrupts
        bcf     intcon,6        ;disable peripheral interrupts
        bsf     status,rp0      ;bank 1
        bcf     pie1,1          ;disable timer 2 interrupts
        bcf     pie1,2          ;disable ccp1 interrupts
        bcf     status,rp0      ;bank 0
        clrf    ccp1con         ;   ccp1 module off
        bsf     status,rp0      ;bank 1
        movlw   0xff            ;decimal 255
        movwf   pr2             ;load period register
        bcf     status,rp0      ;bank 0
        bcf     ccp1con,5       ;clear bit 1 of duty cycle reg
        bcf     ccp1con,4       ;clear bit 0 of duty cycle reg
        movlw   0x7f            ;duty cycle 50 percent
        movwf   ccpr1l          ;bits 9-2 of duty cycle
        movlw   b'00000001'     ;prescaler = 1:4,
        movwf   t2con           ;   tmr2 off
        clrf    tmr2            ;clear tmr2
        movlw   b'00001100'     ;ccp1 pwm mode, ccp1 module on
        movwf   ccp1con
        bsf     t2con,2         ;tmr2 on
```

```
circle   goto    circle        ;done
;
         end
;------------------------------------------------------------
;at blast time, select:
;        memory unprotected
;        watchdog timer disabled (default is enabled)
;        standard crystal (using 4 MHz osc for test) XT
;        power-up timer on
;        brown-out detect on
;============================================================
```

An oscilloscope may be used to observe the output signal. The duty cycle will be 50 percent.

ANALOG OUTPUT - INCREASE/DECREASE BUTTONS - PWM - 8-bit Mode

The next example shows how an adjustable analog output on the CCP1 pin can be created using PWM via TMR2, PR2 and the CCP1 module. The circuit is controlled by an increase (voltage) button and a decrease button. Increase/decrease is proportional to the time the button is pressed (to a maximum of 5 volts at the output or a minimum of 0 volts). The rate of increase/decrease is proportional to the time interval generated by the time delay code (change it if you wish).

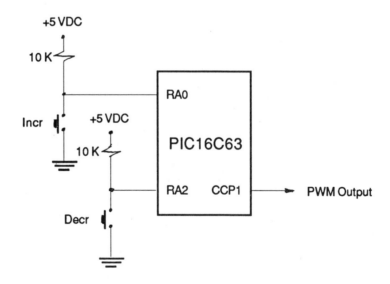

OVERVIEW

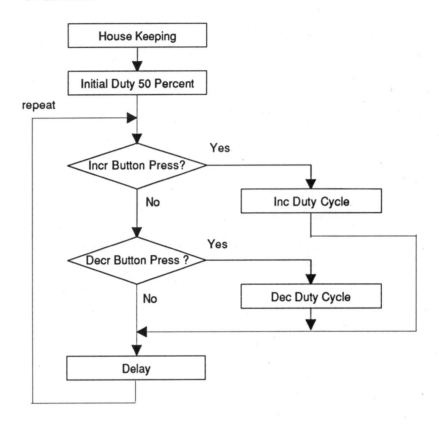

Main Program

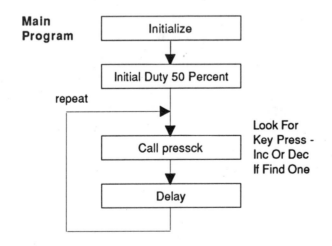

Look For Key Press - Inc Or Dec If Find One

Subroutine

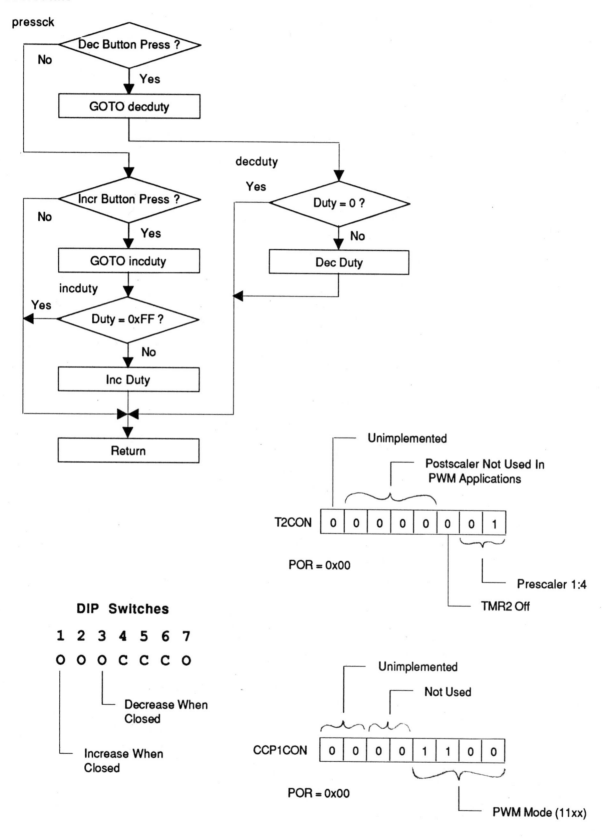

pressck

Dec Button Press ?
No
Yes
GOTO decduty

decduty

Incr Button Press ?
No
Yes
GOTO incduty

Duty = 0 ?
Yes
No
Dec Duty

incduty

Duty = 0xFF ?
Yes
No
Inc Duty

Return

Unimplemented

Postscaler Not Used In
PWM Applications

T2CON | 0 | 0 | 0 | 0 | 0 | 0 | 0 | 1

POR = 0x00

Prescaler 1:4

TMR2 Off

DIP Switches

1 2 3 4 5 6 7

O O O C C C O

Decrease When
Closed

Increase When
Closed

Unimplemented

Not Used

CCP1CON | 0 | 0 | 0 | 0 | 1 | 1 | 0 | 0

POR = 0x00

PWM Mode (11xx)

```
;======CCPPWM.ASM================================11/11/98==
          list    p=16c63
          radix   hex
;-----------------------------------------------------------
;         cpu equates (memory map)
status    equ     0x03
porta     equ     0x05
portc     equ     0x07
intcon    equ     0x0b
tmr2      equ     0x11
t2con     equ     0x12
ccpr1l    equ     0x15
ccp1con   equ     0x17
duty      equ     0x20
mcount    equ     0x21
ncount    equ     0x22
trisa     equ     0x85
trisc     equ     0x87
pie1      equ     0x8c
pr2       equ     0x92
;-----------------------------------------------------------
;         bit equates
z         equ     2
rp0       equ     5
ccp1      equ     2               ;ccp1 bit 2, port C
;-----------------------------------------------------------
          org     0x000
;
start     bsf     status,rp0  ;switch to bank 1
          movlw   b'00000101' ;inputs/outputs
          movwf   trisa
          bcf     trisc,ccp1  ;ccp1 pin output
          bcf     status,rp0  ;switch back to bank 0
          bcf     portc,ccp1  ;ccp1 pin low
          bcf     intcon,7    ;disable global interrupts
          bcf     intcon,6    ;disable peripheral interrupts
          bsf     status,rp0  ;bank 1
          bcf     pie1,1      ;disable timer 2 interrupts
          bcf     pie1,2      ;disable ccp1 interrupts
          bcf     status,rp0  ;bank 0
          clrf    ccp1con     ;ccp1 module off
          bsf     status,rp0  ;bank 1
          movlw   0xff        ;decimal 255
          movwf   pr2         ;load period register
          bcf     status,rp0  ;bank 0
          bcf     ccp1con,5   ;clear bit 1 of duty cycle reg
          bcf     ccp1con,4   ;clear bit 0 of duty cycle reg
          movlw   0x7f        ;initial duty cycle 50 percent
          movwf   duty
          movwf   ccpr1l      ;bits 9-2 of duty cycle
          movlw   b'00000001' ;prescaler = 1:4,
          movwf   t2con       ;    tmr2 off
          clrf    tmr2        ;clear tmr2
```

124

```
        movlw    b'00001100'  ;ccp1 pwm mode, ccp1 module on
        movwf    ccp1con
        bsf      t2con,2       ;tmr2 on
;------------------------------------------------------------
repeat  call     pressck       ;look for incr/decr button press
        movlw    0xff          ;delay 200 milliseconds
        movwf    mcount
loadn   movlw    0xff
        movwf    ncount
decn    decfsz   ncount,f      ;decrement N
        goto     decn          ;again
        decfsz   mcount,f      ;decrement M
        goto     loadn         ;again
        goto     repeat
;------------------------------------------------------------
pressck btfss    porta,2       ;decrease button pressed?
        goto     decduty       ;yes, decrement duty cycle
        btfss    porta,0       ;increase button pressed?
        goto     incduty       ;yes, increment duty cycle
        return
incduty movf     duty,w        ;get duty cycle into W
        sublw    0xff          ;duty cycle=0xff?
        btfsc    status,z
        return
        incf     duty,f        ;increment duty cycle
        movf     duty,w        ;get duty cycle into W
        movwf    ccpr1l        ;duty cycle into ccp register
        return                 ;press check done
decduty movf     duty,w        ;get duty cycle into W
        sublw    0x00          ;duty cycle=0?
        btfsc    status,z
        return
        decf     duty,f        ;decrement duty cycle
        movf     duty,w        ;get duty cycle into W
        movwf    ccpr1l        ;duty cycle into ccp register
        return                 ;press check done
;
        end
;------------------------------------------------------------
;at blast time, select:
;       memory unprotected
;       watchdog timer disabled (default is enabled)
;       standard crystal (using 4 MHz osc for test) XT
;       power-up timer on
;       brown-out detect on
;============================================================
```

An oscilloscope may be used to observe the output signal. The duty cycle will be 50 percent initially. Close the increase switch and observe the results on the scope.

DUTY CYCLE - 10-bit Mode

The duty cycle register is really 10 bits wide, split 8 and 2.

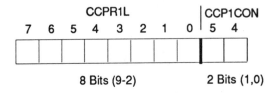

The high 8 bits (bits 9 - 2) are the CCPR1L register. The low 2 bits are bits 1 and 0 of the CCP1CON register. Resolution up to 10 bits is possible.

The most significant 8 bits and least significant 2 bits must be loaded separately requiring a little thought in programming.

Many PWM applications involve incrementing or decrementing the duty cycle. To do this, the current duty cycle value needs to be stored in two file registers and incremented or decremented there. Then a copy of the contents of those registers is transferred to the CCP module to change the duty cycle. In the 10-bit mode, doing this is an extra challenge. For the purpose of incrementing or decrementing, the low 8 bits need to be in an 8-bit register and the two remaining (high) bits should be in a second register. The challenge is that the opposite arrangement is used in the CCP module registers. The high 8 bits are written to the CCPR1L register and the low 2 bits are written to the middle of the CCP1CON register.

Here is an example of 10-bit hardware PWM. The duty cycle is stored in two registers. The low 8 bits are in the duty_lo register. The high 2 bits are in the duty_hi register. A subroutine called "dutychg" moves the bits to their proper places in the CCP module registers.

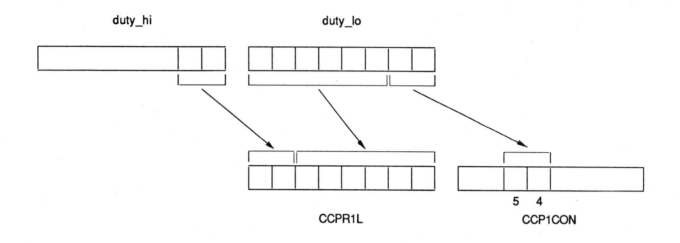

duty_hi   duty_lo

CCPR1L   CCP1CON

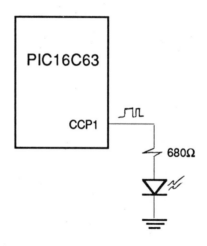

dutychg

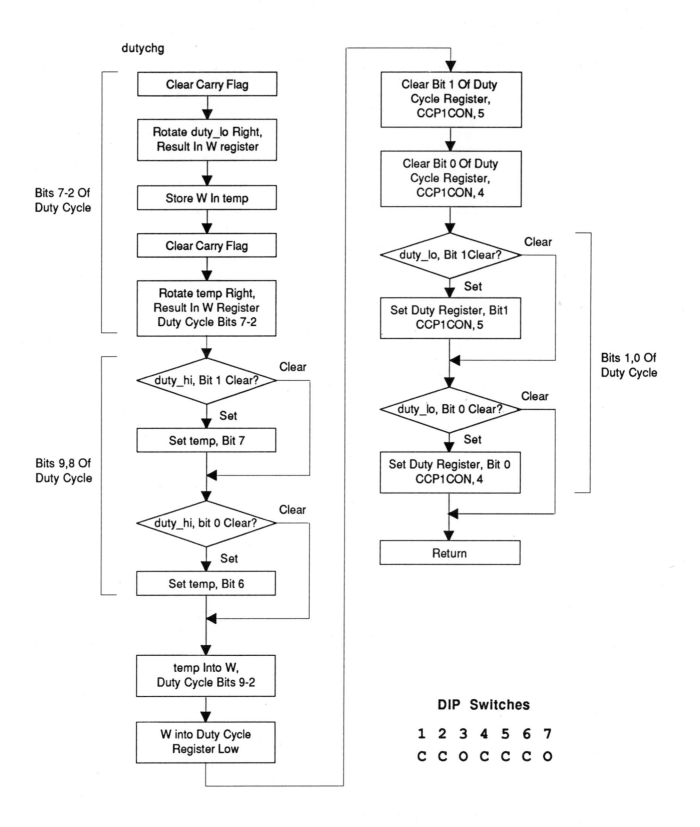

Bits 7-2 Of
Duty Cycle

Clear Carry Flag

Rotate duty_lo Right,
Result In W register

Store W In temp

Clear Carry Flag

Rotate temp Right,
Result In W Register
Duty Cycle Bits 7-2

Bits 9,8 Of
Duty Cycle

duty_hi, Bit 1 Clear? — Clear

Set

Set temp, Bit 7

duty_hi, bit 0 Clear? — Clear

Set

Set temp, Bit 6

temp Into W,
Duty Cycle Bits 9-2

W into Duty Cycle
Register Low

Clear Bit 1 Of Duty
Cycle Register,
CCP1CON, 5

Clear Bit 0 Of Duty
Cycle Register,
CCP1CON, 4

duty_lo, Bit 1 Clear? — Clear

Set

Set Duty Register, Bit1
CCP1CON, 5

duty_lo, Bit 0 Clear? — Clear

Set

Set Duty Register, Bit 0
CCP1CON, 4

Bits 1,0 Of
Duty Cycle

Return

DIP Switches

1	2	3	4	5	6	7
C	C	O	C	C	C	O

128

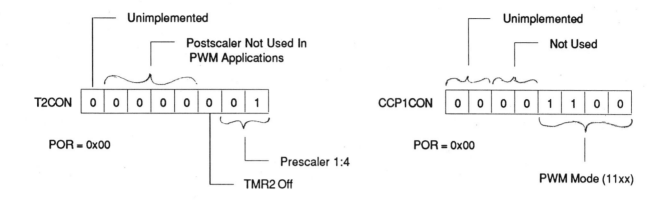

T2CON | 0 | 0 | 0 | 0 | 0 | 0 | 0 | 1

- Unimplemented
- Postscaler Not Used In PWM Applications
- Prescaler 1:4
- TMR2 Off

POR = 0x00

CCP1CON | 0 | 0 | 0 | 0 | 1 | 1 | 0 | 0

- Unimplemented
- Not Used
- PWM Mode (11xx)

POR = 0x00

```
;=======HDWPWMY.ASM================================11/10/98==
        list    p=16c63
        radix   hex
;--------------------------------------------------------------
;       cpu equates (memory map)
status  equ     0x03
portc   equ     0x07
intcon  equ     0x0b
tmr2    equ     0x11
t2con   equ     0x12
ccpr1l  equ     0x15
ccp1con equ     0x17
duty_lo equ     0x20
duty_hi equ     0x21
temp    equ     0x22
trisc   equ     0x87
pie1    equ     0x8c
pr2     equ     0x92
;--------------------------------------------------------------
;       bit equates
c       equ     0
rp0     equ     5
ccp1    equ     2               ;ccp1 bit 2, port C
;--------------------------------------------------------------
        org     0x000
;
start   bsf     status,rp0      ;switch to bank 1
        bcf     trisc,ccp1      ;ccp1 pin output
        bcf     status,rp0      ;switch back to bank 0
        bcf     portc,ccp1      ;ccp1 pin low
        bcf     intcon,7        ;disable global interrupts
        bcf     intcon,6        ;disable peripheral interrupts
        bsf     status,rp0      ;bank 1
        bcf     pie1,1          ;disable timer 2 interrupts
        bcf     pie1,2          ;disable ccp1 interrupts
        bcf     status,rp0      ;bank 0
        clrf    ccp1con         ;ccp1 module off
        bsf     status,rp0      ;bank 1
        movlw   0xff            ;decimal 255
```

```
        movwf   pr2             ;load period register
        bcf     status,rp0      ;bank 0
        movlw   0x00            ;duty cycle 25 percent
        movwf   duty_lo
        movlw   b'00000001'     ;duty cycle hi 2 bits
        movwf   duty_hi
        call    dutychg         ;change duty cycle via subroutine
        movlw   b'00000001'     ;prescaler = 1:4,
        movwf   t2con           ;    tmr2 off
        clrf    tmr2            ;clear tmr2
        movlw   b'00001100'     ;ccp1 pwm mode, ccp1 module on
        movwf   ccp1con
        bsf     t2con,2         ;tmr2 on
circle  goto    circle  ;done
;-------------------------------------------------------------
dutychg bcf     status,c        ;clear carry flag
        rrf     duty_lo,w       ;rotate duty right, result in W
        movwf   temp            ;store in temp
        bcf     status,c        ;clear carry flag
        rrf     temp,f          ;bits 7-2 of duty cycle
        btfsc   duty_hi,1       ;duty cycle hi bit 1 = 1?
        bsf     temp,7          ;yes, set duty register bit 9
        btfsc   duty_hi,0       ;duty cycle hi bit 0 = 1?
        bsf     temp,6          ;yes, set duty register bit 8
        movf    temp,w          ;duty cycle bits 9-2
        movwf   ccpr1l          ;into duty cycle register
        bcf     ccp1con,5       ;clear bit 1 of duty cycle reg
        bcf     ccp1con,4       ;clear bit 0 of duty cycle reg
        btfsc   duty_lo,1       ;duty cycle bit 1 = 1?
        bsf     ccp1con,5       ;yes, set duty register bit 1
        btfsc   duty_lo,0       ;duty cycle bit 0 = 1?
        bsf     ccp1con,4       ;yes, set duty register bit 0
        return
;-------------------------------------------------------------
        end
;-------------------------------------------------------------
;at blast time, select:
;       memory unprotected
;       watchdog timer disabled (default is enabled)
;       standard crystal (using 4 MHz osc for test) XT
;       power-up timer on
;       brown-out detect on
;=============================================================
```

An oscilloscope may be used to observe the output signal. The duty cycle will be 25 percent.

When the program runs, a PWM signal is generated on the CCP1 pin. The duty cycle is 25 percent.

The next challenge is to increment and decrement a register pair where only the least significant 2 bits of the upper register are used. Notice how the increment and decrement instructions affect the zero flag.

- INCF   Z flag set when register contents overflows
- DECF   Z flag set when register contents = 0 (not useful here)

When the lower register is incremented, we need to know when it overflows (0xFF to 0x00) so that a check can be made to see if the upper register should be incremented. We can use the state of the zero flag to tell us.

When the lower register is decremented, we need to know when it underflows (0xFF to 0x00) so that a check can be made to see if the upper register should be decremented. The state of the zero flag won't tell us, so we will have to use a comparison to test for this.

    Increment:

            FF to 00

                 └── Sets Z-flag, increment 2-bit register if not already full

    Decrement:

            00 to FF

                 └── Test via compare, decrement 2-bit register if not already zero

The flow charts which follow show one method for doing this.

Again, the duty cycle is stored in two registers. The low 8 bits are in the duty_lo register. The high 2 bits are in the duty_hi register.

The maximum and minimum values are:

	duty_hi	duty_lo
Maximum	b'00000011'	0xFF
Minimum	b'00000000'	0x00

The increment/decrement program must keep the values controlling the duty cycle within these boundaries.

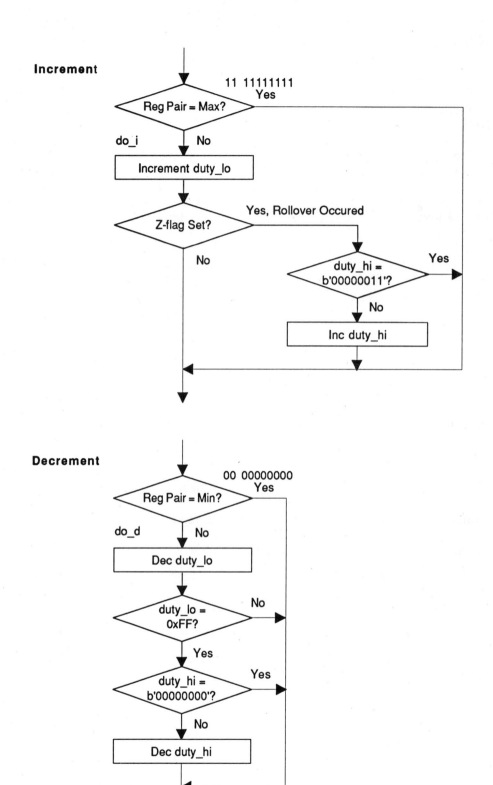

132

```
;------------------------------------------------------------
incduty movf     duty_lo,w    ;test for maximum
        sublw    0xff
        btfss    status,z
        goto     do_i         ;not at maximum
        movf     duty_hi,w
        sublw    b'00000011'  ;compare
        btfsc    status,z
        return                ;at maximum
do_i    incf     duty_lo,f    ;increment
        btfss    status,z
        goto     inc
        movf     duty_hi,w
        sublw    b'00000011'  ;compare
        btfsc    status,z
        goto     inc
        incf     duty_hi,f
inc     call     dutychg      ;change duty cycle
        return                ;press check done
;------------------------------------------------------------
decduty movf     duty_lo,w    ;test for minimum
        sublw    0x00
        btfss    status,z
        goto     do_d         ;not at minimum
        movf     duty_hi,w
        sublw    b'00000000'
        btfsc    status,z
        return                ;at minimum
do_d    decf     duty_lo,f    ;decrement
        movf     duty_lo,w
        sublw    0xff
        btfss    status,z
        goto     dec
        movf     duty_hi,w
        sublw    b'00000000'  ;compare
        btfsc    status,z
        goto     dec
        decf     duty_hi,f
dec     call     dutychg      ;change duty cycle
        return                ;press check done
;------------------------------------------------------------
```

ANALOG OUTPUT - INCREASE/DECREASE BUTTONS - PWM - 10-bit Mode

The next example shows how to generate a PWM output with increase/decrease capability using 10 bits to represent the duty cycle. The rate of increase/decrease is controlled by a software time delay loop. When you test this circuit and program, you can change the delay if you wish.

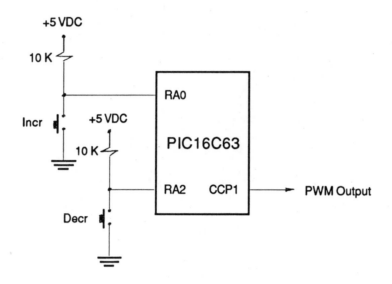

OVERVIEW

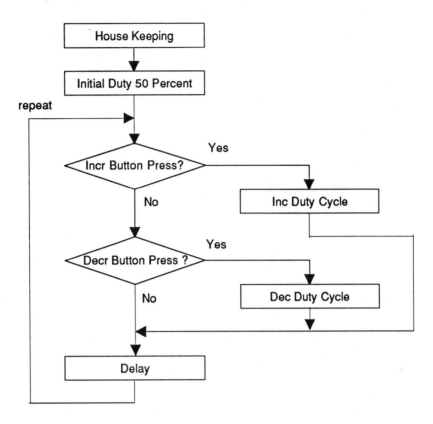

Main Program

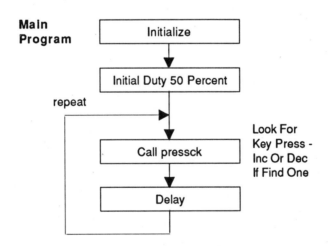

Subroutine

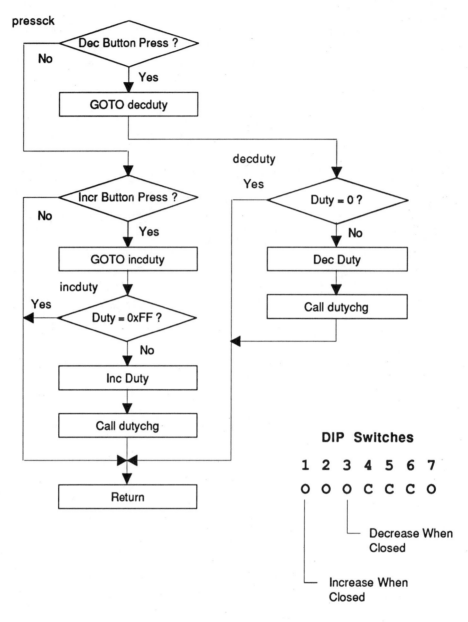

pressck

Dec Button Press ?
- No
- Yes → GOTO decduty

Incr Button Press ?
- No
- Yes → GOTO incduty

incduty

Duty = 0xFF ?
- Yes
- No → Inc Duty → Call dutychg

decduty

Duty = 0 ?
- Yes
- No → Dec Duty → Call dutychg

Return

DIP Switches

1	2	3	4	5	6	7
O	O	O	C	C	C	O

Decrease When Closed

Increase When Closed

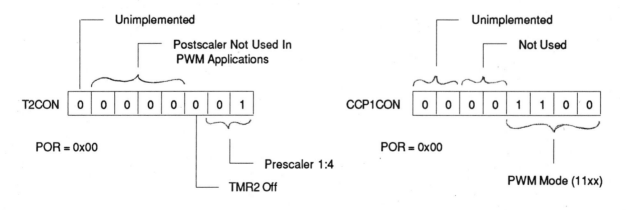

Unimplemented

Postscaler Not Used In PWM Applications

T2CON	0	0	0	0	0	0	0	1

POR = 0x00

Prescaler 1:4

TMR2 Off

Unimplemented

Not Used

CCP1CON	0	0	0	0	1	1	0	0

POR = 0x00

PWM Mode (11xx)

```
;=======CCPPWMX.ASM=============================11/12/98==
          list     p=16c63
          radix    hex
;---------------------------------------------------------
;         cpu equates (memory map)
status    equ      0x03
porta     equ      0x05
portc     equ      0x07
intcon    equ      0x0b
tmr2      equ      0x11
t2con     equ      0x12
ccpr1l    equ      0x15
ccp1con   equ      0x17
duty_lo   equ      0x20
duty_hi   equ      0x21
temp      equ      0x22
mcount    equ      0x23
ncount    equ      0x24
trisa     equ      0x85
trisc     equ      0x87
pie1      equ      0x8c
pr2       equ      0x92
;---------------------------------------------------------
;         bit equates
c         equ      0
z         equ      2
rp0       equ      5
ccp1      equ      2               ;ccp1 bit 2, port C
;---------------------------------------------------------
          org      0x000
;
start     bsf      status,rp0      ;switch to bank 1
          movlw    b'00000101'     ;inputs/outputs
          movwf    trisa
          bcf      trisc,ccp1      ;ccp1 pin output
          bcf      status,rp0      ;switch back to bank 0
          bcf      portc,ccp1      ;ccp1 pin low
          bcf      intcon,7        ;disable global interrupts
          bcf      intcon,6        ;disable peripheral interrupts
          bsf      status,rp0      ;bank 1
          bcf      pie1,1          ;disable timer 2 interrupts
          bcf      pie1,2          ;disable ccp1 interrupts
          bcf      status,rp0      ;bank 0
          clrf     ccp1con         ;ccp1 module off
          bsf      status,rp0      ;bank 1
          movlw    0xff            ;decimal 255
          movwf    pr2             ;load period register
          bcf      status,rp0      ;bank 0
          movlw    0xff            ;duty cycle 50 percent
          movwf    duty_lo
          movlw    b'00000001'     ;duty cycle hi 2 bits
          movwf    duty_hi
          call     dutychg         ;change duty cycle via subroutine
```

```
        movlw    b'00000001'  ;prescaler = 1:4,
        movwf    t2con        ;    tmr2 off
        clrf     tmr2         ;clear tmr2
        movlw    b'00001100'  ;ccp1 pwm mode, ccp1 module on
        movwf    ccp1con
        bsf      t2con,2      ;tmr2 on
;-------------------------------------------------------------
repeat  call     pressck      ;look for incr/decr button press
        movlw    0x7f         ;delay 100 milliseconds
        movwf    mcount
loadn   movlw    0xff
        movwf    ncount
decn    decfsz   ncount,f     ;decrement N
        goto     decn         ;again
        decfsz   mcount,f     ;decrement M
        goto     loadn        ;again
        goto     repeat
;-------------------------------------------------------------
pressck btfss    porta,2      ;decrease button pressed?
        call     decduty      ;yes, decrement duty cycle
        btfss    porta,0      ;increase button pressed?
        call     incduty      ;yes, increment duty cycle
        return
;-------------------------------------------------------------
incduty movf     duty_lo,w    ;test for maximum
        sublw    0xff
        btfss    status,z
        goto     do_i         ;not at maximum
        movf     duty_hi,w
        sublw    b'00000011'  ;compare
        btfsc    status,z
        return                ;at maximum
do_i    incf     duty_lo,f    ;increment
        btfss    status,z
        goto     inc
        movf     duty_hi,w
        sublw    b'00000011'  ;compare
        btfsc    status,z
        goto     inc
        incf     duty_hi,f
inc     call     dutychg      ;change duty cycle
        return                ;press check done
;-------------------------------------------------------------
decduty movf     duty_lo,w    ;test for minimum
        sublw    0x00
        btfss    status,z
        goto     do_d         ;not at minimum
        movf     duty_hi,w
        sublw    b'00000000'
        btfsc    status,z
        return                ;at minimum
do_d    decf     duty_lo,f    ;decrement
        movf     duty_lo,w
        sublw    0xff
```

```
        btfss   status,z
        goto    dec
        movf    duty_hi,w
        sublw   b'00000000'  ;compare
        btfsc   status,z
        goto    dec
        decf    duty_hi,f
dec     call    dutychg      ;change duty cycle
        return               ;press check done
;-----------------------------------------------------------
dutychg bcf     status,c     ;clear carry flag
        rrf     duty_lo,w    ;rotate duty right, result in W
        movwf   temp         ;store in temp
        bcf     status,c     ;clear carry flag
        rrf     temp,f       ;bits 7-2 of duty cycle
        movf    temp,w
        btfsc   duty_hi,1    ;duty cycle hi bit 1 = 1?
        bsf     temp,7       ;yes, set duty register bit 9
        btfsc   duty_hi,0    ;duty cycle hi bit 0 = 1?
        bsf     temp,6       ;yes, set duty register bit 8
        movf    temp,w       ;duty cycle bits 9-2
        movwf   ccpr1l       ;into duty cycle register
        bcf     ccp1con,5    ;clear bit 1 of duty cycle reg
        bcf     ccp1con,4    ;clear bit 0 of duty cycle reg
        btfsc   duty_lo,1    ;duty cycle bit 1 = 1?
        bsf     ccp1con,5    ;yes, set duty register bit 1
        btfsc   duty_lo,0    ;duty cycle bit 0 = 1?
        bsf     ccp1con,4    ;yes, set duty register bit 0
        return
;
        end
;-----------------------------------------------------------
;at blast time, select:
;       memory unprotected
;       watchdog timer disabled (default is enabled)
;       standard crystal (using 4 MHz osc for test) XT
;       power-up timer on
;       brown-out detect on
;===========================================================
```

An oscilloscope may be used to observe the output signal. The duty cycle will be 50 percent initially.

DESIGNING AND BUILDING
YOUR OWN TEST EQUIPMENT

Designing and building your own lab test equipment is a great way to have some fun and learn more about the applications for microcontrollers in projects of your own choosing. The projects presented are not intended to be the ultimate device of their type. They are intended as simple examples which demonstrate PIC'n **Techniques** you can use for your own amazement.

KEYPAD/LCD USER INTERFACE

To add to the fun and to create more useful experiments, we need a user interface which will allow us to key in numbers corresponding to pulse width, frequency, etc. Serial communication, interfacing an alphanumeric LCD, scanning keypads, and double precision arithmetic are explained in PIC'n **Up The Pace**. An interface using a 3x4 telephone keypad (switch matrix) and a 1 line by 16 character alphanumeric display along with a 3-digit decimal to 8-bit binary conversion program are presented there.

Since we are using a 16-bit timer here, we will need 5-digit decimal to 16-bit binary conversion capability. The Decimal Interface chapter in PIC'n **Up The Pace** describes 3-digit decimal to 8-bit binary conversion. The programming example is decentry.asm which includes the routines for scanning the keypad , serial output of the information to be displayed, and decimal-to-binary conversion. Following will be an adaptation of that program. The changes are:

- 5 decimal digits instead of 3.
- 16-bit binary result instead of 8-bit.
- Double precision addition to handle the 16-bit result.
- Runs on PIC16C63 instead of PIC16C84 or PIC16F84 (general purpose file registers start at 0x20).

The hardware for the remaining timing and counting experiments utilizes the '63 on a board used thus far plus the keypad and the PIC/LCD boards described in PIC'n **Up The Pace** (see Appendix D and Appendix E in this book).

Thus, there are three modules and a 5 volt power supply involved.

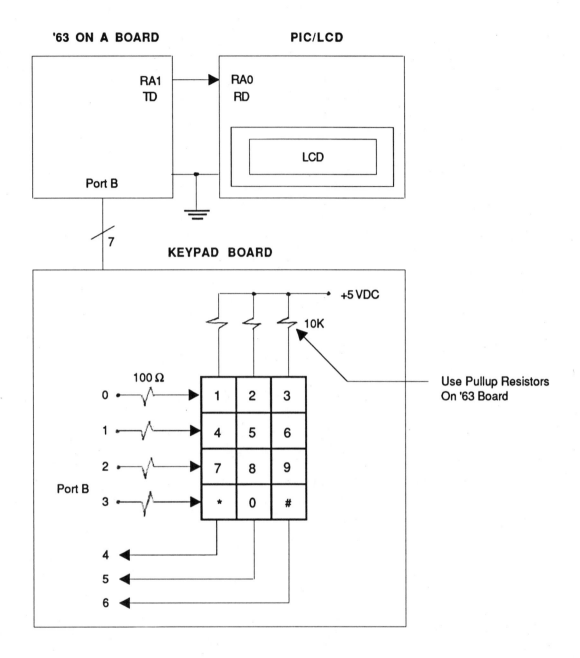

'63 ON A BOARD

PIC/LCD

RA1
TD

RA0
RD

LCD

Port B

KEYPAD BOARD

7

+5 VDC

10K

100 Ω

0

1

2

Port B

3

1	2	3
4	5	6
7	8	9
*	0	#

Use Pullup Resistors
On '63 Board

4

5

6

141

5-digit Decimal To 16-bit Binary Entry Program

The program does some setup and then gets each digit in succession, multiplies by its decimal weight (in binary) and adds it to a register pair which accumulates the total value of the number. The first digit entered is the 10,000's place digit so it is multiplied by 10,000 and added to the addition registers named "numsum". The second digit entered is multiplied by 1,000, and so on, until the binary equivalent of the number has been assembled in the numsum locations.

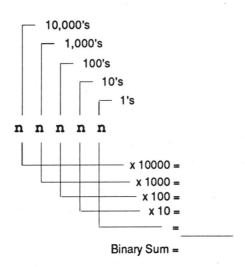

To supress high order zeros, we will need a most significant digit flag for each digit down to 100's. The first non-zero digit encountered will set the flag. From that point on, a zero should be displayed rather than being replaced with a blank.

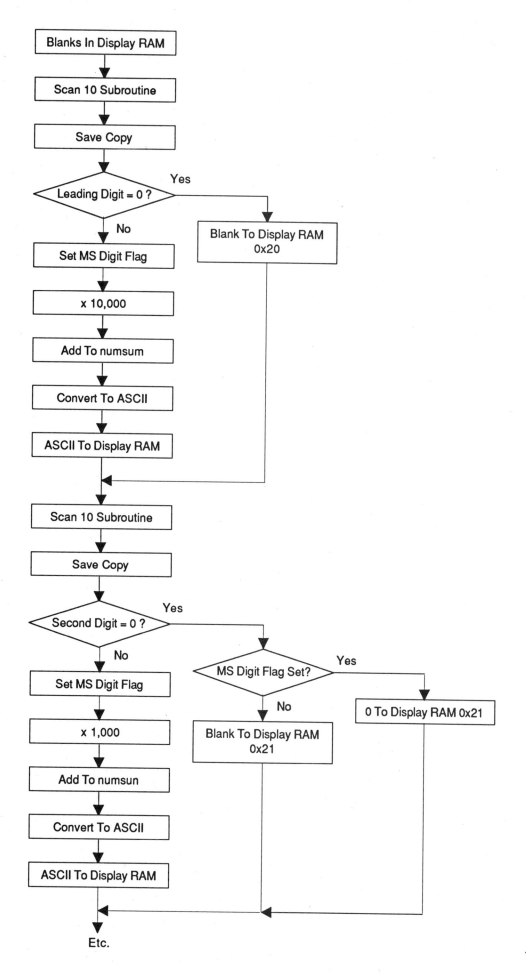

Etc.

```
;======DECENT63.ASM===============================9/21/98==
         list    p=16c63
         radix   hex
;------------------------------------------------------------
;        cpu equates (memory map)
tmr0     equ     0x01
status   equ     0x03
porta    equ     0x05
portb    equ     0x06
intcon   equ     0x0b
sendreg  equ     0x20
count    equ     0x21
instr    equ     0x22
char     equ     0x23
addr     equ     0x24
digctr   equ     0x25
rowctr   equ     0x26
colctr   equ     0x27
rowbits  equ     0x28
colbits  equ     0x29
temp     equ     0x2a
ncount   equ     0x2b
mcount   equ     0x2c
test_n   equ     0x2d
math     equ     0x2e
copy_8xn equ     0x2f
numsuml  equ     0x30
numsumh  equ     0x31
tenthou  equ     0x32
thou     equ     0x33
hund     equ     0x34
ten      equ     0x35
one      equ     0x36
hold     equ     0x37
lobyte   equ     0x38
hibyte   equ     0x39
copylo   equ     0x3a
copyhi   equ     0x3b
flags    equ     0x3c
optreg   equ     0x81
trisa    equ     0x85
trisb    equ     0x86
;------------------------------------------------------------
;        bit equates
c        equ     0
z        equ     2
rp0      equ     5
;------------------------------------------------------------
         org     0x000
;
start    bsf     status,rp0  ;switch to bank 1
         movlw   b'00000000' ;port A outputs
         movwf   trisa
```

144

```
         movlw    b'01110000'  ;port B inputs/outputs
         movwf    trisb
         bcf      status,rp0   ;switch back to bank 0
         bsf      porta,1      ;output mark, bit 1 (serial - LCD)
         bsf      portb,0      ;rows high
         bsf      portb,1
         bsf      portb,2
         bsf      portb,3
         bcf      portb,7      ;unused line low
         call     debounce
         call     debounce
         movlw    0x00         ;blanks to display RAM
         movwf    instr
         call     sndstf       ;send instruction to LCD module
         call     debounce
         movlw    0x01         ;send 16 characters to display
         movwf    instr
         call     sndstf       ;send instruction to LCD module
         call     debounce
         clrf     numsumh      ;clean out
         clrf     numsuml      ;clean out
         clrf     flags
do10000  call     scan10
         movf     digctr,w     ;get 10000's digit
         movwf    tenthou      ;save copy
         sublw    0x00         ;compare - digit=0?
         btfsc    status,z
         goto     tthzero      ;yes
         bsf      flags,0      ;no, this is ms digit
         movf     tenthou,w
         movwf    lobyte
         clrf     hibyte
         call     decmult      ;times 10
         call     decmult      ;times 10
         call     decmult      ;times 10
         call     decmult      ;times 10, result = x10000
         call     addnum       ;add 10000's to num sum registers
         movf     tenthou,w    ;get 10000's digit
         call     hex2asc      ;convert binary digit to ascii
         movwf    char
         movlw    0x20         ;display RAM address
         movwf    addr
         movlw    0x03         ;ascii char follows, send to display RAM
         movwf    instr
         call     sndstf       ;send 10000's digit to display RAM
         call     debounce     ;time delay - debounce switches
do1000   call     scan10
         movf     digctr,w     ;get 1000's digit
         movwf    thou         ;save copy
         sublw    0x00         ;compare - digit=0?
         btfsc    status,z
         goto     thzero       ;yes
         bsf      flags,0      ;no, this could be ms digit
         movf     thou,w
```

```
        movwf    lobyte
        clrf     hibyte
        call     decmult        ;times 10
        call     decmult        ;times 10
        call     decmult        ;times 10, result = x1000
        call     addnum         ;add 1000's to num sum registers
        movf     thou,w         ;get 1000's digit
        call     hex2asc        ;convert binary digit to ascii
        movwf    char
        movlw    0x21           ;display RAM address
        movwf    addr
        movlw    0x03           ;ascii char follows, send to display RAM
        movwf    instr
        call     sndstf         ;send 1000's digit to display RAM
        call     debounce       ;time delay - debounce switches
do100   call     scan10
        movf     digctr,w       ;get 100's digit
        movwf    hund           ;save copy
        sublw    0x00           ;compare - digit=0?
        btfsc    status,z
        goto     hzero          ;yes
        bsf      flags,0        ;no, this could be ms digit
        movf     hund,w
        movwf    lobyte
        clrf     hibyte
        call     decmult        ;times 10
        call     decmult        ;times 10, result = x100
        call     addnum         ;add 100's to num sum registers
        movf     hund,w         ;get 100's digit
        call     hex2asc        ;convert binary digit to ascii
        movwf    char
        movlw    0x22           ;display RAM address
        movwf    addr
        movlw    0x03           ;ascii char follows, send to display RAM
        movwf    instr
        call     sndstf         ;send 100's digit to display RAM
        call     debounce       ;time delay - debounce switches
do10    call     scan10
        movf     digctr,w       ;get 10's digit
        movwf    ten            ;save copy
        sublw    0x00           ;compare - digit=0?
        btfsc    status,z
        goto     tzero          ;yes
        movf     ten,w
        movwf    lobyte
        clrf     hibyte
        call     decmult        ;times 10
        call     addnum         ;add 10's to num sum registers
        movf     ten,w          ;get 10's digit
        call     hex2asc        ;convert binary digit to ascii
        movwf    char
        movlw    0x23           ;display RAM address
        movwf    addr
        movlw    0x03           ;ascii char follows, send to display RAM
```

146

```
        movwf   instr
        call    sndstf          ;send 10's digit to display RAM
        call    debounce        ;time delay - debounce switches
do1     call    scan10
        movf    digctr,w        ;get 1's digit
        movwf   one             ;save copy
        movwf   lobyte
        clrf    hibyte
        call    addnum          ;add 1's to num sum registers
        movf    one,w           ;get one's digit
        call    hex2asc         ;convert binary digit to ascii
        movwf   char
        movlw   0x24            ;display RAM address
        movwf   addr
        movlw   0x03            ;ascii char follows, send to display RAM
        movwf   instr
        call    sndstf          ;send 1's digit to display RAM
        call    debounce
send    movlw   0x01            ;send 16 characters to display
        movwf   instr
        call    sndstf          ;to LCD module
;------------------------------------------------------------
        call    debounce        ;delay, display decimal entry
        call    debounce
        call    debounce
        call    debounce
        call    debounce
        call    debounce
        call    debounce
        call    debounce
        call    debounce
        call    debounce
;------------------------------------------------------------
;display numsum contents high byte first with time delay
        movf    numsumh,w       ;get total high byte
        movwf   char
        movlw   0x04            ;hex byte follows, convert and display
        movwf   instr
        call    sndstf
        call    debounce        ;delay, display high byte
        call    debounce
        call    debounce
        call    debounce
        call    debounce
        call    debounce
        call    debounce
        call    debounce
        call    debounce
        call    debounce
        movf    numsuml,w       ;get total low byte
        movwf   char
        movlw   0x04            ;hex byte follows, convert and display
        movwf   instr
        call    sndstf
```

```
circle  goto    circle      ;done
;----------------------------------------------------------
tthzero movlw   0x20        ;ascii blank
        movwf   char
        movlw   0x20        ;display RAM address
        movwf   addr
        movlw   0x03        ;ascii character to display RAM
        movwf   instr
        call    sndstf
        call    debounce
        goto    do1000
;----------------------------------------------------------
thzero  btfsc   flags,0     ;ms digit entered?
        goto    zeroth      ;yes
        movlw   0x20        ;ascii blank
thchar  movwf   char
        movlw   0x21        ;display RAM address
        movwf   addr
        movlw   0x03        ;ascii character to display RAM
        movwf   instr
        call    sndstf
        call    debounce
        goto    do100
zeroth  movlw   0x30        ;ascii 0
        goto    thchar
;----------------------------------------------------------
hzero   btfsc   flags,0     ;ms digit entered?
        goto    zeroh       ;yes
        movlw   0x20        ;ascii blank
hchar   movwf   char
        movlw   0x22        ;display RAM address
        movwf   addr
        movlw   0x03        ;ascii character to display RAM
        movwf   instr
        call    sndstf
        call    debounce
        goto    do10
zeroh   movlw   0x30        ;ascii 0
        goto    hchar
;----------------------------------------------------------
tzero   btfsc   flags,0     ;ms digit entered?
        goto    zerot       ;yes
        movlw   0x20        ;ascii blank
tchar   movwf   char
        movlw   0x23        ;display RAM address
        movwf   addr
        movlw   0x03        ;ascii character to display RAM
        movwf   instr
        call    sndstf
        call    debounce
        goto    do1
zerot   movlw   0x30        ;ascii 0
        goto    tchar
;----------------------------------------------------------
```

```
;returns with digit in digctr
;
scan10  bsf     portb,0     ;rows high
        bsf     portb,1
        bsf     portb,2
        bsf     portb,3
        clrf    digctr      ;digit counter=0
        bcf     portb,3     ;row=4
        btfss   portb,5     ;test column 2
        return              ;"0" key press
        bsf     portb,3     ;deselect row 4
        movlw   0x01
        movwf   digctr      ;digit counter=1
        movwf   rowctr      ;row counter=1
        movwf   rowbits     ;row bits = 0000 0001
rowout  movf    rowbits,w   ;get row bits
        xorlw   0x0f        ;complement row bits
        movwf   portb       ;output row bits
        movlw   0x01
        movwf   colctr      ;column counter=1
        movlw   0x10        ;0001 0000
        movwf   colbits     ;col=1
tstcol  movf    portb,w     ;read port B
        andlw   0x70        ;mask off rows and bit 7
        movwf   temp        ;columns
        movf    colbits,w   ;get column bits
        xorlw   0x70        ;complement column bits
        subwf   temp,w      ;compare with contents of temp
        btfsc   status,z
        return              ;digit available
lastc   movf    colctr,w    ;get column count
        sublw   0x03
        btfsc   status,z    ;=3 ?
        goto    lastr
        rlf     colbits,f   ;shift column bits
        bcf     colbits,0   ;fix carry flag garbage
        incf    colctr,f
        incf    digctr,f
        goto    tstcol
lastr   movf    rowctr,w    ;get row count
        sublw   0x03
        btfsc   status,z    ;=3 ?
        goto    scan10      ;scan 10 digit keys again
        rlf     rowbits,f   ;shift row bits
        bcf     rowbits,0   ;fix carry flag garbage
        incf    rowctr,f
        incf    digctr,f
        goto    rowout
;-------------------------------------------------------------
debounce movlw  0x02        ;to counter
        movwf   count
dbloop  movlw   0xff        ;M
        movwf   mcount      ;to M counter
loadn   movlw   0xff        ;N
```

```
              movwf   ncount      ;to N counter
decn          decfsz  ncount,f    ;decrement N
              goto    decn        ;again
              decfsz  mcount,f    ;decrement M
              goto    loadn       ;again
              decfsz  count,f
              goto    dbloop      ;thru loop within a loop twice -
;                                 400 milliseconds
              return              ;done
;----------------------------------------------------------
sndstf        movf    instr,w     ;get instruction
              movwf   sendreg     ;to be sent
              call    ser_out     ;to serial out subroutine
              movf    char,w      ;get character or hex byte
              movwf   sendreg     ;to be sent
              call    ser_out     ;to serial out subroutine
              movf    addr,w      ;get address
              movwf   sendreg     ;to be sent
              call    ser_out     ;to serial out subroutine
              return
;----------------------------------------------------------
ser_out       bcf     intcon,5    ;disable tmr0 interrupts
              bcf     intcon,7    ;disable global interrupts
              clrf    tmr0        ;clear timer/counter
              clrwdt              ;clear wdt prep prescaler assign
              bsf     status,rp0  ;to page 1
              movlw   b'11011000' ;set up timer/counter
              movwf   optreg
              bcf     status,rp0  ;back to page 0
              movlw   0x08        ;init shift counter
              movwf   count
              bcf     porta,1     ;start bit
              clrf    tmr0        ;start timer/counter
              bcf     intcon,2    ;clear tmr0 overflow flag
time1         btfss   intcon,2    ;timer overflow?
              goto    time1       ;no
              bcf     intcon,2    ;yes, clear overflow flag
nxtbit        rlf     sendreg,f   ;rotate msb into carry flag
              bcf     porta,1     ;clear port A, bit 1
              btfsc   status,c    ;test carry flag
              bsf     porta,1     ;bit is set
time2         btfss   intcon,2    ;timer overflow?
              goto    time2       ;no
              bcf     intcon,2    ;clear overflow flag
              decfsz  count,f     ;shifted 8?
              goto    nxtbit      ;no
              bsf     porta,1     ;yes, output mark
time3         btfss   intcon,2    ;timer overflow?
              goto    time3       ;no
              return              ;done
;----------------------------------------------------------
;multiply 2-byte binary number by 10 decimal
;enter sub with number in hibyte and lobyte - exit with result
;   in hybyte and lobyte
```

```
;
decmult movf     lobyte,w     ;get low byte
        movwf    copylo       ;store copy
        movf     hibyte,w     ;get high byte
        movwf    copyhi       ;store copy
        bcf      status,c     ;clear carry flag
        rlf      lobyte,f     ;rotate low byte
        rlf      hibyte,f     ;rotate high byte
        bcf      status,c     ;clear carry flag
        rlf      lobyte,f     ;rotate low byte
        rlf      hibyte,f     ;rotate high byte
        movf     copylo,w     ;fetch low byte
        addwf    lobyte,f     ;add low bytes
        btfss    status,c     ;carry set?
        goto     contin       ;no, continue
        incf     hibyte,f     ;yes, add 1 to hi byte
contin  movf     copyhi,w     ;fetch high byte
        addwf    hibyte,f     ;add high bytes
        bcf      status,c     ;clear carry flag
        rlf      lobyte,f     ;rotate low byte
        rlf      hibyte,f     ;rotate high byte
        return
;----------------------------------------------------------
;add digit to numsum registers - enter with digit in hibyte
;    and lobyte
;
addnum  movf     lobyte,w     ;fetch low byte
        addwf    numsuml,f    ;add low bytes, result in numsuml
        btfsc    status,c     ;carry set?
        incf     numsumh,f    ;yes, add 1 to msb result
        movf     hibyte,w     ;fetch high byte
        addwf    numsumh,f    ;add high bytes, result in numsumh
        return
;----------------------------------------------------------
;enter with hex digit in w
;
hex2asc movwf    hold         ;store copy of hex digit
        sublw    0x09         ;subtract w from 1 less than 0x0a
        btfss    status,c     ;carry flag set if w < 0x0a
        goto     add37
        goto     add30
add37   movf     hold,w       ;get hex digit
        addlw    0x37
        return                ;return with ascii in w
add30   movf     hold,w       ;get hex digit
        addlw    0x30
        return                ;return with ascii in w
;----------------------------------------------------------
        end
;----------------------------------------------------------
;at blast time, select:
;       memory unprotected
;       watchdog timer disabled (default is enabled)
;       standard crystal (using 4 MHz osc for test) XT
```

```
;          power-up timer on
;          brown-out detect on
;================================================================
```

Using The 5-digit Decimal To 16-bit Binary Entry Program

- Power up the '63 and PIC/LCD boards
- LCD will display "HELLO" briefly and then go blank.
- Key in 5 digits (including leading zeros)
- 0 - must key in 5 zeros
- Range of numbers is 0 to 65535.

The number keyed in will be displayed and will be in the "numsum" registers. The most significant byte will be displayed on completion of a time delay followed by the least significant byte after a second time delay.

Examples:

```
------------------------------------------------
Key In        Hex        High Byte    Low Byte
------------------------------------------------
00000       0x0000       0000 0000    0000 0000
00015       0x000F       0000 0000    0000 1111
00016       0x0010       0000 0000    0001 0000
65535       0xFFFF       1111 1111    1111 1111
65536       0x0000       0000 0000    0000 0000
12345       0x3039       0011 0000    0011 1001
```

The resulting number may be loaded into a counter or used for set point comparison or whatever.

Hit the reset switch on both the '63 board and PIC/LCD board between entries.

DIGITAL PULSE GENERATOR

The object here is to be able to key in the desired pulse width in microseconds and to have that pulse output when the "ready" switch is opened. The 5-digit decimal number keyed in must be displayed on the LCD and converted to 16-bit binary for use in the compare register to determine the pulse width. The pulse is output via the CCP1 pin and is terminated when the contents of timer 1 match the contents of the compare register. The pulse is positive going.

The range of possible pulse widths is 25 to 65,535 microseconds. The range could be extended to longer pulses by using an external clock providing 1 millisecond or 1 second pulses (as examples).

Two programs are combined to accomplish this. They are:

- Pulse generator (one128.asm).
- Keypad/LCD user interface (decent63.asm).

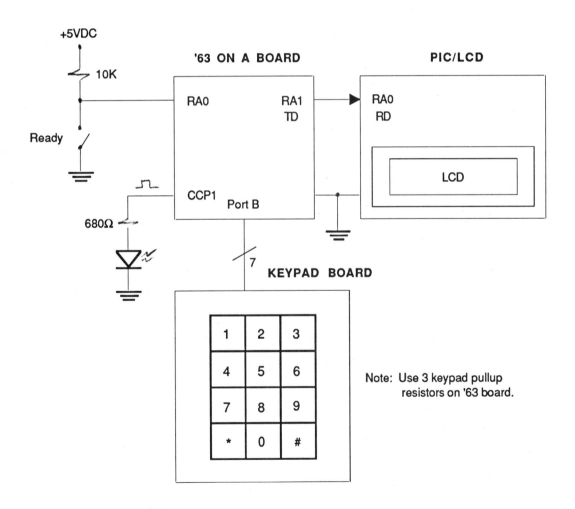

Note: Use 3 keypad pullup resistors on '63 board.

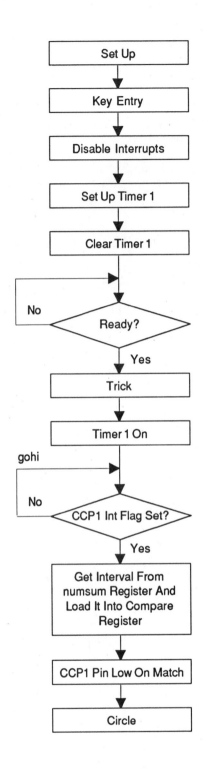

```
            ┌──────────────────────┐
            │       Set Up         │
            └──────────┬───────────┘
                       ▼
            ┌──────────────────────┐
            │     Key Entry        │
            └──────────┬───────────┘
                       ▼
            ┌──────────────────────┐
            │  Disable Interrupts  │
            └──────────┬───────────┘
                       ▼
            ┌──────────────────────┐
            │    Set Up Timer 1    │
            └──────────┬───────────┘
                       ▼
            ┌──────────────────────┐
            │    Clear Timer 1     │
            └──────────┬───────────┘
                       ▼
      No           ╱ Ready? ╲
      ◄───────────◄           ►
                   ╲         ╱
                       │ Yes
                       ▼
            ┌──────────────────────┐
            │        Trick         │
            └──────────┬───────────┘
                       ▼
            ┌──────────────────────┐
            │     Timer 1 On       │
            └──────────┬───────────┘
   gohi
      No        ╱ CCP1 Int Flag Set? ╲
      ◄────────◄                       ►
                ╲                     ╱
                       │ Yes
                       ▼
            ┌──────────────────────┐
            │   Get Interval From  │
            │  numsum Register And │
            │  Load It Into Compare│
            │       Register       │
            └──────────┬───────────┘
                       ▼
            ┌──────────────────────┐
            │ CCP1 Pin Low On Match│
            └──────────┬───────────┘
                       ▼
            ┌──────────────────────┐
            │       Circle         │
            └──────────────────────┘
```

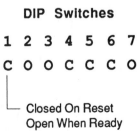

DIP Switches

1 2 3 4 5 6 7

C O O C C C O

└── Closed On Reset
    Open When Ready

154

```
;======PULSGEN.ASM===============================9/28/98==
        list    p=16c63
        radix   hex
;-------------------------------------------------------------
;       cpu equates (memory map)
tmr0    equ     0x01
status  equ     0x03
porta   equ     0x05
portb   equ     0x06
portc   equ     0x07
intcon  equ     0x0b
pir1    equ     0x0c
tmr1l   equ     0x0e
tmr1h   equ     0x0f
t1con   equ     0x10
ccpr1l  equ     0x15
ccpr1h  equ     0x16
ccp1con equ     0x17
sendreg equ     0x20
count   equ     0x21
instr   equ     0x22
char    equ     0x23
addr    equ     0x24
digctr  equ     0x25
rowctr  equ     0x26
colctr  equ     0x27
rowbits equ     0x28
colbits equ     0x29
temp    equ     0x2a
ncount  equ     0x2b
mcount  equ     0x2c
test_n  equ     0x2d
math    equ     0x2e
copy_8xn equ    0x2f
numsuml equ     0x30
numsumh equ     0x31
tenthou equ     .0x32
thou    equ     0x33
hund    equ     0x34
ten     equ     0x35
one     equ     0x36
hold    equ     0x37
lobyte  equ     0x38
hibyte  equ     0x39
copylo  equ     0x3a
copyhi  equ     0x3b
flags   equ     0x3c
optreg  equ     0x81
trisa   equ     0x85
trisb   equ     0x86
trisc   equ     0x87
pie1    equ     0x8c
;-------------------------------------------------------------
```

```
;       bit equates
c       equ     0
z       equ     2
rp0     equ     5
ccp1    equ     2               ;ccp1 bit 2, port C
;------------------------------------------------------------
        org     0x000
;
start   bsf     status,rp0      ;switch to bank 1
        movlw   b'00000001'     ;port A inputs/outputs
        movwf   trisa
        bsf     trisa,0         ;port A, bit 0 input
        movlw   b'01110000'     ;port B inputs/outputs
        movwf   trisb
        bcf     trisc,ccp1      ;ccp1 pin output
        bcf     status,rp0      ;switch back to bank 0
        bcf     portc,ccp1      ;ccp1 pin low
        bsf     porta,1         ;output mark, bit 1 (serial - LCD)
        bsf     portb,0         ;rows high
        bsf     portb,1
        bsf     portb,2
        bsf     portb,3
        bcf     portb,7         ;unused line low
        call    debounce
        call    debounce
        movlw   0x00            ;blanks to display RAM
        movwf   instr
        call    sndstf          ;send instruction to LCD module
        call    debounce
        movlw   0x01            ;send 16 characters to display
        movwf   instr
        call    sndstf          ;send instruction to LCD module
        call    debounce
        clrf    numsumh         ;clean out
        clrf    numsuml         ;clean out
        clrf    flags
do10000 call    scan10
        movf    digctr,w        ;get 10000's digit
        movwf   tenthou         ;save copy
        sublw   0x00            ;compare - digit=0?
        btfsc   status,z
        goto    tthzero         ;yes
        bsf     flags,0         ;no, this is ms digit
        movf    tenthou,w
        movwf   lobyte
        clrf    hibyte
        call    decmult         ;times 10
        call    decmult         ;times 10
        call    decmult         ;times 10
        call    decmult         ;times 10, result = x10000
        call    addnum          ;add 10000's to num sum registers
        movf    tenthou,w       ;get 10000's digit
        call    hex2asc         ;convert binary digit to ascii
        movwf   char
```

```
          movlw     0x20           ;display RAM address
          movwf     addr
          movlw     0x03           ;ascii char follows, send to display RAM
          movwf     instr
          call      sndstf         ;send 10000's digit to display RAM
          call      debounce       ;time delay - debounce switches
do1000    call      scan10
          movf      digctr,w       ;get 1000's digit
          movwf     thou           ;save copy
          sublw     0x00           ;compare - digit=0?
          btfsc     status,z
          goto      thzero         ;yes
          bsf       flags,0        ;no, this could be ms digit
          movf      thou,w
          movwf     lobyte
          clrf      hibyte
          call      decmult        ;times 10
          call      decmult        ;times 10
          call      decmult        ;times 10, result = x1000
          call      addnum         ;add 1000's to num sum registers
          movf      thou,w         ;get 1000's digit
          call      hex2asc        ;convert binary digit to ascii
          movwf     char
          movlw     0x21           ;display RAM address
          movwf     addr
          movlw     0x03           ;ascii char follows, send to display RAM
          movwf     instr
          call      sndstf         ;send 1000's digit to display RAM
          call      debounce       ;time delay - debounce switches
do100     call      scan10
          movf      digctr,w       ;get 100's digit
          movwf     hund           ;save copy
          sublw     0x00           ;compare - digit=0?
          btfsc     status,z
          goto      hzero          ;yes
          bsf       flags,0        ;no, this could be ms digit
          movf      hund,w
          movwf     lobyte
          clrf      hibyte
          call      decmult        ;times 10
          call      decmult        ;times 10, result = x100
          call      addnum         ;add 100's to num sum registers
          movf      hund,w         ;get 100's digit
          call      hex2asc        ;convert binary digit to ascii
          movwf     char
          movlw     0x22           ;display RAM address
          movwf     addr
          movlw     0x03           ;ascii char follows, send to display RAM
          movwf     instr
          call      sndstf         ;send 100's digit to display RAM
          call      debounce       ;time delay - debounce switches
do10      call      scan10
          movf      digctr,w       ;get 10's digit
          movwf     ten            ;save copy
```

```
        sublw     0x00          ;compare - digit=0?
        btfsc     status,z
        goto      tzero         ;yes
        movf      ten,w
        movwf     lobyte
        clrf      hibyte
        call      decmult       ;times 10
        call      addnum        ;add 10's to num sum registers
        movf      ten,w         ;get 10's digit
        call      hex2asc       ;convert binary digit to ascii
        movwf     char
        movlw     0x23          ;display RAM address
        movwf     addr
        movlw     0x03          ;ascii char follows, send to display RAM
        movwf     instr
        call      sndstf        ;send 10's digit to display RAM
        call      debounce      ;time delay - debounce switches
do1     call      scan10
        movf      digctr,w      ;get 1's digit
        movwf     one           ;save copy
        movwf     lobyte
        clrf      hibyte
        call      addnum        ;add 1's to num sum registers
        movf      one,w         ;get one's digit
        call      hex2asc       ;convert binary digit to ascii
        movwf     char
        movlw     0x24          ;display RAM address
        movwf     addr
        movlw     0x03          ;ascii char follows, send to display RAM
        movwf     instr
        call      sndstf        ;send 1's digit to display RAM
        call      debounce
send    movlw     0x01          ;send 16 characters to display
        movwf     instr
        call      sndstf        ;to LCD module
        call      debounce      ;delay, display decimal entry
;-------------------------------------------------------
        bcf       intcon,7      ;disable global interrupts
        bcf       intcon,6      ;disable peripheral interrupts
        bsf       status,rp0    ;bank 1
        bcf       pie1,0        ;disable timer 1 interrupts
        bcf       pie1,2        ;disable ccp1 interrupts
        bcf       status,rp0    ;bank 0
        bcf       pir1,2        ;clear ccp1 interrupt flag
        clrf      ccp1con       ;ccp1 module off
        movlw     b'00000000'   ;tmr1 prescaler and tmr1 setup,
        movwf     t1con         ;   tmr1 off
        clrf      tmr1h         ;clear timer 1 high
        clrf      tmr1l         ;clear timer 1 low
ready   btfss     porta,0       ;ready?
        goto      ready         ;not yet
trick   clrf      ccpr1h        ;clear compare register high
        movlw     0x01          ;load compare register low
        movwf     ccpr1l
```

```
          movlw    b'00001000'  ;ccp1 compare mode, ccp1 pin high
          movwf    ccp1con      ;   on match, ccp1 module on,
                                 ;   ccp1 pin low
          bsf      t1con,0      ;timer 1 on
gohi      btfss    pir1,2       ;ccp1 interrupt flag set?
          goto     gohi         ;not yet
          movf     numsumh,w    ;get interval high byte
          movwf    ccpr1h       ;load compare register high
          movf     numsuml,w    ;get interval low byte
          movwf    ccpr1l       ;load compare register low
          bsf      ccp1con,0    ;ccp1 pin low on match
circle    goto     circle       ;done
;---------------------------------------------------------------
tthzero   movlw    0x20         ;ascii blank
          movwf    char
          movlw    0x20         ;display RAM address
          movwf    addr
          movlw    0x03         ;ascii character to display RAM
          movwf    instr
          call     sndstf
          call     debounce
          goto     do1000
;---------------------------------------------------------------
thzero    btfsc    flags,0      ;ms digit entered?
          goto     zeroth       ;yes
          movlw    0x20         ;ascii blank
thchar    movwf    char
          movlw    0x21         ;display RAM address
          movwf    addr
          movlw    0x03         ;ascii character to display RAM
          movwf    instr
          call     sndstf
          call     debounce
          goto     do100
zeroth    movlw    0x30         ;ascii 0
          goto     thchar
;---------------------------------------------------------------
hzero     btfsc    flags,0      ;ms digit entered?
          goto     zeroh        ;yes
          movlw    0x20         ;ascii blank
hchar     movwf    char
          movlw    0x22         ;display RAM address
          movwf    addr
          movlw    0x03         ;ascii character to display RAM
          movwf    instr
          call     sndstf
          call     debounce
          goto     do10
zeroh     movlw    0x30         ;ascii 0
          goto     hchar
;---------------------------------------------------------------
tzero     btfsc    flags,0      ;ms digit entered?
          goto     zerot        ;yes
          movlw    0x20         ;ascii blank
```

159

```
tchar     movwf    char
          movlw    0x23        ;display RAM address
          movwf    addr
          movlw    0x03        ;ascii character to display RAM
          movwf    instr
          call     sndstf
          call     debounce
          goto     do1
zerot     movlw    0x30        ;ascii 0
          goto     tchar
;-------------------------------------------------------------
;returns with digit in digctr
;
scan10    bsf      portb,0     ;rows high
          bsf      portb,1
          bsf      portb,2
          bsf      portb,3
          clrf     digctr      ;digit counter=0
          bcf      portb,3     ;row=4
          btfss    portb,5     ;test column 2
          return               ;"0" key press
          bsf      portb,3     ;deselect row 4
          movlw    0x01
          movwf    digctr      ;digit counter=1
          movwf    rowctr      ;row counter=1
          movwf    rowbits     ;row bits = 0000 0001
rowout    movf     rowbits,w   ;get row bits
          xorlw    0x0f        ;complement row bits
          movwf    portb       ;output row bits
          movlw    0x01
          movwf    colctr      ;column counter=1
          movlw    0x10        ;0001 0000
          movwf    colbits     ;col=1
tstcol    movf     portb,w     ;read port B
          andlw    0x70        ;mask off rows and bit 7
          movwf    temp        ;columns
          movf     colbits,w   ;get column bits
          xorlw    0x70        ;complement column bits
          subwf    temp,w      ;compare with contents of temp
          btfsc    status,z
          return               ;digit available
lastc     movf     colctr,w    ;get column count
          sublw    0x03
          btfsc    status,z     ;=3 ?
          goto     lastr
          rlf      colbits,f   ;shift column bits
          bcf      colbits,0   ;fix carry flag garbage
          incf     colctr,f
          incf     digctr,f
          goto     tstcol
lastr     movf     rowctr,w    ;get row count
          sublw    0x03
          btfsc    status,z     ;=3 ?
          goto     scan10      ;scan 10 digit keys again
```

```
        rlf     rowbits,f   ;shift row bits
        bcf     rowbits,0   ;fix carry flag garbage
        incf    rowctr,f
        incf    digctr,f
        goto    rowout
;------------------------------------------------------------
debounce movlw  0x02        ;to counter
        movwf   count
dbloop  movlw   0xff        ;M
        movwf   mcount      ;to M counter
loadn   movlw   0xff        ;N
        movwf   ncount      ;to N counter
decn    decfsz  ncount,f    ;decrement N
        goto    decn        ;again
        decfsz  mcount,f    ;decrement M
        goto    loadn       ;again
        decfsz  count,f
        goto    dbloop      ;thru loop within a loop twice -
;                               400 milliseconds
        return              ;done
;------------------------------------------------------------
sndstf  movf    instr,w     ;get instruction
        movwf   sendreg     ;to be sent
        call    ser_out     ;to serial out subroutine
        movf    char,w      ;get character or hex byte
        movwf   sendreg     ;to be sent
        call    ser_out     ;to serial out subroutine
        movf    addr,w      ;get address
        movwf   sendreg     ;to be sent
        call    ser_out     ;to serial out subroutine
        return
;------------------------------------------------------------
ser_out bcf     intcon,5    ;disable tmr0 interrupts
        bcf     intcon,7    ;disable global interrupts
        clrf    tmr0        ;clear timer/counter
        clrwdt              ;clear wdt prep prescaler assign
        bsf     status,rp0  ;to page 1
        movlw   b'11011000' ;set up timer/counter
        movwf   optreg
        bcf     status,rp0  ;back to page 0
        movlw   0x08        ;init shift counter
        movwf   count
        bcf     porta,1     ;start bit
        clrf    tmr0        ;start timer/counter
        bcf     intcon,2    ;clear tmr0 overflow flag
time1   btfss   intcon,2    ;timer overflow?
        goto    time1       ;no
        bcf     intcon,2    ;yes, clear overflow flag
nxtbit  rlf     sendreg,f   ;rotate msb into carry flag
        bcf     porta,1     ;clear port A, bit 1
        btfsc   status,c    ;test carry flag
        bsf     porta,1     ;bit is set
time2   btfss   intcon,2    ;timer overflow?
        goto    time2       ;no
```

```
        bcf       intcon,2      ;clear overflow flag
        decfsz    count,f       ;shifted 8?
        goto      nxtbit        ;no
        bsf       porta,1       ;yes, output mark
time3   btfss     intcon,2      ;timer overflow?
        goto      time3         ;no
        return                  ;done
;----------------------------------------------------------------
;multiply 2-byte binary number by 10 decimal
;enter sub with number in hibyte and lobyte - exit with result
;    in hybyte and lobyte
;
decmult movf      lobyte,w      ;get low byte
        movwf     copylo        ;store copy
        movf      hibyte,w      ;get high byte
        movwf     copyhi        ;store copy
        bcf       status,c      ;clear carry flag
        rlf       lobyte,f      ;rotate low byte
        rlf       hibyte,f      ;rotate high byte
        bcf       status,c      ;clear carry flag
        rlf       lobyte,f      ;rotate low byte
        rlf       hibyte,f      ;rotate high byte
        movf      copylo,w      ;fetch low byte
        addwf     lobyte,f      ;add low bytes
        btfss     status,c      ;carry set?
        goto      contin        ;no, continue
        incf      hibyte,f      ;yes, add 1 to hi byte
contin  movf      copyhi,w      ;fetch high byte
        addwf     hibyte,f      ;add high bytes
        bcf       status,c      ;clear carry flag
        rlf       lobyte,f      ;rotate low byte
        rlf       hibyte,f      ;rotate high byte
        return
;----------------------------------------------------------
;add digit to numsum registers - enter with digit in hibyte
;    and lobyte
;
addnum  movf      lobyte,w      ;fetch low byte
        addwf     numsuml,f     ;add low bytes, result in numsuml
        btfsc     status,c      ;carry set?
        incf      numsumh,f     ;yes, add 1 to msb result
        movf      hibyte,w      ;fetch high byte
        addwf     numsumh,f     ;add high bytes, result in numsumh
        return
;----------------------------------------------------------
;enter with hex digit in w
;
hex2asc movwf     hold          ;store copy of hex digit
        sublw     0x09          ;subtract w from 1 less than 0x0a
        btfss     status,c      ;carry flag set if w < 0x0a
        goto      add37
        goto      add30
add37   movf      hold,w        ;get hex digit
        addlw     0x37
```

162

```
        return              ;return with ascii in w
add30   movf    hold,w      ;get hex digit
        addlw   0x30
        return              ;return with ascii in w
;----------------------------------------------------------------
        end
;----------------------------------------------------------------
;at blast time, select:
;       memory unprotected
;       watchdog timer disabled (default is enabled)
;       standard crystal (using 4 MHz osc for test) XT
;       power-up timer on
;       brown-out detect on
;================================================================
```

This device may be tested by using a PIC16F84 to measure pulse width. An example was given earlier which measures pulse width up to 255 microseconds (pgentst.asm). This program may be modified to measure pulse widths covering the range of the device (25 to 65,535 microseconds).

Notice that short pulses can not be seen with the eye. I can't see a 1,000 microsecond pulse, but I can see a 5,000 microsecond pulse.

Procedure:

    1) In preparation for power-up:
         "ready" switch on '63 closed.
    2) Power-up '63.
    3) Key in the pulse width (microseconds).
    4) Open the "ready" switch on the '63.
    5) Observe interval via LED or PIC16F84 circuit or storage oscilloscope.

DIGITAL FREQUENCY GENERATOR

Building a frequency generator is more fun and the output can be observed more easily using an oscilloscope. The object here is to be able to key in the desired pulse width (time the output is high or low) in microseconds. The 5-digit decimal number keyed in must be displayed on the LCD and converted to 16-bit binary for use in the compare register to determine the pulse width. The signal is output via the CCP1 pin. The signal changes level when the contents of timer 1 match the contents of the compare register. Each time a match occurs, the interval value is added to the compare register and the process is repeated.

The range of possible pulse widths is 25 to 65,535 microseconds which translates to a frequency range of 7.6 Hz to 20 KHz. The range could be extended to lower frequencies by using an external clock providing 1 millisecond or 1 second pulses (as examples). The upper frequency limit is largely determined by the PIC16C63 clock oscillator frequency which gets divided to generate the output signal. The software overhead also is a factor in determining the maximum frequency attainable. So - for lower frequencies, use a slower time base. For higher frequencies, use a faster clock oscillator for the PIC16C63.

Two programs are combined to accomplish this. They are:

- Frequency generator (freeadd.asm).
- Keypad/LCD user interface (decent63.asm).

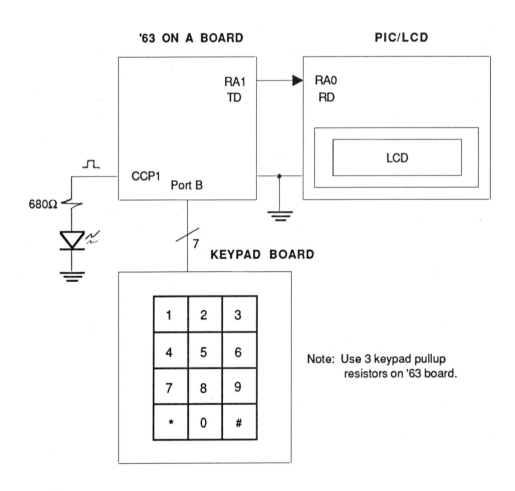

164

Main Program

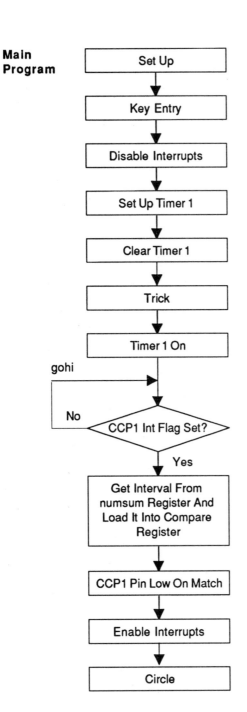

Set Up

Key Entry

Disable Interrupts

Set Up Timer 1

Clear Timer 1

Trick

Timer 1 On

gohi

No

CCP1 Int Flag Set?

Yes

Get Interval From numsum Register And Load It Into Compare Register

CCP1 Pin Low On Match

Enable Interrupts

Circle

Interrupt Service Routine

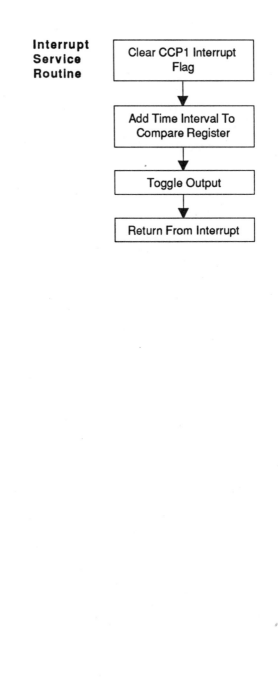

Clear CCP1 Interrupt Flag

Add Time Interval To Compare Register

Toggle Output

Return From Interrupt

DIP Switches

1	2	3	4	5	6	7
O	O	O	C	C	C	O

```
;======FREQGEN.ASM==================================9/28/98==
        list    p=16c63
        radix   hex
;-------------------------------------------------------------
;       cpu equates (memory map)
tmr0     equ       0x01
status   equ       0x03
porta    equ       0x05
portb    equ       0x06
portc    equ       0x07
intcon   equ       0x0b
pir1     equ       0x0c
tmr1l    equ       0x0e
tmr1h    equ       0x0f
t1con    equ       0x10
ccpr1l   equ       0x15
ccpr1h   equ       0x16
ccp1con  equ       0x17
sendreg  equ       0x20
count    equ       0x21
instr    equ       0x22
char     equ       0x23
addr     equ       0x24
digctr   equ       0x25
rowctr   equ       0x26
colctr   equ       0x27
rowbits  equ       0x28
colbits  equ       0x29
temp     equ       0x2a
ncount   equ       0x2b
mcount   equ       0x2c
test_n   equ       0x2d
math     equ       0x2e
copy_8xn equ       0x2f
numsuml  equ       0x30
numsumh  equ       0x31
tenthou  equ       0x32
thou     equ       0x33
hund     equ       0x34
ten      equ       0x35
one      equ       0x36
hold     equ       0x37
lobyte   equ       0x38
hibyte   equ       0x39
copylo   equ       0x3a
copyhi   equ       0x3b
flags    equ       0x3c
;
lsb2     equ       0x3d
msb2     equ       0x3e
;
optreg   equ       0x81
trisa    equ       0x85
```

```
trisb     equ     0x86
trisc     equ     0x87
pie1      equ     0x8c
;------------------------------------------------------------
;         bit equates
c         equ     0
z         equ     2
rp0       equ     5
ccp1      equ     2           ;ccp1 bit 2, port C
;------------------------------------------------------------
          org     0x000
          goto    start       ;skip over location pointed to by
                              ;    interrupt vector
          org     0x004
          goto    iserv
;
start     bsf     status,rp0  ;switch to bank 1
          movlw   b'00000000' ;port A outputs
          movwf   trisa
          movlw   b'01110000' ;port B inputs/outputs
          movwf   trisb
          bcf     trisc,ccp1  ;ccp1 pin output
          bcf     status,rp0  ;switch back to bank 0
          bcf     portc,ccp1  ;ccp1 pin low
          bsf     porta,1     ;output mark, bit 1 (serial - LCD)
          bsf     portb,0     ;rows high
          bsf     portb,1
          bsf     portb,2
          bsf     portb,3
          bcf     portb,7     ;unused line low
          call    debounce
          call    debounce
          movlw   0x00        ;blanks to display RAM
          movwf   instr
          call    sndstf      ;send instruction to LCD module
          call    debounce
          movlw   0x01        ;send 16 characters to display
          movwf   instr
          call    sndstf      ;send instruction to LCD module
          call    debounce
          clrf    numsumh      ;clean out
          clrf    numsuml      ;clean out
          clrf    flags
do10000   call    scan10
          movf    digctr,w    ;get 10000's digit
          movwf   tenthou     ;save copy
          sublw   0x00        ;compare - digit=0?
          btfsc   status,z
          goto    tthzero     ;yes
          bsf     flags,0     ;no, this is ms digit
          movf    tenthou,w
          movwf   lobyte
          clrf    hibyte
          call    decmult     ;times 10
```

```
        call    decmult         ;times 10
        call    decmult         ;times 10
        call    decmult         ;times 10, result = x10000
        call    addnum          ;add 10000's to num sum registers
        movf    tenthou,w       ;get 10000's digit
        call    hex2asc         ;convert binary digit to ascii
        movwf   char
        movlw   0x20            ;display RAM address
        movwf   addr
        movlw   0x03            ;ascii char follows, send to display RAM
        movwf   instr
        call    sndstf          ;send 10000's digit to display RAM
        call    debounce        ;time delay - debounce switches
do1000  call    scan10
        movf    digctr,w        ;get 1000's digit
        movwf   thou            ;save copy
        sublw   0x00            ;compare - digit=0?
        btfsc   status,z
        goto    thzero          ;yes
        bsf     flags,0         ;no, this could be ms digit
        movf    thou,w
        movwf   lobyte
        clrf    hibyte
        call    decmult         ;times 10
        call    decmult         ;times 10
        call    decmult         ;times 10, result = x1000
        call    addnum          ;add 1000's to num sum registers
        movf    thou,w          ;get 1000's digit
        call    hex2asc         ;convert binary digit to ascii
        movwf   char
        movlw   0x21            ;display RAM address
        movwf   addr
        movlw   0x03            ;ascii char follows, send to display RAM
        movwf   instr
        call    sndstf          ;send 1000's digit to display RAM
        call    debounce        ;time delay - debounce switches
do100   call    scan10
        movf    digctr,w        ;get 100's digit
        movwf   hund            ;save copy
        sublw   0x00            ;compare - digit=0?
        btfsc   status,z
        goto    hzero           ;yes
        bsf     flags,0         ;no, this could be ms digit
        movf    hund,w
        movwf   lobyte
        clrf    hibyte
        call    decmult         ;times 10
        call    decmult         ;times 10, result = x100
        call    addnum          ;add 100's to num sum registers
        movf    hund,w          ;get 100's digit
        call    hex2asc         ;convert binary digit to ascii
        movwf   char
        movlw   0x22            ;display RAM address
        movwf   addr
```

168

```
            movlw    0x03           ;ascii char follows, send to display RAM
            movwf    instr
            call     sndstf         ;send 100's digit to display RAM
            call     debounce       ;time delay - debounce switches
do10        call     scan10
            movf     digctr,w       ;get 10's digit
            movwf    ten            ;save copy
            sublw    0x00           ;compare - digit=0?
            btfsc    status,z
            goto     tzero          ;yes
            movf     ten,w
            movwf    lobyte
            clrf     hibyte
            call     decmult        ;times 10
            call     addnum         ;add 10's to num sum registers
            movf     ten,w          ;get 10's digit
            call     hex2asc        ;convert binary digit to ascii
            movwf    char
            movlw    0x23           ;display RAM address
            movwf    addr
            movlw    0x03           ;ascii char follows, send to display RAM
            movwf    instr
            call     sndstf         ;send 10's digit to display RAM
            call     debounce       ;time delay - debounce switches
do1         call     scan10
            movf     digctr,w       ;get 1's digit
            movwf    one            ;save copy
            movwf    lobyte
            clrf     hibyte
            call     addnum         ;add 1's to num sum registers
            movf     one,w          ;get one's digit
            call     hex2asc        ;convert binary digit to ascii
            movwf    char
            movlw    0x24           ;display RAM address
            movwf    addr
            movlw    0x03           ;ascii char follows, send to display RAM
            movwf    instr
            call     sndstf         ;send 1's digit to display RAM
            call     debounce
send        movlw    0x01           ;send 16 characters to display
            movwf    instr
            call     sndstf         ;to LCD module
            call     debounce       ;delay, display decimal entry
;------------------------------------------------------------
            bcf      intcon,7       ;disable global interrupts
            bcf      intcon,6       ;disable peripheral interrupts
            bsf      status,rp0     ;bank 1
            bcf      pie1,0         ;disable timer 1 interrupts
            bcf      pie1,2         ;disable ccp1 interrupts
            bcf      status,rp0     ;bank 0
            bcf      pir1,2         ;clear ccp1 interrupt flag
            clrf     ccp1con        ;ccp1 module off
            movlw    b'00000000'    ;tmr1 prescaler and tmr1 setup,
            movwf    t1con          ;   tmr1 off
```

169

```
        clrf    tmr1h       ;clear timer 1 high
        clrf    tmr1l       ;clear timer 1 low
trick   clrf    ccpr1h      ;clear compare register high
        movlw   0x01        ;load compare register low
        movwf   ccpr1l
        movlw   b'00001000' ;ccp1 compare mode, ccp1 pin high
        movwf   ccp1con     ;    on match, ccp1 module on,
                            ;    ccp1 pin low
        bsf     t1con,0     ;timer 1 on
gohi    btfss   pir1,2      ;ccp1 interrupt flag set?
        goto    gohi        ;not yet
        movf    numsumh,w   ;get interval high byte
        movwf   ccpr1h      ;load compare register high
        movf    numsuml,w   ;get interval low byte
        movwf   ccpr1l      ;load compare register low
        bsf     ccp1con,0   ;ccp1 pin low on match
        bsf     intcon,7    ;enable global interrupts
        bsf     intcon,6    ;enable peripheral interrupts
        bsf     status,rp0  ;bank 1
        bsf     pie1,2      ;enable ccp1 compare interrupt
        bcf     status,rp0  ;bank 0
circle  goto    circle      ;done
;-----------------------------------------------------------
tthzero movlw   0x20        ;ascii blank
        movwf   char
        movlw   0x20        ;display RAM address
        movwf   addr
        movlw   0x03        ;ascii character to display RAM
        movwf   instr
        call    sndstf
        call    debounce
        goto    do1000
;-----------------------------------------------------------
thzero  btfsc   flags,0     ;ms digit entered?
        goto    zeroth      ;yes
        movlw   0x20        ;ascii blank
thchar  movwf   char
        movlw   0x21        ;display RAM address
        movwf   addr
        movlw   0x03        ;ascii character to display RAM
        movwf   instr
        call    sndstf
        call    debounce
        goto    do100
zeroth  movlw   0x30        ;ascii 0
        goto    thchar
;-----------------------------------------------------------
hzero   btfsc   flags,0     ;ms digit entered?
        goto    zeroh       ;yes
        movlw   0x20        ;ascii blank
hchar   movwf   char
        movlw   0x22        ;display RAM address
        movwf   addr
        movlw   0x03        ;ascii character to display RAM
```

```
        movwf    instr
        call     sndstf
        call     debounce
        goto     do10
zeroh   movlw    0x30         ;ascii 0
        goto     hchar
;-------------------------------------------------------------
tzero   btfsc    flags,0      ;ms digit entered?
        goto     zerot        ;yes
        movlw    0x20         ;ascii blank
tchar   movwf    char
        movlw    0x23         ;display RAM address
        movwf    addr
        movlw    0x03         ;ascii character to display RAM
        movwf    instr
        call     sndstf
        call     debounce
        goto     do1
zerot   movlw    0x30         ;ascii 0
        goto     tchar
;-------------------------------------------------------------
;returns with digit in digctr
;
scan10  bsf      portb,0      ;rows high
        bsf      portb,1
        bsf      portb,2
        bsf      portb,3
        clrf     digctr       ;digit counter=0
        bcf      portb,3      ;row=4
        btfss    portb,5      ;test column 2
        return                ;"0" key press
        bsf      portb,3      ;deselect row 4
        movlw    0x01
        movwf    digctr       ;digit counter=1
        movwf    rowctr       ;row counter=1
        movwf    rowbits      ;row bits = 0000 0001
rowout  movf     rowbits,w    ;get row bits
        xorlw    0x0f         ;complement row bits
        movwf    portb        ;output row bits
        movlw    0x01
        movwf    colctr       ;column counter=1
        movlw    0x10         ;0001 0000
        movwf    colbits      ;col=1
tstcol  movf     portb,w      ;read port B
        andlw    0x70         ;mask off rows and bit 7
        movwf    temp         ;columns
        movf     colbits,w    ;get column bits
        xorlw    0x70         ;complement column bits
        subwf    temp,w       ;compare with contents of temp
        btfsc    status,z
        return                ;digit available
lastc   movf     colctr,w     ;get column count
        sublw    0x03
        btfsc    status,z     ;=3 ?
```

```
        goto    lastr
        rlf     colbits,f    ;shift column bits
        bcf     colbits,0    ;fix carry flag garbage
        incf    colctr,f
        incf    digctr,f
        goto    tstcol
lastr   movf    rowctr,w     ;get row count
        sublw   0x03
        btfsc   status,z     ;=3 ?
        goto    scan10       ;scan 10 digit keys again
        rlf     rowbits,f    ;shift row bits
        bcf     rowbits,0    ;fix carry flag garbage
        incf    rowctr,f
        incf    digctr,f
        goto    rowout
;--------------------------------------------------------------
debounce movlw  0x02         ;to counter
        movwf   count
dbloop  movlw   0xff         ;M
        movwf   mcount       ;to M counter
loadn   movlw   0xff         ;N
        movwf   ncount       ;to N counter
decn    decfsz  ncount,f     ;decrement N
        goto    decn         ;again
        decfsz  mcount,f     ;decrement M
        goto    loadn        ;again
        decfsz  count,f
        goto    dbloop       ;thru loop within a loop twice -
;                             400 milliseconds
        return               ;done
;--------------------------------------------------------------
sndstf  movf    instr,w      ;get instruction
        movwf   sendreg      ;to be sent
        call    ser_out      ;to serial out subroutine
        movf    char,w       ;get character or hex byte
        movwf   sendreg      ;to be sent
        call    ser_out      ;to serial out subroutine
        movf    addr,w       ;get address
        movwf   sendreg      ;to be sent
        call    ser_out      ;to serial out subroutine
        return
;--------------------------------------------------------------
ser_out bcf     intcon,5     ;disable tmr0 interrupts
        bcf     intcon,7     ;disable global interrupts
        clrf    tmr0         ;clear timer/counter
        clrwdt               ;clear wdt prep prescaler assign
        bsf     status,rp0   ;to page 1
        movlw   b'11011000'  ;set up timer/counter
        movwf   optreg
        bcf     status,rp0   ;back to page 0
        movlw   0x08         ;init shift counter
        movwf   count
        bcf     porta,1      ;start bit
        clrf    tmr0         ;start timer/counter
```

```
            bcf      intcon,2      ;clear tmr0 overflow flag
time1       btfss    intcon,2      ;timer overflow?
            goto     time1         ;no
            bcf      intcon,2      ;yes, clear overflow flag
nxtbit      rlf      sendreg,f     ;rotate msb into carry flag
            bcf      porta,1       ;clear port A, bit 1
            btfsc    status,c      ;test carry flag
            bsf      porta,1       ;bit is set
time2       btfss    intcon,2      ;timer overflow?
            goto     time2         ;no
            bcf      intcon,2      ;clear overflow flag
            decfsz   count,f       ;shifted 8?
            goto     nxtbit        ;no
            bsf      porta,1       ;yes, output mark
time3       btfss    intcon,2      ;timer overflow?
            goto     time3         ;no
            return                 ;done
;----------------------------------------------------------------
;multiply 2-byte binary number by 10 decimal
;enter sub with number in hibyte and lobyte - exit with result
;    in hybyte and lobyte
;
decmult     movf     lobyte,w      ;get low byte
            movwf    copylo        ;store copy
            movf     hibyte,w      ;get high byte
            movwf    copyhi        ;store copy
            bcf      status,c      ;clear carry flag
            rlf      lobyte,f      ;rotate low byte
            rlf      hibyte,f      ;rotate high byte
            bcf      status,c      ;clear carry flag
            rlf      lobyte,f      ;rotate low byte
            rlf      hibyte,f      ;rotate high byte
            movf     copylo,w      ;fetch low byte
            addwf    lobyte,f      ;add low bytes
            btfss    status,c      ;carry set?
            goto     contin        ;no, continue
            incf     hibyte,f      ;yes, add 1 to hi byte
contin      movf     copyhi,w      ;fetch high byte
            addwf    hibyte,f      ;add high bytes
            bcf      status,c      ;clear carry flag
            rlf      lobyte,f      ;rotate low byte
            rlf      hibyte,f      ;rotate high byte
            return
;-------------------------------------------------------------
;add digit to numsum registers - enter with digit in hibyte
;    and lobyte
;
addnum      movf     lobyte,w      ;fetch low byte
            addwf    numsuml,f     ;add low bytes, result in numsuml
            btfsc    status,c      ;carry set?
            incf     numsumh,f     ;yes, add 1 to msb result
            movf     hibyte,w      ;fetch high byte
            addwf    numsumh,f     ;add high bytes, result in numsumh
            return
```

```
;------------------------------------------------------------
;enter with hex digit in w
;
hex2asc movwf    hold          ;store copy of hex digit
        sublw    0x09          ;subtract w from 1 less than 0x0a
        btfss    status,c      ;carry flag set if w < 0x0a
        goto     add37
        goto     add30
add37   movf     hold,w        ;get hex digit
        addlw    0x37
        return                 ;return with ascii in w
add30   movf     hold,w        ;get hex digit
        addlw    0x30
        return                 ;return with ascii in w
;------------------------------------------------------------
iserv   bcf      pir1,2        ;clear ccp1 interrupt flag,
                               ;   enable further interrupts
dbladd  movf     numsuml,w     ;fetch interval low
        addwf    lsb2,f        ;add low bytes, result in lsb2
        btfsc    status,c      ;carry set?
        incf     msb2,f        ;yes, add 1 to msb result
        movf     numsumh,w     ;fetch interval high
        addwf    msb2,f        ;add high bytes, result in msb2
        movf     msb2,w        ;load compare register high
        movwf    ccpr1h
        movf     lsb2,w        ;load compare register low
        movwf    ccpr1l
        btfss    ccp1con,0     ;control bit status?
        goto     sbit          ;bit is clear
cbit    bcf      ccp1con,0     ;clear control bit
        nop                    ;delay 1 cycle to equalize paths
        retfie                 ;return from interrupt
sbit    bsf      ccp1con,0     ;set control bit
        retfie                 ;return from interrupt
;------------------------------------------------------------
        end
;------------------------------------------------------------
;at blast time, select:
;       memory unprotected
;       watchdog timer disabled (default is enabled)
;       standard crystal (using 4 MHz osc for test) XT
;       power-up timer on
;       brown-out detect on
;============================================================
```

With an oscilloscope connected to the output, key in various pulse widths from 25 to 65,535 microseconds and observe the output signal. Try keying in 20 and 65,536 microseconds. What happens and why?

Procedure:

1) Power-up '63.
2) Key in the pulse width of the output signal in microseconds.
3) Observe the output using an oscilloscope.

TIME INTERVAL MEASUREMENT INSTRUMENT

This instrument will measure time intervals from approximately 25 microseconds to 65,535 microseconds. The internal instruction clock is used as the known frequency which is a big factor in determining the range. A clock oscillator of much higher frequency would be needed to measure shorter time intervals (impractical) and a slower clock oscillator is needed to measure lower frequencies (no problem). A selection of two time bases (internal instruction clock or external clock selected via a switch and software) could be used to extend the range of this instrument. You might like to try it.

The measurement portion of the software works like pdccp.asm. The 16-bit result is converted to 5-digit BCD. The digits are converted to ASCII for display purposes. High order zeros are suppressed.

Several programs are combined to accomplish this. They are:

- Period measurement (pdccp.asm).
- Keypad/LCD user interface (decent63.asm).
- 16-bit binary to 5-digit BCD - range 0x0000 to 0xFFFF from PIC'n Up The Pace (dblb2dy.asm).

The format chosen for displaying the decimal result is:

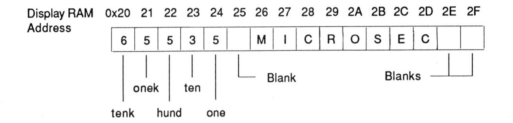

176

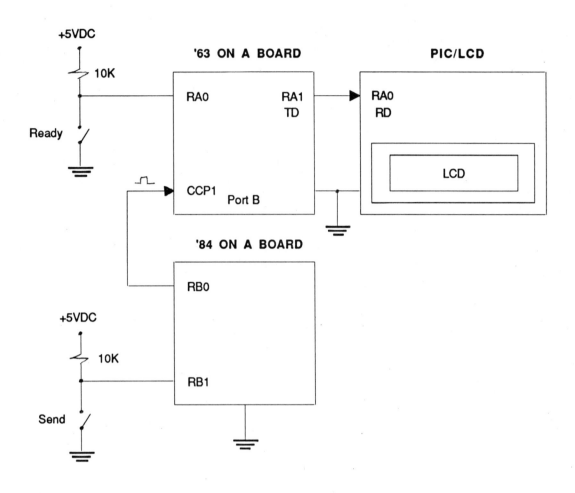

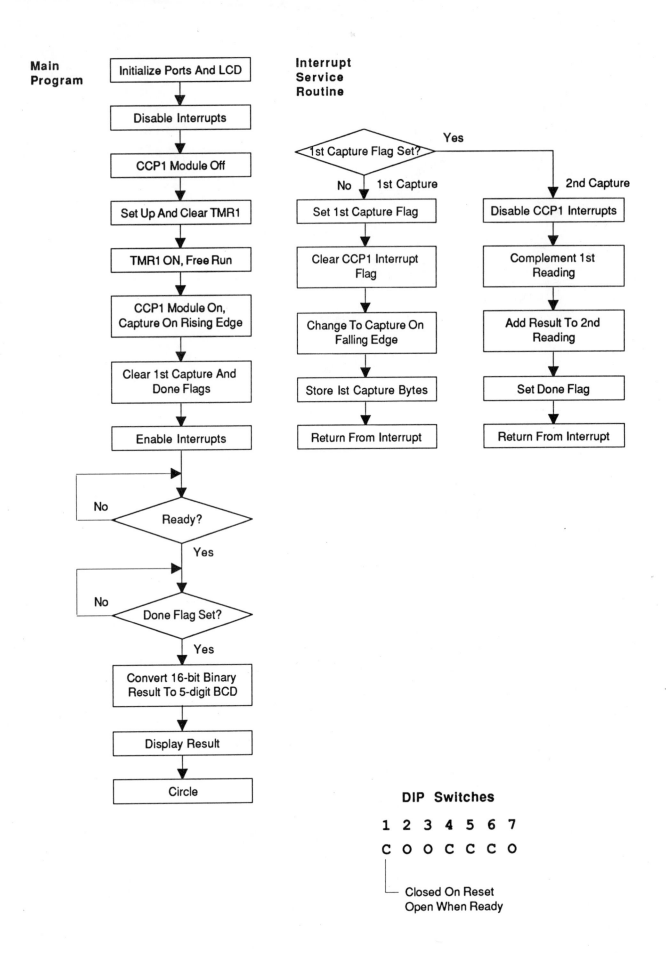

Main Program

Initialize Ports And LCD

Disable Interrupts

CCP1 Module Off

Set Up And Clear TMR1

TMR1 ON, Free Run

CCP1 Module On, Capture On Rising Edge

Clear 1st Capture And Done Flags

Enable Interrupts

Ready? — No

Yes

Done Flag Set? — No

Yes

Convert 16-bit Binary Result To 5-digit BCD

Display Result

Circle

Interrupt Service Routine

1st Capture Flag Set? — Yes

No — 1st Capture

Set 1st Capture Flag

Clear CCP1 Interrupt Flag

Change To Capture On Falling Edge

Store Ist Capture Bytes

Return From Interrupt

2nd Capture

Disable CCP1 Interrupts

Complement 1st Reading

Add Result To 2nd Reading

Set Done Flag

Return From Interrupt

DIP Switches

1	2	3	4	5	6	7
C	O	O	C	C	C	O

Closed On Reset
Open When Ready

```
;=======PDCK.ASM===================================9/29/98==
         list    p=16c63
         radix   hex
;-------------------------------------------------------------
;timer 1 and ccp1 module - period measurement demo - lcd
;    timer 1 free running
;    capture at start and end of period pulse
;-------------------------------------------------------------
;        cpu equates (memory map)
indf     equ     0x00
tmr0     equ     0x01
pc       equ     0x02
status   equ     0x03
fsr      equ     0x04
porta    equ     0x05
portc    equ     0x07
intcon   equ     0x0b
pir1     equ     0x0c
tmr1l    equ     0x0e
tmr1h    equ     0x0f
t1con    equ     0x10
ccpr1l   equ     0x15
ccpr1h   equ     0x16
ccp1con  equ     0x17
tenk     equ     0x20
onek     equ     0x21
hund     equ     0x22
ten      equ     0x23
one      equ     0x24
sendreg  equ     0x25
count    equ     0x26
instr    equ     0x27
char     equ     0x28
addr     equ     0x29
ncount   equ     0x2a
mcount   equ     0x2b
hold     equ     0x2c
index    equ     0x2d
dig_ctr  equ     0x2e
lsb1     equ     0x2f
msb1     equ     0x30
lsb2     equ     0x31
msb2     equ     0x32
flags    equ     0x33          ;done 3, 1st capture 2, overflow 1,
                               ;    ms digit 0
one_hi   equ     0x34
one_lo   equ     0x35
optreg   equ     0x81
trisa    equ     0x85
trisc    equ     0x87
pie1     equ     0x8c
;-------------------------------------------------------------
;        bit equates
```

```
c        equ     0
ovflw    equ     1
z        equ     2
rp0      equ     5
ccp1     equ     2               ;ccp1 bit 2, port C
;------------------------------------------------------------
         org     0x000
         goto    start           ;skip over location pointed to by
                                 ;   interrupt vector and tables
         org     0x004
         goto    iserv
;------------------------------------------------------------
tbl_lo   addwf   pc,f            ;add index to program counter
         retlw   0x10            ;10,000 decimal
         retlw   0xe8            ;1,000 decimal
         retlw   0x64            ;100 decimal
         retlw   0x0a            ;10 decimal
;------------------------------------------------------------
tbl_hi   addwf   pc,f            ;add index to program counter
         retlw   0x27            ;10,000 decimal
         retlw   0x03            ;1,000 decimal
         retlw   0x00            ;100 decimal
         retlw   0x00            ;10 decimal
;------------------------------------------------------------
start    bsf     status,rp0      ;switch to bank 1
         movlw   b'00000001'     ;port A inputs/outputs
         movwf   trisa
         bsf     trisc,ccp1      ;ccp1 pin input
         bcf     status,rp0      ;switch back to bank 0
         bsf     porta,1         ;output mark, bit 1 (serial - LCD)
         call    debounce
         call    debounce
         movlw   0x00            ;blanks to display RAM
         movwf   instr
         call    sndstf          ;send instruction to LCD module
         call    debounce
         movlw   0x01            ;send 16 characters to display
         movwf   instr
         call    sndstf          ;send instruction to LCD module
         call    debounce
;------------------------------------------------------------
         bcf     intcon,7        ;disable global interrupts
         bcf     intcon,6        ;disable peripheral interrupts
         bsf     status,rp0      ;bank 1
         bcf     pie1,0          ;disable timer 1 interrupts
         bcf     pie1,2          ;disable ccp1 interrupts
         bcf     status,rp0      ;bank 0
         bcf     pir1,2          ;clear ccp1 interrupt flag
         clrf    ccp1con         ;ccp1 module off
         movlw   b'00000000'     ;tmr1 prescaler and tmr1 setup,
         movwf   t1con           ;   tmr1 off
         clrf    tmr1h           ;clear timer 1 high
         clrf    tmr1l           ;clear timer 1 low
         bsf     t1con,0         ;timer 1 on, free running
```

180

```
        movlw    b'00000101'  ;capture on rising edge, ccp1
        movwf    ccp1con      ;    module on
        bcf      flags,2      ;clear 1st capture flag
        bcf      flags,3      ;clear done flag
        bsf      intcon,7     ;enable global interrupts
        bsf      intcon,6     ;enable peripheral interrupts
        bsf      status,rp0   ;bank 1
        bsf      pie1,2       ;enable ccp1 interrupts
        bcf      status,rp0   ;bank 0
ready   btfss    porta,0      ;ready?
        goto     ready
done    btfss    flags,3      ;done?
        goto     done
;------------------------------------------------------
;period high byte in msb2
;period low byte in lsb2;
;
;convert 16-bit binary time interval to 5-digit bcd
        call     dblb2d       ;call conversion subroutine
;send digits to display ram
        bcf      flags,0      ;clear ms digit flag
dotenk  movf     tenk,w       ;get 10000's digit
        sublw    0x00         ;compare - digit=0?
        btfsc    status,z
        goto     tthzero      ;yes
        bsf      flags,0      ;no, this is ms digit
        movf     tenk,w       ;get 10000's digit
        call     hex2asc      ;convert binary digit to ascii
        movwf    char
        movlw    0x20         ;display RAM address
        movwf    addr
        movlw    0x03         ;ascii char follows, send to display RAM
        movwf    instr
        call     sndstf       ;send 10000's digit to display RAM
        call     debounce     ;time delay
doonek  movf     onek,w       ;get 1000's digit
        sublw    0x00         ;compare - digit=0?
        btfsc    status,z
        goto     thzero       ;yes
        bsf      flags,0      ;no, this could be ms digit
        movf     onek,w       ;get 1000's digit
        call     hex2asc      ;convert binary digit to ascii
        movwf    char
        movlw    0x21         ;display RAM address
        movwf    addr
        movlw    0x03         ;ascii char follows, send to display RAM
        movwf    instr
        call     sndstf       ;send 1000's digit to display RAM
        call     debounce     ;time delay
dohund  movf     hund,w       ;get 100's digit
        sublw    0x00         ;compare - digit=0?
        btfsc    status,z
        goto     hzero        ;yes
        movf     hund,w       ;get 100's digit
```

```
            call     hex2asc      ;convert binary digit to ascii
            movwf    char
            movlw    0x22         ;display RAM address
            movwf    addr
            movlw    0x03         ;ascii char follows, send to display RAM
            movwf    instr
            call     sndstf       ;send 100's digit to display RAM
            call     debounce     ;time delay
doten       movf     ten,w        ;get 10's digit
            sublw    0x00         ;compare - digit=0?
            btfsc    status,z
            goto     tzero        ;yes
            movf     ten,w        ;get 10's digit
            call     hex2asc      ;convert binary digit to ascii
            movwf    char
            movlw    0x23         ;display RAM address
            movwf    addr
            movlw    0x03         ;ascii char follows, send to display RAM
            movwf    instr
            call     sndstf       ;send 10's digit to display RAM
            call     debounce     ;time delay
doone       movf     one,w        ;get 1's digit
            call     hex2asc      ;convert binary digit to ascii
            movwf    char
            movlw    0x24         ;display RAM address
            movwf    addr
            movlw    0x03         ;ascii char follows, send to display RAM
            movwf    instr
            call     sndstf       ;send 1's digit to display RAM
            call     debounce
;send time units to display ram
m           movlw    0x6d         ;ascii m
            movwf    char
            movlw    0x26         ;display RAM address
            movwf    addr
            movlw    0x03         ;ascii character to display RAM
            movwf    instr
            call     sndstf
            call     debounce
i           movlw    0x69         ;ascii i
            movwf    char
            movlw    0x27         ;display RAM address
            movwf    addr
            movlw    0x03         ;ascii character to display RAM
            movwf    instr
            call     sndstf
            call     debounce
cee1        movlw    0x63         ;ascii c
            movwf    char
            movlw    0x28         ;display RAM address
            movwf    addr
            movlw    0x03         ;ascii character to display RAM
            movwf    instr
            call     sndstf
```

```
          call     debounce
r         movlw    0x72          ;ascii r
          movwf    char
          movlw    0x29          ;display RAM address
          movwf    addr
          movlw    0x03          ;ascii character to display RAM
          movwf    instr
          call     sndstf
          call     debounce
o         movlw    0x6f          ;ascii o
          movwf    char
          movlw    0x2a          ;display RAM address
          movwf    addr
          movlw    0x03          ;ascii character to display RAM
          movwf    instr
          call     sndstf
          call     debounce
s         movlw    0x73          ;ascii s
          movwf    char
          movlw    0x2b          ;display RAM address
          movwf    addr
          movlw    0x03          ;ascii character to display RAM
          movwf    instr
          call     sndstf
          call     debounce
e         movlw    0x65          ;ascii e
          movwf    char
          movlw    0x2c          ;display RAM address
          movwf    addr
          movlw    0x03          ;ascii character to display RAM
          movwf    instr
          call     sndstf
          call     debounce
cee2      movlw    0x63          ;ascii c
          movwf    char
          movlw    0x2d          ;display RAM address
          movwf    addr
          movlw    0x03          ;ascii character to display RAM
          movwf    instr
          call     sndstf
          call     debounce
send      movlw    0x01          ;send 16 characters to display
          movwf    instr
          call     sndstf        ;to LCD module
circle    goto     circle        ;done
;-----------------------------------------------------------------
iserv     btfsc    flags,2       ;1st capture flag set?
          goto     cap2          ;yes, goto 2nd capture
          bsf      flags,2       ;no, set 1st capture flag
          bcf      pir1,2        ;clear ccp1 interrupt flag,
                                 ;   enable second interrupt
          bcf      ccp1con,0     ;second capture on falling edge
          movf     ccpr1h,w      ;get 1st capture high
          movwf    one_hi        ;store
```

```
        movf    ccpr1l,w    ;get 1st capture low
        movwf   one_lo      ;store
        retfie
cap2    bsf     status,rp0  ;bank 1
        bcf     pie1,2      ;disable ccp1 interrupts
        bcf     status,rp0  ;bank 0
        comf    one_hi,f    ;complement 1st capture high
        comf    one_lo,f    ;complement 1st capture low
        movf    ccpr1h,w    ;get 2nd capture high
        movwf   msb2        ;store
        movf    ccpr1l,w    ;get 2nd capture low
        movwf   lsb2        ;store
dbladd  movf    one_lo,w    ;fetch complement of 1st low
        addwf   lsb2,f      ;add low bytes, result in lsb2
        btfsc   status,c    ;carry set?
        incf    msb2,f      ;yes, add 1 to msb result
        movf    one_hi,w    ;fetch complement of 1st high
        addwf   msb2,f      ;add high bytes, result in msb2
        bsf     flags,3     ;set "done" flag
        retfie
;-----------------------------------------------------------
debounce movlw  0x02        ;to counter
        movwf   count
dbloop  movlw   0xff        ;M
        movwf   mcount      ;to M counter
loadn   movlw   0xff        ;N
        movwf   ncount      ;to N counter
decn    decfsz  ncount,f    ;decrement N
        goto    decn        ;again
        decfsz  mcount,f    ;decrement M
        goto    loadn       ;again
        decfsz  count,f
        goto    dbloop      ;thru loop within a loop twice -
;                               400 milliseconds
        return              ;done
;-----------------------------------------------------------
sndstf  movf    instr,w     ;get instruction
        movwf   sendreg     ;to be sent
        call    ser_out     ;to serial out subroutine
        movf    char,w      ;get character or hex byte
        movwf   sendreg     ;to be sent
        call    ser_out     ;to serial out subroutine
        movf    addr,w      ;get address
        movwf   sendreg     ;to be sent
        call    ser_out     ;to serial out subroutine
        return
;-----------------------------------------------------------
ser_out bcf     intcon,5    ;disable tmr0 interrupts
        bcf     intcon,7    ;disable global interrupts
        clrf    tmr0        ;clear timer/counter
        clrwdt              ;clear wdt prep prescaler assign
        bsf     status,rp0  ;to page 1
        movlw   b'11011000' ;set up timer/counter
        movwf   optreg
```

184

```
          bcf       status,rp0     ;back to page 0
          movlw     0x08           ;init shift counter
          movwf     count
          bcf       porta,1        ;start bit
          clrf      tmr0           ;start timer/counter
          bcf       intcon,2       ;clear tmr0 overflow flag
time1     btfss     intcon,2       ;timer overflow?
          goto      time1          ;no
          bcf       intcon,2       ;yes, clear overflow flag
nxtbit    rlf       sendreg,f      ;rotate msb into carry flag
          bcf       porta,1        ;clear port A, bit 1
          btfsc     status,c       ;test carry flag
          bsf       porta,1        ;bit is set
time2     btfss     intcon,2       ;timer overflow?
          goto      time2          ;no
          bcf       intcon,2       ;clear overflow flag
          decfsz    count,f        ;shifted 8?
          goto      nxtbit         ;no
          bsf       porta,1        ;yes, output mark
time3     btfss     intcon,2       ;timer overflow?
          goto      time3          ;no
          return                   ;done
;------------------------------------------------------------
;enter with hex digit in w
;
hex2asc   movwf     hold           ;store copy of hex digit
          sublw     0x09           ;subtract w from 1 less than 0x0a
          btfss     status,c       ;carry flag set if w < 0x0a
          goto      add37
          goto      add30
add37     movf      hold,w         ;get hex digit
          addlw     0x37
          return                   ;return with ascii in w
add30     movf      hold,w         ;get hex digit
          addlw     0x30
          return                   ;return with ascii in w
;------------------------------------------------------------
tthzero   movlw     0x20           ;ascii blank
          movwf     char
          movlw     0x20           ;display RAM address
          movwf     addr
          movlw     0x03           ;ascii character to display RAM
          movwf     instr
          call      sndstf
          call      debounce
          goto      doonek
;------------------------------------------------------------
thzero    btfsc     flags,0        ;ms digit entered?
          goto      zeroth         ;yes
          movlw     0x20           ;ascii blank
thchar    movwf     char
          movlw     0x21           ;display RAM address
          movwf     addr
          movlw     0x03           ;ascii character to display RAM
```

```
        movwf   instr
        call    sndstf
        call    debounce
        goto    dohund
zeroth  movlw   0x30            ;ascii 0
        goto    thchar
;----------------------------------------------------------------
hzero   btfsc   flags,0         ;ms digit entered?
        goto    zeroh           ;yes
        movlw   0x20            ;ascii blank
hchar   movwf   char
        movlw   0x22            ;display RAM address
        movwf   addr
        movlw   0x03            ;ascii character to display RAM
        movwf   instr
        call    sndstf
        call    debounce
        goto    doten
zeroh   movlw   0x30            ;ascii 0
        goto    hchar
;----------------------------------------------------------------
tzero   btfsc   flags,0         ;ms digit entered?
        goto    zerot           ;yes
        movlw   0x20            ;ascii blank
tchar   movwf   char
        movlw   0x23            ;display RAM address
        movwf   addr
        movlw   0x03            ;ascii character to display RAM
        movwf   instr
        call    sndstf
        call    debounce
        goto    doone
zerot   movlw   0x30            ;ascii 0
        goto    tchar
;----------------------------------------------------------------
;16-bit binary to 5-digit bcd conversion
;
dblb2d  clrf    tenk
        clrf    onek
        clrf    hund
        clrf    ten
        clrf    one
        clrf    index
        clrf    dig_ctr
        bcf     flags,ovflw
subtr   movf    index,w         ;get current index into W
        call    tbl_lo          ;get ls chunk for subtraction
        movwf   lsb1
        movf    index,w         ;get current index into W
        call    tbl_hi          ;get ms chunk for subtraction
        movwf   msb1
        call    dblsub          ;to double precision subtraction
        btfsc   status,c        ;test carry flag
        goto    incdig
```

186

```
        movlw    0x20           ;load base address of table
        movwf    fsr
        movf     index,w        ;get index
        addwf    fsr,f          ;add offset
        movf     dig_ctr,w      ;get digit counter contents
        movwf    indf           ;store at digit loc (indexed)
        movf     index,w        ;get index
        call     tbl_lo         ;get ls chunk for addition
        movwf    lsb1
        movf     index,w        ;get index
        call     tbl_hi         ;get ms chunk for addition
        movwf    msb1
        bcf      flags,ovflw
        call     dblplus        ;to double precision addition
        movf     index,w        ;get index
        sublw    0x03           ;index=3?
        btfsc    status,z
        goto     finish
        incf     index,f        ;increment digit index
        clrf     dig_ctr
        goto     subtr
;--------------------------------------------------------------
incdig  incf     dig_ctr,f      ;increment digit counter
        goto     subtr
;--------------------------------------------------------------
finish  movf     lsb2,w         ;get 1's=remainder
        movwf    one
        return                  ;done
;--------------------------------------------------------------
dblsub  bcf      flags,ovflw    ;clear overflow flag
        comf     lsb1,f         ;2's complement stuff
        comf     msb1,f
        movf     lsb1,w
        addlw    0x01
        movwf    lsb1
        btfsc    status,c
        incf     msb1,f
dblplus movf     lsb1,w
        addwf    lsb2,f         ;add low bytes
        btfsc    status,c
        bsf      flags,ovflw    ;indicate overflow occured
        movf     msb1,w
        addwf    msb2,f         ;add high bytes
        btfss    flags,ovflw
        goto     dblx
        btfsc    status,c
        goto     dbl1
        movlw    0x01
        addwf    msb2,f
        goto     dblx
dbl1    incf     msb2,f
dblx    return
;--------------------------------------------------------------
        end
```

```
;---------------------------------------------------------------
;at blast time, select:
;       memory unprotected
;       watchdog timer disabled (default is enabled)
;       standard crystal (using 4 MHz osc for test) XT
;       power-up timer on
;       brown-out detect on
;===============================================================
```

Procedure:

    1) In preparation for power-up:
        A) "Ready" switch on '63 closed.
        B) "Send" switch on '84 closed.
    2) Power-up both '84 and '63.
    3) Open the "ready" switch on the '63.
    4) Open the "send" switch on '84.
    5) The number of microseconds the incoming pulse was high will be displayed.

FREQUENCY MEASUREMENT INSTRUMENT

This instrument will measure frequencies from 100 Hz (0.1 KHz) to 655.4 KHz. The sample time is 0.1 second which is a big factor in determining the range. A shorter sample time is required for higher frequencies and a longer sample time is needed to measure lower frequencies. Switch selectable sample times (via code blocks) could be used to extend the range of this instrument. You might like to try it.

The measurement portion of the software works like freq.asm. The 16-bit result is converted to 5-digit BCD. The least significant digit is rounded off. Then the remaining digits are converted to ASCII for display purposes. High order zeros are suppressed and the decimal point is inserted.

Several programs are combined to accomplish this. They are:

- Frequency measurement (freq.asm).
- Keypad/LCD user interface (decent63.asm).
- 16-bit binary to 5-digit BCD - range 0x0000 to 0xFFFF from PIC'**n Up The Pace**
  (dblb2dy.asm).
- Round off least significant digit - modified decrnd.asm from PIC'**n Up The Pace**
  for one digit.

The format chosen for displaying the decimal result is:

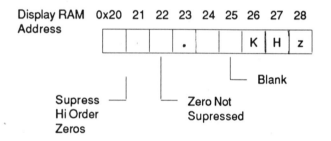

```
100 KHz signal in

10,000 pulses  = 100,000  pulses  = 100.0 KHz
  0.1 second              second

Round off least significant digit.
Place decimal point.
```

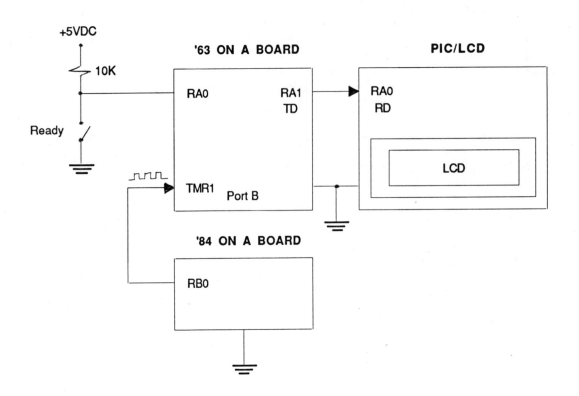

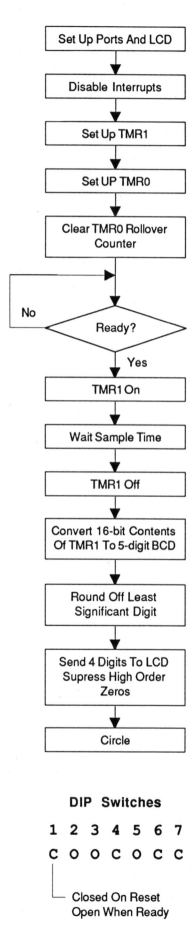

DIP Switches

1	2	3	4	5	6	7
C	O	O	C	O	C	C

Closed On Reset
Open When Ready

Once the frequency is in decimal form, it should be rounded off as the measurement is accurate to within approximately 0.1 KHz.

Example: 107.98   108.0

We will round off the decimal result to the nearest tenth of a KHz.

A little thought reveals that the rounding process can ripple back all the way to the most significant digit (see example above). The round off routine rounds off the least significant digit. It does not clean up trash left in it's place because that information will not be displayed.

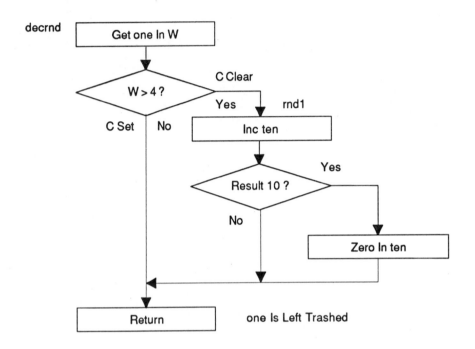

```
;=======FREQCK.ASM==================================9/29/98==
        list    p=16c63
        radix   hex
;------------------------------------------------------------
;frequency measurement demo - lcd
;       gate via tmr0, internal clock, prescaler 1:1
;------------------------------------------------------------
;       cpu equates (memory map)
indf    equ     0x00
tmr0    equ     0x01
pc      equ     0x02
status  equ     0x03
fsr     equ     0x04
porta   equ     0x05
portc   equ     0x07
intcon  equ     0x0b
tmr1l   equ     0x0e
tmr1h   equ     0x0f
t1con   equ     0x10
```

```
tenk      equ     0x20
onek      equ     0x21
hund      equ     0x22
ten       equ     0x23
one       equ     0x24
sendreg   equ     0x25
count     equ     0x26
instr     equ     0x27
char      equ     0x28
addr      equ     0x29
ncount    equ     0x2a
mcount    equ     0x2b
hold      equ     0x2c
index     equ     0x2d
dig_ctr   equ     0x2e
lsb1      equ     0x2f
msb1      equ     0x30
lsb2      equ     0x31
msb2      equ     0x32
flags     equ     0x33
optreg    equ     0x81
trisa     equ     0x85
trisc     equ     0x87
pie1      equ     0x8c
;------------------------------------------------------------
;         bit equates
c         equ     0
ovflw     equ     1
z         equ     2
rp0       equ     5
;------------------------------------------------------------
          org     0x000
;
          goto    start           ;jump over tables
;------------------------------------------------------------
tbl_lo    addwf   pc,f            ;add index to program counter
          retlw   0x10            ;10,000 decimal
          retlw   0xe8            ;1,000 decimal
          retlw   0x64            ;100 decimal
          retlw   0x0a            ;10 decimal
;------------------------------------------------------------
tbl_hi    addwf   pc,f            ;add index to program counter
          retlw   0x27            ;10,000 decimal
          retlw   0x03            ;1,000 decimal
          retlw   0x00            ;100 decimal
          retlw   0x00            ;10 decimal
;------------------------------------------------------------
start     bsf     status,rp0      ;switch to bank 1
          movlw   b'00000001'     ;port A inputs/outputs
          movwf   trisa
          bsf     trisc,0         ;port C, bit 0 input, tmr1 input
          bcf     status,rp0      ;switch back to bank 0
          bsf     porta,1         ;output mark, bit 1 (serial - LCD)
          call    debounce
```

```
        call     debounce
        movlw    0x00          ;blanks to display RAM
        movwf    instr
        call     sndstf        ;send instruction to LCD module
        call     debounce
        movlw    0x01          ;send 16 characters to display
        movwf    instr
        call     sndstf        ;send instruction to LCD module
        call     debounce
;----------------------------------------------------------------
        bcf      intcon,7      ;disable global interrupts
        bcf      intcon,6      ;disable peripheral interrupts
        bcf      intcon,5      ;disable timer 0 interrupts
        bsf      status,rp0    ;bank 1
        bcf      pie1,0        ;disable tmr1 interrupt
        bcf      status,rp0    ;bank 0
        movlw    b'00000010'   ;prescaler and tmr1 setup,
        movwf    t1con         ;   tmr1 off
        clrf     tmr1h         ;clear timer 1 high
        clrf     tmr1l         ;clear timer 1 low, clear prescaler
        clrf     tmr0          ;clear timer 0
        clrwdt                 ;clr WDT, prep prescaler assign
        bsf      status,rp0    ;bank 1
        movlw    b'11011111'   ;set up timer 0
        movwf    optreg
        bcf      status,rp0    ;bank 0
        clrf     count         ;clear tmr0 rollover counter
ready   btfss    porta,0       ;ready?
        goto     ready
        bsf      t1con,0       ;turn on timer 1
        clrf     tmr0          ;clear timer 0
        bcf      intcon,2      ;clear timer 0 interrupt flag
oflow1  btfss    intcon,2      ;timer 0 overflow?
        goto     oflow1        ;not yet
        bcf      intcon,2      ;clear timer 0 interrupt flag
        incf     count,f       ;inc timer 0 overflow counter
        movf     count,w       ;compare
        sublw    0xff          ;decimal 255
        btfss    status,z      ;test z flag, skip next instruction
                               ;   if flag is set
        goto     oflow1        ;again
oflow2  btfss    intcon,2      ;timer 0 overflow?
        goto     oflow2        ;not yet
        bcf      intcon,2      ;clear tmr0 interrupt flag
        incf     count,f       ;inc timer 0 overflow counter
        movf     count,w       ;compare
        sublw    0x86          ;decimal 134
        btfss    status,z      ;test z flag, skip next instruction
                               ;   if flag is set
        goto     oflow2        ;again
        clrf     tmr0          ;clear timer 0
t128    btfss    tmr0,7        ;look for timer 1 = 128
        goto     t128
t32     btfss    tmr0,5        ;look for timer 1 = 128+32=160
```

194

```
          goto     t32
          bcf      t1con,0     ;stop timer 1
;----------------------------------------------------------
;prep for calling conversion subroutine
          movf     tmr1h,w     ;get timer 1 high
          movwf    msb2
          movf     tmr1l,w     ;get timer 1 low
          movwf    lsb2
          call     dblb2d      ;call conversion subroutine
;round off 1's digit
          call     decrnd      ;call round off subroutine
;send digits to display ram
          bcf      flags,0     ;clear ms digit flag
dotenk    movf     tenk,w      ;get 10000's digit
          sublw    0x00        ;compare - digit=0?
          btfsc    status,z
          goto     tthzero     ;yes
          bsf      flags,0     ;no, this is ms digit
          movf     tenk,w      ;get 10000's digit
          call     hex2asc     ;convert binary digit to ascii
          movwf    char
          movlw    0x20        ;display RAM address
          movwf    addr
          movlw    0x03        ;ascii char follows, send to display RAM
          movwf    instr
          call     sndstf      ;send 10000's digit to display RAM
          call     debounce    ;time delay
doonek    movf     onek,w      ;get 1000's digit
          sublw    0x00        ;compare - digit=0?
          btfsc    status,z
          goto     thzero      ;yes
          movf     onek,w      ;get 1000's digit
          call     hex2asc     ;convert binary digit to ascii
          movwf    char
          movlw    0x21        ;display RAM address
          movwf    addr
          movlw    0x03        ;ascii char follows, send to display RAM
          movwf    instr
          call     sndstf      ;send 1000's digit to display RAM
          call     debounce    ;time delay
dohund    movf     hund,w      ;get 100's digit
          call     hex2asc     ;convert binary digit to ascii
          movwf    char
          movlw    0x22        ;display RAM address
          movwf    addr
          movlw    0x03        ;ascii char follows, send to display RAM
          movwf    instr
          call     sndstf      ;send 100's digit to display RAM
          call     debounce    ;time delay
doten     movf     ten,w       ;get 10's digit
          call     hex2asc     ;convert binary digit to ascii
          movwf    char
          movlw    0x24        ;display RAM address
          movwf    addr
```

```
              movlw    0x03         ;ascii char follows, send to display RAM
              movwf    instr
              call     sndstf       ;send 10's digit to display RAM
              call     debounce
;send decimal point and frequency units to display ram
decpt    movlw    0x2e         ;ascii decimal point
              movwf    char
              movlw    0x23         ;display RAM address
              movwf    addr
              movlw    0x03         ;ascii character to display RAM
              movwf    instr
              call     sndstf
              call     debounce
k             movlw    0x4b         ;ascii K
              movwf    char
              movlw    0x26         ;display RAM address
              movwf    addr
              movlw    0x03         ;ascii character to display RAM
              movwf    instr
              call     sndstf
              call     debounce
h             movlw    0x48         ;ascii H
              movwf    char
              movlw    0x27         ;display RAM address
              movwf    addr
              movlw    0x03         ;ascii character to display RAM
              movwf    instr
              call     sndstf
              call     debounce
zee         movlw    0x7a         ;ascii z
              movwf    char
              movlw    0x28         ;display RAM address
              movwf    addr
              movlw    0x03         ;ascii character to display RAM
              movwf    instr
              call     sndstf
              call     debounce
send       movlw    0x01         ;send 16 characters to display
              movwf    instr
              call     sndstf       ;to LCD module
circle    goto     circle       ;done
;--------------------------------------------------------------
debounce movlw    0x02         ;to counter
              movwf    count
dbloop   movlw    0xff         ;M
              movwf    mcount       ;to M counter
loadn     movlw    0xff         ;N
              movwf    ncount       ;to N counter
decn       decfsz   ncount,f     ;decrement N
              goto     decn         ;again
              decfsz   mcount,f     ;decrement M
              goto     loadn        ;again
              decfsz   count,f
              goto     dbloop       ;thru loop within a loop twice -
;                                            400 milliseconds
```

```
        return                  ;done
;--------------------------------------------------------------
sndstf  movf    instr,w         ;get instruction
        movwf   sendreg         ;to be sent
        call    ser_out         ;to serial out subroutine
        movf    char,w          ;get character or hex byte
        movwf   sendreg         ;to be sent
        call    ser_out         ;to serial out subroutine
        movf    addr,w          ;get address
        movwf   sendreg         ;to be sent
        call    ser_out         ;to serial out subroutine
        return
;--------------------------------------------------------------
ser_out bcf     intcon,5        ;disable tmr0 interrupts
        bcf     intcon,7        ;disable global interrupts
        clrf    tmr0            ;clear timer/counter
        clrwdt                  ;clear wdt prep prescaler assign
        bsf     status,rp0      ;to page 1
        movlw   b'11011000'     ;set up timer/counter
        movwf   optreg
        bcf     status,rp0      ;back to page 0
        movlw   0x08            ;init shift counter
        movwf   count
        bcf     porta,1         ;start bit
        clrf    tmr0            ;start timer/counter
        bcf     intcon,2        ;clear tmr0 overflow flag
time1   btfss   intcon,2        ;timer overflow?
        goto    time1           ;no
        bcf     intcon,2        ;yes, clear overflow flag
nxtbit  rlf     sendreg,f       ;rotate msb into carry flag
        bcf     porta,1         ;clear port A, bit 1
        btfsc   status,c        ;test carry flag
        bsf     porta,1         ;bit is set
time2   btfss   intcon,2        ;timer overflow?
        goto    time2           ;no
        bcf     intcon,2        ;clear overflow flag
        decfsz  count,f         ;shifted 8?
        goto    nxtbit          ;no
        bsf     porta,1         ;yes, output mark
time3   btfss   intcon,2        ;timer overflow?
        goto    time3           ;no
        return                  ;done
;--------------------------------------------------------------
;enter with hex digit in w
;
hex2asc movwf   hold            ;store copy of hex digit
        sublw   0x09            ;subtract w from 1 less than 0x0a
        btfss   status,c        ;carry flag set if w < 0x0a
        goto    add37
        goto    add30
add37   movf    hold,w          ;get hex digit
        addlw   0x37
        return                  ;return with ascii in w
```

```
add30     movf    hold,w      ;get hex digit
          addlw   0x30
          return              ;return with ascii in w
;------------------------------------------------------------
tthzero   movlw   0x20        ;ascii blank
          movwf   char
          movlw   0x20        ;display RAM address
          movwf   addr
          movlw   0x03        ;ascii character to display RAM
          movwf   instr
          call    sndstf
          call    debounce
          goto    doonek
;------------------------------------------------------------
thzero    btfsc   flags,0     ;ms digit entered?
          goto    zeroth      ;yes
          movlw   0x20        ;ascii blank
thchar    movwf   char
          movlw   0x21        ;display RAM address
          movwf   addr
          movlw   0x03        ;ascii character to display RAM
          movwf   instr
          call    sndstf
          call    debounce
          goto    dohund
zeroth    movlw   0x30        ;ascii 0
          goto    thchar
;------------------------------------------------------------
;16-bit binary to 5-digit bcd conversion
;
dblb2d    clrf    tenk
          clrf    onek
          clrf    hund
          clrf    ten
          clrf    one
          clrf    index
          clrf    dig_ctr
          bcf     flags,ovflw
subtr     movf    index,w     ;get current index into W
          call    tbl_lo      ;get ls chunk for subtraction
          movwf   lsb1
          movf    index,w     ;get current index into W
          call    tbl_hi      ;get ms chunk for subtraction
          movwf   msb1
          call    dblsub      ;to double precision subtraction
          btfsc   status,c    ;test carry flag
          goto    incdig
          movlw   0x20        ;load base address of table
          movwf   fsr
          movf    index,w     ;get index
          addwf   fsr,f       ;add offset
          movf    dig_ctr,w   ;get digit counter contents
          movwf   indf        ;store at digit loc (indexed)
          movf    index,w     ;get index
```

```
        call    tbl_lo          ;get ls chunk for addition
        movwf   lsb1
        movf    index,w         ;get index
        call    tbl_hi          ;get ms chunk for addition
        movwf   msb1
        bcf     flags,ovflw
        call    dblplus         ;to double precision addition
        movf    index,w         ;get index
        sublw   0x03            ;index=3?
        btfsc   status,z
        goto    finish
        incf    index,f         ;increment digit index
        clrf    dig_ctr
        goto    subtr
;------------------------------------------------------------
incdig  incf    dig_ctr,f       ;increment digit counter
        goto    subtr
;------------------------------------------------------------
finish  movf    lsb2,w          ;get 1's=remainder
        movwf   one
        return                  ;done
;------------------------------------------------------------
dblsub  bcf     flags,ovflw     ;clear overflow flag
        comf    lsb1,f          ;2's complement stuff
        comf    msb1,f
        movf    lsb1,w
        addlw   0x01
        movwf   lsb1
        btfsc   status,c
        incf    msb1,f
dblplus movf    lsb1,w
        addwf   lsb2,f          ;add low bytes
        btfsc   status,c
        bsf     flags,ovflw     ;indicate overflow occured
        movf    msb1,w
        addwf   msb2,f          ;add high bytes
        btfss   flags,ovflw
        goto    dblx
        btfsc   status,c
        goto    dbl1
        movlw   0x01
        addwf   msb2,f
        goto    dblx
dbl1    incf    msb2,f
dblx    return
;------------------------------------------------------------
;decimal roundoff subroutine
;rounds off the least significant digit of a
;   5-digit decimal number
;the contents of file register one are left as trash
;
decrnd  movf    one,w           ;get one into W
        sublw   0x04            ;subtract W from 4, result in W
        btfss   status,c
```

```
              goto     rnd1           ;if carry clear, round
              return
rnd1          incf     ten,f
              movf     ten,w          ;compare
              sublw    0x0a           ;result 10 decimal?
              btfss    status,z
              return                  ;not 10
              clrf     ten
              return
;-----------------------------------------------------------
              end
;-----------------------------------------------------------
;at blast time, select:
;      memory unprotected
;      watchdog timer disabled (default is enabled)
;      standard crystal (using 4 MHz osc for test) XT
;      power-up timer on
;      brown-out detect on
;===========================================================
```

Procedure:

    1) In preparation for power-up:
        A) "Ready" switch on '63 closed.
        B) "Send" switch on '84 closed.
    2) Power-up both '84 and '63.
    3) Open the "ready" switch on the '63.
    4) The frequency of the incoming signal will be displayed in KHz.

Try measuring frequencies from 0.1 to 655.4 KHz. The "ready" switch is not really necessary. Once under way, new measurements may be taken by resetting the '63.

You will doubtless think of ways to improve this instrument and I would encourage you to do so. My suggestions would include:

- Loop back to sample the input on a periodic basis.
- Shorten the "debounce" time delay" which was used here to make it easy to show the commonality between the instrument programs. There is no keypad in this application, so there are no switches to debounce. A delay is required to allow the PIC/LCD module to send 16 characters to the display. 5 milliseconds should do the trick.
- Add range switching by adding switching and sample time code modules.

CREATING YOUR OWN COMBINATION SIGNAL GENERATOR AND INSTRUMENT

There is lots of opportunity to expand on what you have learned by designing and building your own combination device. You have probably noticed that the hardware involved in the four signal generator/instruments is almost identical. The keypad is not used in the two measurement instruments, but it is not in the way either. It has two function keys that are not being used (so far). We have talked about selectable time bases and selectable sample times. A third PIC16 could be used to generate multiple time bases and the '63 could tell the third PIC16 what to do. HMMmmmmm ....

TALKING TO A PIC16 WITH A PC
VIA A WINDOWS TERMINAL PROGRAM

Having the ability to talk to a PIC-controlled black box using an MS-DOS(tm) based computer (PC) running a built-in terminal program under Windows (tm) opens up an area of interesting possibilities. The PC can:

- Send data or a command.
- Receive status information.
- Receive data - display data on-screen, print data, save data file, massage data with a spreadsheet program, graph data, do math manipulation, etc.

Windows 3.x has a built-in terminal program called "Terminal" (tm) and Windows 95 includes "HyperTerminal" (tm). Terminal can easily set up a serial port such as COM2 and use it to communicate with a PIC-based black box. It is not necessary to learn a programming language for the PC although doing so will enable you to create more sophisticated applications. The PC provides the on-screen user interface, file storage on disk, and printer plus data manipulation, graphing and display capabilities. The PIC-based black box provides the controller, data acquisition system, instrument or whatever device you want to dream up.

What is a terminal? The term comes from the days of the teletype when a terminal looked like a typewriter and was used to send and receive messages. For our purposes, "Terminal" which comes with Windows 3.x allows sending or receiving single characters or complete files. "HyperTerminal" under Windows 95 is dumbed down slightly and is note capable of assigning a file name prior to receiving the file. It also no provision for clearing the buffer which clears the screen. Only Terminal will work for our purposes.

So what about Windows 95 users? Fortunately, there is a very simple solution! Copy Terminal from your old PC and put the copy on your hard drive of your Windows 95 machine. All that is involved is to copy the file terminal.exe to a floppy disk and carry it over to the 95 machine.

- 1) Insert the disk in the A drive.
- 2) Open My Computer by double clicking on it's icon.
- 3) In the dialog box, double click on 3 1/2 Floppy [A:].
- 4) In the box, click on and drag the Terminal icon over to the desktop.
- 5) Double click on the Terminal icon and a dialog box will appear allowing you to select the serial port you want to use with Terminal (usually COM 2).

Double click on the Terminal icon when you want to use it.

It's as simple as that!

As you may already know, the Windows 3.x and Windows 95 user interfaces are distinctly different, so there will be two separate descriptions where Microsoft Works (tm) is used.

"U-TURN" EXPERIMENT

The experiment that follows is an easy way to become familiar with terminal programs and to get a feel for how the PC end of things will work when connected to a PIC-controlled black box.

You will need an ultra-simple piece of test equipment made from a 9-pin female D-subminiature solder cup connector and a short piece of wire. The wire connects pins 2 and 3.

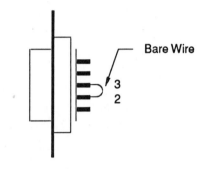

9-pin Female D-subminiature
Solder Cup Connector

The objective is to send stuff out a PC serial port on the transmit data (T_D) line and to have it make a U-turn and come right back in on the receive data line (R_D) of the same port.

We will discuss hardware later. Now we will work toward understanding the PC Terminal program and what can be done with it.

The first objective is to open the Terminal program and select a group of settings which will work for our applications, and save the file (settings) so we don't have to go through the setup procedure each time we want to do something.

The second objective is to use the "U-turn" connector and send and receive a single character at a time.

The third objective is to use the Windows built-in text editor Notepad to create a text file and save it.

The forth objective is to use the "U-turn" connector and send/receive a file created in Notepad.

A note for Windows 3.x users - in Program Manager, double click on the Accessories icon, then double click on the Terminal icon to activate Terminal

First, we will create a communications setup file for use in our experiments. Double click on the Terminal icon. The "Terminal" window will appear. It will be labeled "Terminal-(Untitled)".

```
┌───┬──────────────────────────────────────────────────────┐
│ ─ │            Terminal - (Untitled)                     │
├───┴────────┬────────┬──────────┬────────┬─────────┬──────┤
│    File    │  Edit  │ Settings │ Phone  │Transfers│ Help │
├────────────┴────────┴──────────┴────────┴─────────┴──────┤
│ █                                                        │
│  \                                                       │
│   \                                                      │
│    \                                                     │
│     \___ Blinking Cursor                                 │
│                                                          │
│                                                          │
│                                                          │
│                                                          │
│                                                          │
└──────────────────────────────────────────────────────────┘
```

We will create a setup file for use in our experiments.

Settings>Terminal Emulation.

> Dialog box - select "DEC VT-100 (ANSI)" (default setting).

Settings>Terminal preferences.

> Dialog box - deselect "Local Echo" (default setting).
> All other settings - default OK.

Settings>Communications.

> Dialog box - select following options:

```
Baud rate         1200 (default)
Data bits         8
Stop bits         1
Parity            None
Flow control      None
Connector         COM 2 *
Parity check      Deselect
Carrier check     Deselect

* The serial port you are going to use (usually COM 2).
```

File>Save.

> Name the file per the DOS file naming conventions with the extension ".trm' which indicates the file is a terminal file.

There is a difference between 3.x and 95 here. On my 3.1 machine, my Terminal file with the saved settings comes up as the default file when I open Terminal. On my 95 machine, the Terminal - [untitled] file is the default file. I have to open Terminal and File>Open to select my file with the saved settings.

Now strike a letter key. Nothing happens. The screen displays characters received, <u>NOT</u> characters sent.

Turn off your computer. Install the "U-turn" connector at the serial port you are going to use. Generally this will be COM 2 as most systems have the mouse connected to COM 1. Turn on your computer. Open the settings file you just created in Terminal. The Terminal window should now be open, blank, and a cursor should be blinking in the upper left hand corner. Now type any character. The character will appear on-screen where the cursor was. The character displayed is actually the character <u>received</u> by the terminal program. If you type the letter "a", it will be transmitted out the COM 2 serial port on the T_D line, make a U-turn, come back in the same serial port on the R_D line and will be displayed on the screen. Note that the character sent is not displayed, the character received is. They happen to be the same in this case because of the U-turn.

To clear the screen: Edit>Clear buffer.

To view a text file: Transfers>View Text File.

    Dialog box.

To send a text file: Transfers>Send Text File

    Dialog box.

        Clicking "OK" causes the file to be sent.

To receive text file: Transfers>Receive Text File

    Dialog box.

        The incoming file must be named using MS-DOS file naming conventions. Use the ".txt" file name extension.

    U-turn connector - only the last line of the file will appear on screen.

To create a text file:

    Use Notepad.
    Saved file is stored in the Windows directory. Terminal can access it.

Using the U-turn connector, you can experiment with sending a file.

Create a test file in Notepad and save it (DOS-style file name, .txt).
Open your settings file in "Terminal".
Transfers>Send Text File.
Highlight the name of your file.
Click "OK". This causes the file to be sent. It will make a U-turn and appear on-screen (file received is displayed).

PC-TO-PC "2-LANE HIGHWAY" EXPERIMENT

If you have two PCs available, you might like to do the following experiment to learn more about serial communication between two PCs, both running Terminal. A cable will be required to connect the two serial ports. The simplest possible cable which will work consists of two data lines (one for each direction) and a ground line.

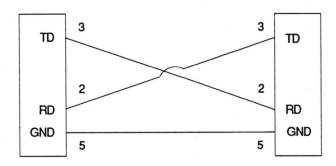

Cable Assembly

Notice that the transmit data (T_D) line on computer 1 is connected to the receive data (R_D) line on computer 2 and visa versa. You can easily make your own cable assembly using two 9-pin female D-subminiature connectors and three lengths of wire. Keep the cable as short as possible (8 feet works for me).

Both computers must communicate using the same settings for baud rate, etc. You can start by using the settings used previously in the setup examples.

```
Baud rate        1200(default)
Data bits        8
Parity           None
Stop bits        1
Flow control     None
```

The first objective is to establish bi-directional communication between two computers.

The second objective is to create a file in computer 1 and send it over our simple serial link to computer 2. Name the file created in computer 1 using the DOS file naming rules with the file name extension ".txt" (text file). The file name will not be transmitted. Only the file contents (text) will be. The file to be received in computer 2 must be named in computer 2 prior to its being received. The same name can be used that is used in computer 1 or a different one can be assigned (whatever works for you to keep it all straight). Once received, the text file can be moved, saved, printed or whatever needs to be done.

We will assume both computers are running Terminal.

To establish bi-directional communication, connect the computers via the serial cable, turn both of them on and bring up Terminal with your settings file in each. When you have the Terminal window open in each computer, type a character in one of the computers. It will appear on the screen of the other computer. Now do the reverse. After you have played a little, clean off the screen in each computer by:

> Edit>Clear Buffer.

Next, we will send a file from one computer to the other. The numbers designate which computer the operation takes place in.

1) Create a test file in Notepad and save it (DOS-style file name, .txt).
1) Open your settings file in "Terminal".
1) Transfers>Send Text File.

> Highlight the name of your file.
> Do NOT click "OK".

2) Open your settings file in "Terminal".
2) Transfers>Receive Text File.
2) Type file name in dialog box. Click "OK".
2) The window will be blank and there will be a new menu bar at the bottom. Computer 2 is now sitting there waiting to receive the file from computer 1.
1) Click "OK" in the Send Text File dialog box. This sends the file out the serial port.
2) The text received from computer 1 will appear on the screen.
2) Click "Stop" on the menu bar at the bottom of the window to get out of the receive mode.
2) To transfer the text somewhere else:
> Use Edit>Copy
> or
> Close "Terminal" and open "Notepad". Open your file.
> Do whatever you want with the text.

IMPORTING A TEXT FILE INTO A SPREADSHEET PROGRAM

As part of our experiments with PIC black boxes, it will be useful to squirt data from the PIC16 into the PC and import it into a spreadsheet program for two possible purposes. One is to graph the data. The other is to manipulate the data.

The data should be arranged in columns. As an example for experimentation, let's create some bogus time vs. temperature data in Notepad and save the file. Use tabs to create the data columns.

Time	Temp
1	4.5
2	6.0
3	3.0

Highlight the data in the columns (not the column headings) and copy them as a block using Edit>Copy.

Close Notepad.

The Works screens/interface differ for Windows 3.x vs. 95.

Windows 3.x

Open Microsoft Works (tm) and:

- 1) Select "spreadsheet". "Sheet 1 " will appear and cell A1 will be highlighted.

	A	B	C	
1				
2				
3				
4				

- 2) Paste the data (Edit>Paste) in cell A-1. The time data will appear in column A and the temperature data will appear in column B.

	A	B	C	
1	1	4.5		
2	2	6		
3	3	3		
4				

- 3) Charts>Create New Chart. The result will be a meaningless bar chart.
- 4) Edit>Series. In the dialog box:

```
┌──────────────────────────────────────────────────┐
│  Value [Y] Series                                  │
│                                                    │
│      1st :  ┌──────────────┐                       │
│            │ B1:B3         │                       │
│             └──────────────┘                       │
│      2nd :  ┌──────────────┐                       │
│            │              │                        │
│             └──────────────┘                       │
│  Category [X] Series :  ┌────────────────────────┐ │
│                         │                        │ │
│                          └────────────────────────┘│
└──────────────────────────────────────────────────┘
```

Click OK.
A meaningful bar chart will appear.
- 4) Gallery>Line. In the dialog box:
      Select number 2.
      Click OK.
- 5) Edit>Titles. In the Dialog box:

```
┌──────────────────────────────────────────────────────┐
│       Chart Title :  ┌────────────────────────────┐    │
│                      │ TEMP vs. TIME              │    │
│                       └────────────────────────────┘   │
│         Subtitle :   ┌────────────────────────────┐    │
│                      │                            │    │
│                       └────────────────────────────┘   │
│  Horizontal [X] Axis :  ┌────────────────────────────┐ │
│                         │ Time                       │ │
│                          └────────────────────────────┘│
│    Vertical [Y] Axis :  ┌────────────────────────────┐ │
│                         │ Temp                       │ │
│                          └────────────────────────────┘│
│  Right Vertical Axis :  ┌────────────────────────────┐ │
│                         │                            │ │
│                          └────────────────────────────┘│
└──────────────────────────────────────────────────────┘
```

The resulting graph follows:

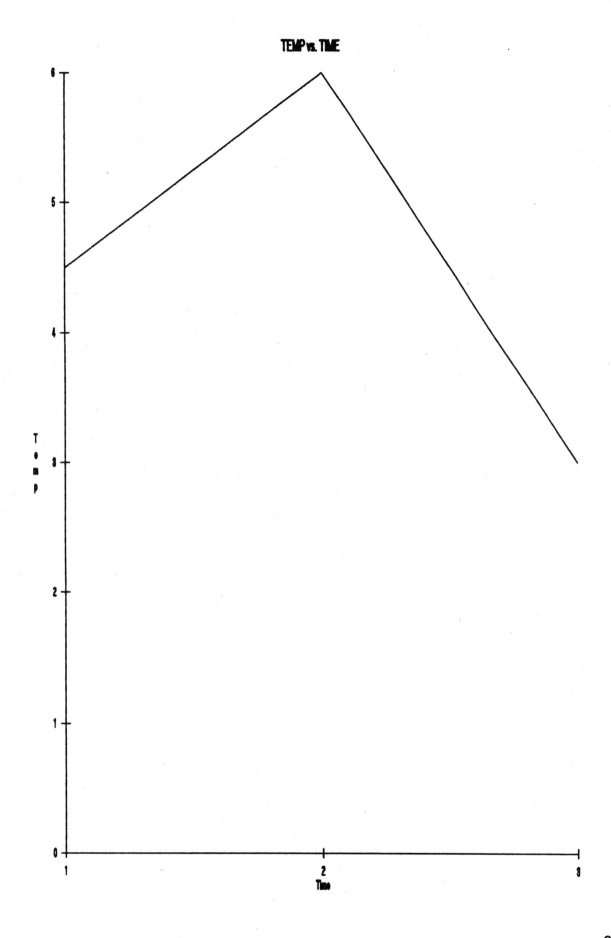

TEMP vs. TIME

Windows 95

Open Microsoft Works and:

- 1) With the Works Tools tab selected, select "spreadsheet".
  "Unsaved sheet 1" will appear and cell A1 will be highlighted.

	A	B	C	
1				
2				
3				
4				

- 2) Paste the data (Edit>Paste) in cell A-1. The time
  data will appear in column A and the temperature data will appear in column B.

	A	B	C	
1	1	4.5		
2	2	6		
3	3	3		
4				

- 3) Tools>Create New Chart. The result will be a meaningless bar chart on the
  right side of a dialog box and a matrix of graph pictures on the left.
- 4) With the Basic Options tab selected (default), click on the line graph symbol
  with two lines (top row, second from the right in the matrix) in the dialog box.
  The result will be a meaningless line graph.
- 5) With the Advanced Options tab selected, a dialog box appears with your
  graph on the right side and three rows of buttons on the left under the
  heading "How is your spreadsheet data organized?".
  1) Which way does your series go? Select "down" (default).
  2) First row contains: Select "A category" (default).
  3) First column contains: Select "Category labels".
  A meaningful line graph will appear!
- 6) Click "OK".

• 7) Edit Titles

```
┌─────────────────────────────────────────────────────────────┐
│                                 ┌───────────────────────────┐ │
│          Chart Title :          │ TEMP vs. TIME             │ │
│                                 └───────────────────────────┘ │
│                                 ┌───────────────────────────┐ │
│  Horizontal [X] Axis :          │ Time                      │ │
│                                 └───────────────────────────┘ │
│                                 ┌───────────────────────────┐ │
│    Vertical [Y] Axis :          │ Temp                      │ │
│                                 └───────────────────────────┘ │
└─────────────────────────────────────────────────────────────┘
```

• 11) Click "OK".

The resulting graph follows:

TEMP vs. TIME

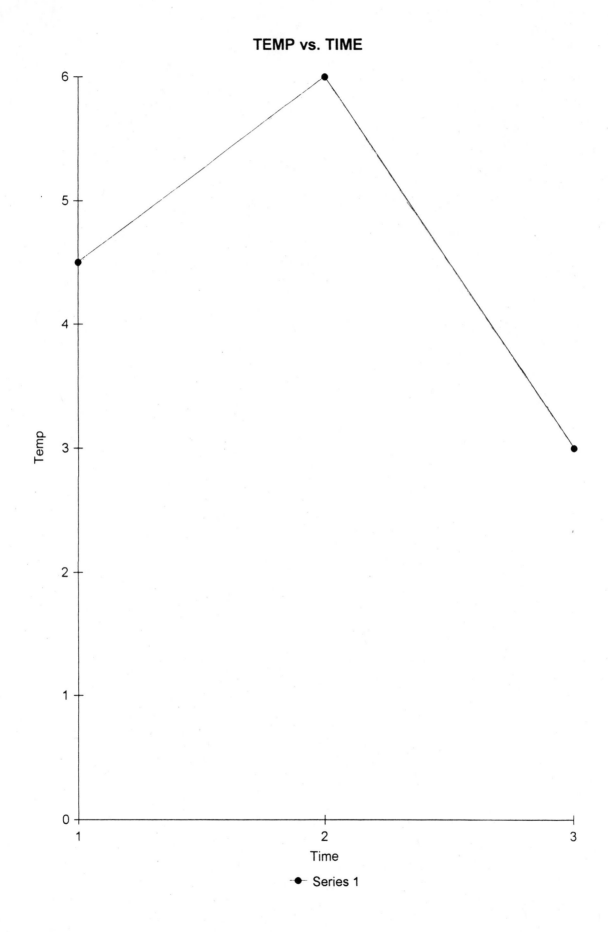

PC/PIC

Serial communications between two PIC16s is described in PIC'n Up The Pace. We will use that information as a basis for our project here which is to get a PC to talk to a PIC16 and visa versa. The only changes required are to use a standard baud rate compatible with PC serial communications and to transmit least significant bit first. After making the necessary code modifications and verifying them by having one PIC16 talk with another, we will experiment by replacing the transmitting '84 on a board with a PC. Then we will reverse rolls and let the transmitting '84 on a board send data to the PC.

PC Baud Rates

Baud rate is defined as the number of bits transmitted per second. The baud rates available for serial communication via a PC using Terminal are:

```
          ----------
          Baud Rates
          ----------
               110
               300
               600
             1,200
             2,400
             4,800
             9,600
            19,200
```

We will modify the serial input and output routines described in PIC'n Up The Pace for use in PC applications. These routines were designed to make programming and use of TMR0 easy, not to run at some standard baud rate. Now they must conform to the standard.

A serial output subroutine called "ser_out" is described and used in the experiments in PIC'n Up The Pace. I used a bit time of 256 internal clock cycles just to make using TMR0 easy. A PIC16F84 coupled with a 4.0 MHz clock oscillator has an internal clock frequency of 1.0 MHz (divide by 4). An internal clock cycle is, then, 1 microsecond long. 256 internal clock cycles equals 256 microseconds equals the time to transmit one bit. One bit per 256 microseconds works out to be 3906 baud. This is a non-standard baud rate. Since we need to use a standard baud rate, we will redefine the bit time (width) accordingly and change the TMR0 code to suit.

Slowing the baud rate would require counting to a number larger than 256. It is easier to speed up the baud rate and use a number less than 256. The next fastest standard baud rate is 4,800.

$$1 \text{ bit width} = \frac{1}{4,800} \text{ sec} = 208.3 \text{ } \mu\text{sec}$$

use 0xD0

half bit = 0x68

The use of TMR0 is explained in **Easy** PIC'n. To generate the desired baud rate (4800), TMR0 must be loaded with a number each time a time interval is generated. TMR0 counts up meaning it is incremented by the PIC16's internal instruction cycle clock in this application. TMR0 overflows when the count reaches 0xFF and rolls over to 0x00. The timer must be loaded with a value equal to 0xFF minus the number of pulses required to generate the required time interval.

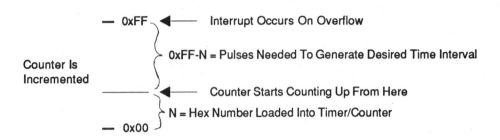

We will bump these numbers by 0x1 to compensate for the time (1 microsecond) required to execute the MOVLW instruction used to define the number.

```
                    -------------------
                     Full Bit   Half Bit
                    -------------------
        0xFF-N        0x68        0xD0
             N        0x97        0x2f
     Use N =          0x98        0x30
```

Another change is that TMR0 was used in the free running mode in the ser_in routine. this worked because the number of pulses required was 256. TMR0 was cleared to start it (CLRF TMR0) followed by letting it roll over each time the count reached 256. This time, we must load the counter for each time interval.

PC Serial Communications - Least Significant Bit First

PCs transmit and receive the least significant bit first. The serial routines "ser_out" and "ser_in" used in PIC'n **Up The Pace** communicate most significant bit first. Changing the RLF instruction operating on the receive register and send register to RRF takes care of that.

The two modified and renamed subroutines follow. "ser_in" is renamed "rcv4800" and "ser_out" is renamed "snd4800".

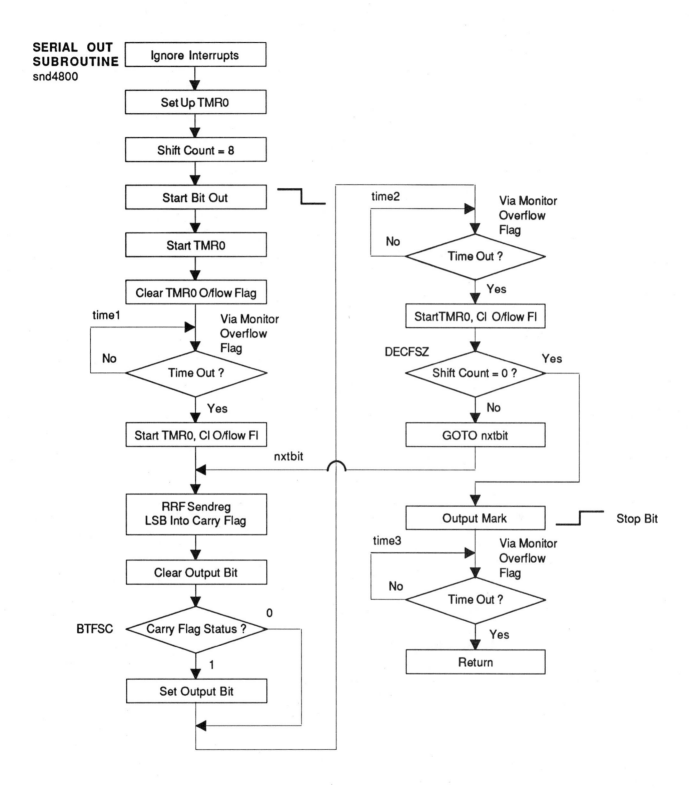

SERIAL OUT SUBROUTINE
snd4800

Ignore Interrupts

Set Up TMR0

Shift Count = 8

Start Bit Out

Start TMR0

Clear TMR0 O/flow Flag

time1

Via Monitor Overflow Flag

No

Time Out ?

Yes

Start TMR0, Cl O/flow Fl

nxtbit

RRF Sendreg LSB Into Carry Flag

Clear Output Bit

BTFSC

Carry Flag Status ?

0

1

Set Output Bit

time2

Via Monitor Overflow Flag

No

Time Out ?

Yes

StartTMR0, Cl O/flow Fl

DECFSZ

Shift Count = 0 ?

Yes

No

GOTO nxtbit

Output Mark

Stop Bit

time3

Via Monitor Overflow Flag

No

Time Out ?

Yes

Return

```
;======SND4800.ASM================================5/2/98==
        list    p=16f84
        radix   hex
;-----------------------------------------------------------
;       cpu equates (memory map)
tmr0    equ     0x01
status  equ     0x03
porta   equ     0x05
intcon  equ     0x0b
sendreg equ     0x0c
count   equ     0x0d
optreg  equ     0x81
trisa   equ     0x85
;-----------------------------------------------------------
;       bit equates
c       equ     0
rp0     equ     5
;-----------------------------------------------------------
        org     0x000
;
start   bsf     status,rp0  ;switch to bank 1
        movlw   b'00000100' ;port A inputs/outputs
        movwf   trisa
        bcf     status,rp0  ;switch back to bank 0
        bsf     porta,1     ;output mark, bit 1
        movlw   b'01000001' ;ASCII "A" to be sent
        movwf   sendreg     ;store
switch  btfsc   porta,2     ;start send?
        goto    switch      ;not yet
        call    snd4800     ;to serial out subroutine
circle  goto    circle      ;done
;-----------------------------------------------------------
snd4800 bcf     intcon,5    ;disable tmr0 interrupts
        bcf     intcon,7    ;disable global interrupts
        clrf    tmr0        ;clear timer/counter
        clrwdt              ;clear wdt prep prescaler assign
        bsf     status,rp0  ;to page 1
        movlw   b'11011000' ;set up timer/counter
        movwf   optreg
        bcf     status,rp0  ;back to page 0
        movlw   0x08        ;init shift counter
        movwf   count
        bcf     porta,1     ;start bit
        movlw   0x30        ;define N for timer
        movwf   tmr0        ;start timer/counter
        bcf     intcon,2    ;clear tmr0 overflow flag
time1   btfss   intcon,2    ;timer overflow?
        goto    time1       ;no
        movlw   0x30        ;yes, define N for timer
        movwf   tmr0        ;start timer/counter
        bcf     intcon,2    ;clear overflow flag
nxtbit  rrf     sendreg,f   ;rotate lsb into carry flag
        bcf     porta,1     ;clear port A, bit 1
        btfsc   status,c    ;test carry flag
```

216

```
        bsf     porta,1      ;bit is set
time2   btfss   intcon,2     ;timer overflow?
        goto    time2        ;no
        movlw   0x30         ;yes, define N for timer
        movwf   tmr0         ;start timer/counter
        bcf     intcon,2     ;clear overflow flag
        decfsz  count,f      ;shifted 8?
        goto    nxtbit       ;no
        bsf     porta,1      ;yes, output mark
time3   btfss   intcon,2     ;timer overflow?
        goto    time3        ;no
        return               ;yes, done
;-------------------------------------------------------------
        end
;-------------------------------------------------------------
;at blast time, select:
;       memory unprotected
;       watchdog timer disabled (default is enabled)
;       standard crystal (using 4 MHz osc for test) XT
;       power-up timer on
;=============================================================
```

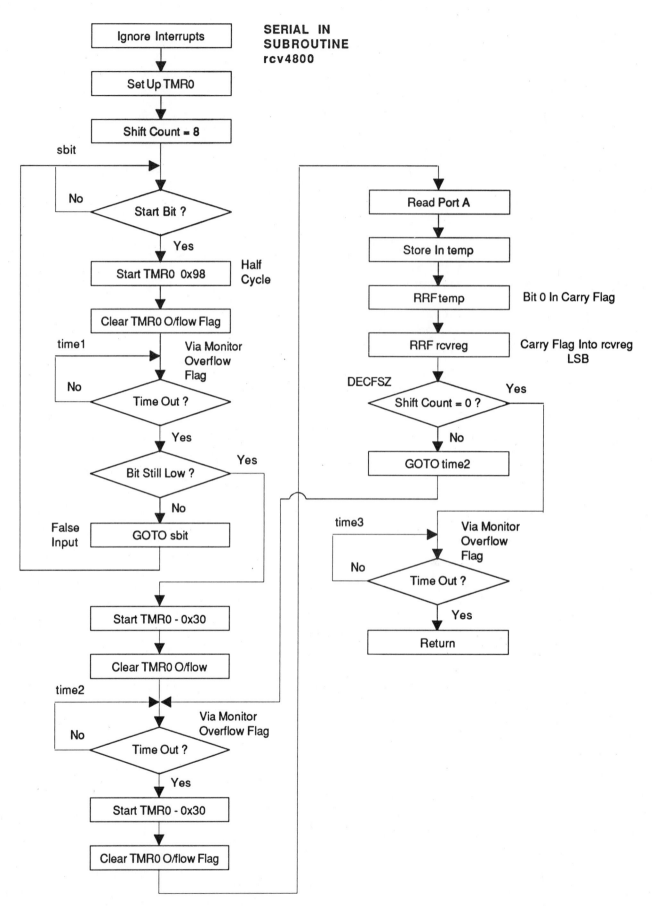

SERIAL IN
SUBROUTINE
rcv4800

Ignore Interrupts

Set Up TMR0

Shift Count = 8

sbit

Start Bit ?   No

Yes

Start TMR0 0x98   Half Cycle

Clear TMR0 O/flow Flag

time1   Via Monitor Overflow Flag

Time Out ?   No

Yes

Bit Still Low ?   Yes

No

False Input   GOTO sbit

Start TMR0 - 0x30

Clear TMR0 O/flow

time2   Via Monitor Overflow Flag

Time Out ?   No

Yes

Start TMR0 - 0x30

Clear TMR0 O/flow Flag

Read Port A

Store In temp

RRF temp   Bit 0 In Carry Flag

RRF rcvreg   Carry Flag Into rcvreg LSB

DECFSZ

Shift Count = 0 ?   Yes

No

GOTO time2

time3   Via Monitor Overflow Flag

Time Out ?   No

Yes

Return

218

```
;=======RCV4800.ASM=================================5/2/98==
          list     p=16f84
          radix    hex
;-------------------------------------------------------------
;         cpu equates (memory map)
tmr0      equ      0x01
status    equ      0x03
porta     equ      0x05
portb     equ      0x06
intcon    equ      0x0b
rcvreg    equ      0x0c
count     equ      0x0d
temp      equ      0x0e
optreg    equ      0x81
trisa     equ      0x85
trisb     equ      0x86
;-------------------------------------------------------------
;         bit equates
rp0       equ      5
;-------------------------------------------------------------
          org      0x000
;
start     bsf      status,rp0   ;switch to bank 1
          movlw    b'00000101'  ;port A inputs/outputs
          movwf    trisa
          movlw    b'00000000'  ;port B outputs
          movwf    trisb
          bcf      status,rp0   ;back to bank 0
          clrf     portb
          clrf     rcvreg
switch    btfsc    porta,2      ;operator ready to receive?
          goto     switch       ;no
          call     rcv4800      ;yes, to serial in subroutine
          movf     rcvreg,w     ;get byte received
          movwf    portb        ;display via LEDs
circle    goto     circle       ;done
;-------------------------------------------------------------
rcv4800   bcf      intcon,5     ;disable tmr0 interrupts
          bcf      intcon,7     ;disable global interrupts
          clrf     tmr0         ;clear timer/counter
          clrwdt                ;clear wdt prep prescaler assign
          bsf      status,rp0   ;to page 1
          movlw    b'11011000'  ;set up timer/counter
          movwf    optreg
          bcf      status,rp0   ;back to page 0
          movlw    0x08         ;init shift counter
          movwf    count
sbit      btfsc    porta,0      ;look for start bit
          goto     sbit         ;mark
          movlw    0x98         ;start bit received, half bit time
          movwf    tmr0         ;load and start timer/counter
          bcf      intcon,2     ;clear tmr0 overflow flag
time1     btfss    intcon,2     ;timer overflow?
```

```
            goto     time1            ;no
            btfsc    porta,0          ;start bit still low?
            goto     sbit             ;false start, go back
            movlw    0x30             ;real, define N for timer
            movwf    tmr0             ;start timer/ctr - bit time
            bcf      intcon,2         ;clear tmr0 overflow flag
time2       btfss    intcon,2         ;timer overflow?
            goto     time2            ;no
            movlw    0x30             ;yes, define N for timer
            movwf    tmr0             ;start timer/ctr
            bcf      intcon,2         ;clear tmr0 overflow flag
            movf     porta,w          ;read port A
            movwf    temp             ;store
            rrf      temp,f           ;rotate bit 0 into carry flag
            rrf      rcvreg,f         ;rotate carry into rcvreg bit 7
            decfsz   count,f          ;shifted 8?
            goto     time2            ;no
time3       btfss    intcon,2         ;timer overflow?
            goto     time3            ;no
            return                    ;yes, byte received
;----------------------------------------------------------------
            end
;----------------------------------------------------------------
;at blast time, select:
;       memory unprotected
;       watchdog timer disabled (default is enabled)
;       standard crystal (using 4 MHz osc for test) XT
;       power-up timer on
;================================================================
```

`PIC-TO-PIC SERIAL COMMUNICATION AT 4800 BAUD, LSB FIRST

To verify that our our serial communication hardware and software works, we will get a couple of PIC16s to talk to each other. Actually, we'll do part of the job by getting one PIC16 to talk while the other listens. We'll see if the listener understood what the talker said. This is just like the experiment in PIC'n Up The Pace with the exception of baud rate and moving data LSB first.

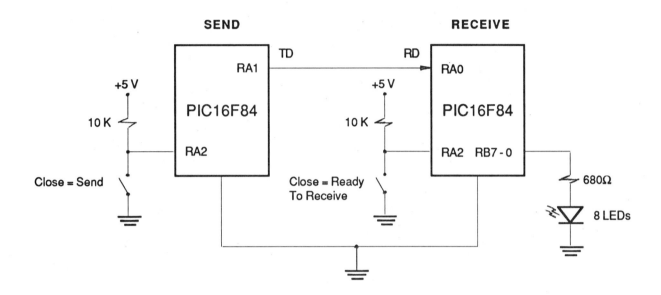

Two '84 on a board modules may be used for this experiment.

Both PIC16s are PIC16F84s with 4.0 MHz clock oscillators. For the transmitting chip, port A, bit 1 is used to transmit. The receiver uses port A, bit 0 to receive. Both transmitter and receiver will use TMR0 for timing.

SEND MAIN

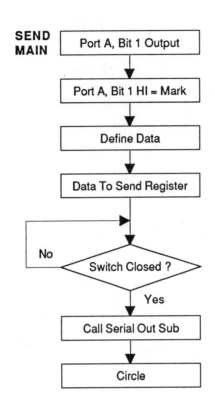

Port A, Bit 1 Output

↓

Port A, Bit 1 HI = Mark

↓

Define Data

↓

Data To Send Register

↓

No ← Switch Closed ?

Yes ↓

Call Serial Out Sub

↓

Circle

RECEIVE MAIN

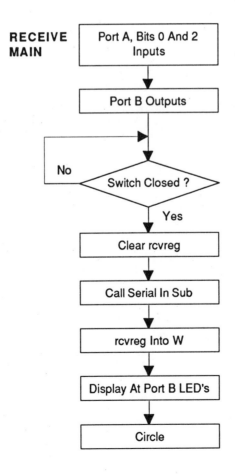

Port A, Bits 0 And 2 Inputs

↓

Port B Outputs

↓

No ← Switch Closed ?

Yes ↓

Clear rcvreg

↓

Call Serial In Sub

↓

rcvreg Into W

↓

Display At Port B LED's

↓

Circle

To run the programs (snd4800.asm and rcv4800.asm):

Run "send" first with switch off (RA2) - establish proper level on TD = mark.
Run "receive" second with switch off (RA2) - get ready to receive.
     Stabilize, then switch on = ready.
Send switch on.
LEDs on the receive circuit will display the byte received.

RS-232 INTERFACE FOR PIC16

My objective here is to give you just enough information about RS-232 to make it possible to build a simple hardware interface between a PC serial port and a PIC16. A MAX233 RS-232 converter IC from MAXIM will be used to develop the 9 volts or so required to transfer data per the RS-232 standard. Among other things, an RS-232 converter chip is an inverter. There is an RS-232 converter chip inside the PC which inverts data going both ways. It is desirable to use one at the PIC16 end too so that everything comes out right (see diagram on following page).

RS-232 CONVERTER

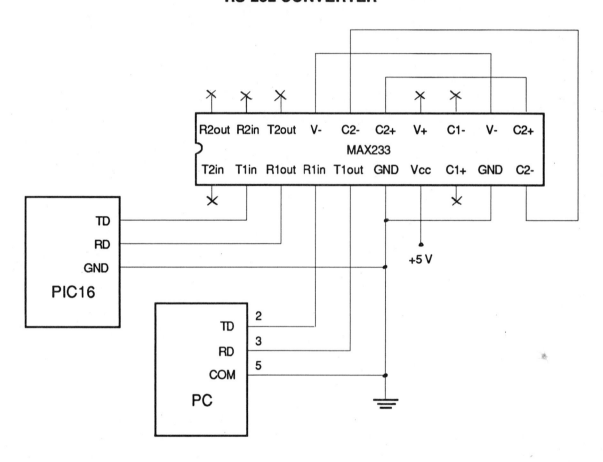

The connections between the PC, cable, RS-232 converter and PIC16 are:

RS-232
CONVERTER

Note that only the wires used between the PC and RS-232 converter board in a particular experiment are shown in the drawings that follow in this book. The third wire in the cable described in the "2-lane highway" experiment will not interfere.

The pin-functions for PC RS-232 serial connectors of interest here are:

```
------------------------------------
     Function          9-pin*  25-pin
------------------------------------
Transmitted data (TD)    3        2
Received data (RD)       2        3
Common                   5        7

* Shown in this book
```

The cable is the same one used for the PC-to-PC experiments. Note that transmit on one end goes to receive on the other end.

To test your RS-232 converter, use a wire to connect the PIC16 transmit and receive terminals (R1out and T1in) on the converter board. With the converter board connected to the PC via cable, a character sent using the PC terminal program will (should) appear on screen as was the case with the "U-turn" experiment.

PC-TO-PIC SERIAL COMMUNICATION

To verify that our our serial communication hardware and software works, we will get a PC to talk to a PIC16. We'll see if the listener (PIC16) understood what the talker (PC) said. This is just like the experiment in **PIC'n Up The Pace** with the exception of baud rate and moving data LSB first.

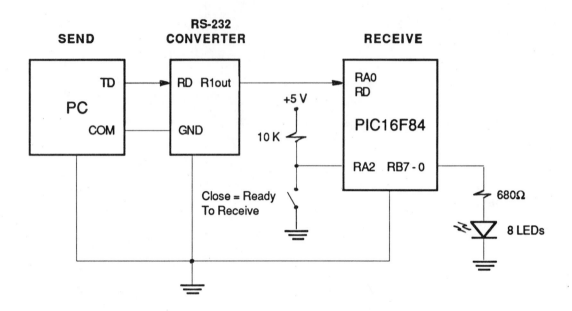

An '84 on a board module may be used for this experiment.

The PIC16F84 is connected to a 4.0 MHz clock oscillator, uses port A, bit 0 to receive, and uses TMR0 for timing. "rcv4800.asm" is the program used for receiving.

To run PC to PIC16:

PC on, Terminal program set up as in previous examples except 4800 baud.
Run "receive" program with switch off (RA2) - get ready to receive.
    Stabilize, then switch on = ready.
Send switch on.
Type "A".
"01000001" (ASCII "A") should appear on the LEDs.

PIC-TO-PC SERIAL COMMUNICATION

Next, we will get a PIC16 to talk to a PC. Again, we'll see if the listener (PC this time) understood what the talker (PIC) said. And again, this is just like the experiment in PIC'n Up The Pace with the exception of baud rate and moving data LSB first.

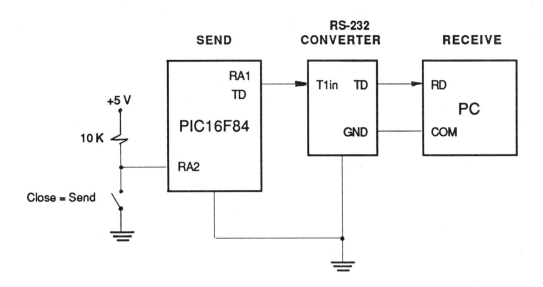

An '84 on a board module may be used for this experiment.

The PIC16F84 is connected to a 4.0 MHz clock oscillator, uses port A, bit 1 to transmit, and uses TMR0 for timing. "snd4800.asm" is the program used for transmitting.

To run the program:

Power-up the PIC16 board.
Power-up the PC.
Set up the Terminal program as in previous examples except 4800 baud.
Run "send" first with switch off (RA2) - establish proper level on TD = mark.
Send switch on.
An "A" should appear on the screen of the PC.

Code For Formatting PIC16 Data On A PC Screen

Three ASCII control characters are useful for controlling the placement of ASCII alphanumeric characters on the screen of the PC as they are received. This is important because we want the information to be readable and also because we will want data to be formatted to be saved as a useful text file. The three ASCII control characters are:

```
Carriage return     CR     00001101     0x0D
Line feed           LF     00001010     0x0A
Horizontal tab      HT     00001001     0x09
```

As you probably already know, carriage return causes placement of characters on the screen to move to the extreme left side. Line feed causes characters to be placed on the next line down the screen. Horizontal tab means tab over to the right. Theses terms come from the teletype days. The binary codes for these functions must be built into PIC16 code sent to the PC so that the data displayed will make sense to humans.

We will use two sample programs to illustrate how this works. The first one uses straight line code and the binary codes for the ASCII text characters. The second example uses a lookup table for the ASCII characters and a loop with a counter to access them. In the second example, the ASCII alpha characters are defined using an easier technique (example: a'B').

```
;=======FORMAT1.ASM================================5/2/98==
        list    p=16f84
        radix   hex
;------------------------------------------------------------
;       cpu equates (memory map)
tmr0    equ     0x01
status  equ     0x03
porta   equ     0x05
intcon  equ     0x0b
sendreg equ     0x0c
count   equ     0x0d
optreg  equ     0x81
trisa   equ     0x85
;------------------------------------------------------------
;       bit equates
c       equ     0
rp0     equ     5
;------------------------------------------------------------
        org     0x000
;
start   bsf     status,rp0  ;switch to bank 1
        movlw   b'00000100' ;port A inputs/outputs
        movwf   trisa
        bcf     status,rp0  ;switch back to bank 0
        bsf     porta,1     ;output mark, bit 1
switch  btfsc   porta,2     ;start send?
        goto    switch      ;not yet
        movlw   b'01000001' ;ASCII "A" to be sent
        movwf   sendreg     ;store
```

```
          call      snd4800      ;to serial out subroutine
          movlw     b'00001001'  ;tab
          movwf     sendreg      ;store
          call      snd4800      ;to serial out subroutine
          movlw     b'01000010'  ;ASCII "B" to be sent
          movwf     sendreg      ;store
          call      snd4800      ;to serial out subroutine
          movlw     b'00001101'  ;carriage return
          movwf     sendreg      ;store
          call      snd4800      ;to serial out subroutine
          movlw     b'00001010'  ;line feed
          movwf     sendreg      ;store
          call      snd4800      ;to serial out subroutine
          movlw     b'01100011'  ;ASCII "c" to be sent
          movwf     sendreg      ;store
          call      snd4800      ;to serial out subroutine
          movlw     b'00001001'  ;tab
          movwf     sendreg      ;store
          call      snd4800      ;to serial out subroutine
          movlw     b'01100100'  ;ASCII "d" to be sent
          movwf     sendreg      ;store
          call      snd4800      ;to serial out subroutine
circle    goto      circle       ;done
;----------------------------------------------------------
snd4800   bcf       intcon,5     ;disable tmr0 interrupts
          bcf       intcon,7     ;disable global interrupts
          clrf      tmr0         ;clear timer/counter
          clrwdt                 ;clear wdt prep prescaler assign
          bsf       status,rp0   ;to page 1
          movlw     b'11011000'  ;set up timer/counter
          movwf     optreg
          bcf       status,rp0   ;back to page 0
          movlw     0x08         ;init shift counter
          movwf     count
          bcf       porta,1      ;start bit
          movlw     0x30         ;define N for timer
          movwf     tmr0         ;start timer/counter
          bcf       intcon,2     ;clear tmr0 overflow flag
time1     btfss     intcon,2     ;timer overflow?
          goto      time1        ;no
          movlw     0x30         ;yes, define N for timer
          movwf     tmr0         ;start timer/counter
          bcf       intcon,2     ;clear overflow flag
nxtbit    rrf       sendreg,f    ;rotate lsb into carry flag
          bcf       porta,1      ;clear port A, bit 1
          btfsc     status,c     ;test carry flag
          bsf       porta,1      ;bit is set
time2     btfss     intcon,2     ;timer overflow?
          goto      time2        ;no
          movlw     0x30         ;yes, define N for timer
          movwf     tmr0         ;start timer/counter
          bcf       intcon,2     ;clear overflow flag
          decfsz    count,f      ;shifted 8?
          goto      nxtbit       ;no
```

```
        bsf     porta,1      ;yes, output mark
time3   btfss   intcon,2     ;timer overflow?
        goto    time3        ;no
        return               ;yes, done
;----------------------------------------------------------------
        end
;----------------------------------------------------------------
;at blast time, select:
;       memory unprotected
;       watchdog timer disabled (default is enabled)
;       standard crystal (using 4 MHz osc for test) XT
;       power-up timer on
;================================================================
```

The second sample program works like this:

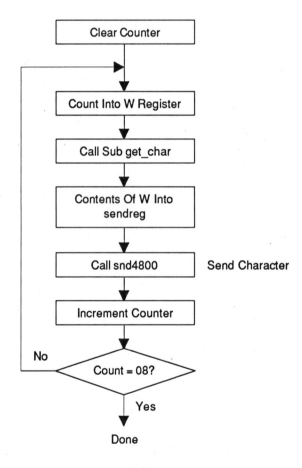

The program adds the counter contents to the program counter to jump into the table of ASCII characters. A comparison is made via subtracting the current count from the maximum count and testing the Z-flag. If the Z-flag is set, the result of subtraction is zero meaning the count is at maximum.

```
;======FORMAT2.ASM================================5/4/98==
          list     p=16f84
          radix    hex
;--------------------------------------------------------
;         cpu equates (memory map)
tmr0      equ      0x01
pc        equ      0x02
status    equ      0x03
porta     equ      0x05
intcon    equ      0x0b
sendreg   equ      0x0c
count     equ      0x0d
ctr       equ      0x0e
optreg    equ      0x81
trisa     equ      0x85
;--------------------------------------------------------
;         bit equates
c         equ      0
rp0       equ      5
;--------------------------------------------------------
          org      0x000
;
start     bsf      status,rp0   ;switch to bank 1
          movlw    b'00000100'  ;port A inputs/outputs
          movwf    trisa
          bcf      status,rp0   ;switch back to bank 0
          bsf      porta,1      ;output mark, bit 1
switch    btfsc    porta,2      ;start send?
          goto     switch       ;not yet
          clrf     ctr          ;zero counter
charout   movf     ctr,w        ;get count = offest
          call     getchar      ;get character from table
          movwf    sendreg      ;store
          call     snd4800      ;to serial out subroutine
          incf     ctr,f        ;increment counter
          movf     ctr,w        ;contents of counter into w
          sublw    0x08         ;subtract 8 from w - compare
          btfss    status,2     ;test z-flag, skip next instruction
;                                 if result 1 meaning counter=8
          goto     charout      ;not done yet
circle    goto     circle       ;done
;--------------------------------------------------------
getchar   addwf    pc,f         ;add offset to program counter
          retlw    a'A'         ;ASCII "A" to be sent
          retlw    b'00001001'  ;tab
          retlw    a'B'         ;ASCII "B" to be sent
          retlw    b'00001101'  ;carriage return
          retlw    b'00001010'  ;line feed
          retlw    a'c'         ;ASCII "c" to be sent
          retlw    b'00001001'  ;tab
          retlw    a'd'         ;ASCII "d" to be sent
;--------------------------------------------------------
snd4800   bcf      intcon,5     ;disable tmr0 interrupts
          bcf      intcon,7     ;disable global interrupts
```

```
        clrf    tmr0            ;clear timer/counter
        clrwdt                  ;clear wdt prep prescaler assign
        bsf     status,rp0      ;to page 1
        movlw   b'11011000'     ;set up timer/counter
        movwf   optreg
        bcf     status,rp0      ;back to page 0
        movlw   0x08            ;init shift counter
        movwf   count
        bcf     porta,1         ;start bit
        movlw   0x30            ;define N for timer
        movwf   tmr0            ;start timer/counter
        bcf     intcon,2        ;clear tmr0 overflow flag
time1   btfss   intcon,2        ;timer overflow?
        goto    time1           ;no
        movlw   0x30            ;yes, define N for timer
        movwf   tmr0            ;start timer/counter
        bcf     intcon,2        ;clear overflow flag
nxtbit  rrf     sendreg,f       ;rotate lsb into carry flag
        bcf     porta,1         ;clear port A, bit 1
        btfsc   status,c        ;test carry flag
        bsf     porta,1         ;bit is set
time2   btfss   intcon,2        ;timer overflow?
        goto    time2           ;no
        movlw   0x30            ;yes, define N for timer
        movwf   tmr0            ;start timer/counter
        bcf     intcon,2        ;clear overflow flag
        decfsz  count,f         ;shifted 8?
        goto    nxtbit          ;no
        bsf     porta,1         ;yes, output mark
time3   btfss   intcon,2        ;timer overflow?
        goto    time3           ;no
        return                  ;yes, done
;---------------------------------------------------------------
        end
;---------------------------------------------------------------
;at blast time, select:
;       memory unprotected
;       watchdog timer disabled (default is enabled)
;       standard crystal (using 4 MHz osc for test) XT
;       power-up timer on
;===============================================================
```

PC-TO-PIC/LCD

Sending one ASCII character at a time and sending a group of characters (text file) to a PIC16-controlled LCD will serve to illustrate how a PC may be used to control and/or send data to a PIC16-controlled device of your own design. We will use the PIC/LCD module described in **PIC'n Up The Pace** and we will modify the program from **PIC'n Up The Pace** called lcdslv.asm to control it. We will need our cable and RS-232 converter. These blocks may be connected as follows:

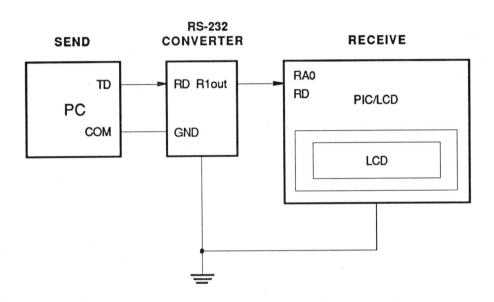

My list of functions the slave should perform under direction of the PC is:

- Display "HELLO" at power-on.
- Display "TEST" on command.
- Blank display.
- Place a single ASCII character in any one of 16 display RAM locations.
- Send the contents of display RAM to the display.

There are lots of ways to do this. My solution follows. You may want to modify mine for your own use or to do it a different way altogether.

Any time something is sent to the display, the instruction must be included to tell the slave what to do. Sometimes there will be an ASCII character or hex byte to be sent. Sometimes an address (RAM location) must be specified. I decided the easiest way to do this is always send 3 bytes at a time even if only 1 or 2 are needed. This makes the software simpler at the flow chart level.

Packets - 3 bytes (2nd and 3rd may be garbage).

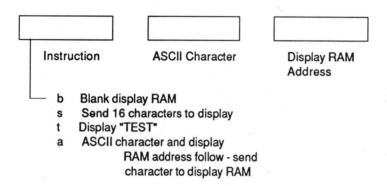

The program lcdslv.asm must be modified to operate at 4800 baud by substituting the subroutine rcv4800.asm. The display hex byte portion of the program has been deleted.

The instruction bytes used in lcdslv.asm are 0x00, 0x01, etc. which are easy to recognize in hexadecimal. The corresponding ASCII characters are ^@ and ^A where "^" denotes use of the control key. To make all this a little more PC-friendly and also to make it possible to use the normal characters which can be created (used) in a text file, we will change the control characters to ASCII letters.

```
-------------------------------------------------------------
Character                Function
-------------------------------------------------------------
    b          Fill  display RAM with blanks
    s          Send 16 characters to display
    t          Display "TEST"
    a          ASCII character and display RAM address follow
```

These changes have been made to the program.

You will also need to know the ASCII equivalents of the hexadecimal display RAM addresses.

```
-----------------------
Hex              ASCII
-----------------------
0x20             space, blank
0x21             !
0x22             "
0x23             #
0x24             $
0x25             %
0x26             &
0x27             '   apostrophe
0x28             (
0x29             )
0x2A             *
0x2B             +
0x2C             ,   comma
0x2D             -   dash,hyphen
0x2E             .   period
0x2F             /
```

```
;======PCLCD.ASM================================5/19/98==
        list    p=16f84
        radix   hex
;--------------------------------------------------------
;       cpu equates (memory map)
indf    equ     0x00
tmr0    equ     0x01
status  equ     0x03
fsr     equ     0x04
porta   equ     0x05
portb   equ     0x06
intcon  equ     0x0b
count1  equ     0x14
count2  equ     0x15
rcvreg  equ     0x16
count   equ     0x17
temp    equ     0x18
instr   equ     0x19
char    equ     0x1a
addr    equ     0x1b
optreg  equ     0x81
trisa   equ     0x85
trisb   equ     0x86
;--------------------------------------------------------
;       bit equates
z       equ     2
rp0     equ     5
;--------------------------------------------------------
        org     0x000
;
```

```
start    bsf      status,rp0  ;switch to bank 1
         movlw    b'00000001' ;port A inputs/outputs
         movwf    trisa
         movlw    b'00000000' ;port B outputs
         movwf    trisb
         bcf      status,rp0  ;back to bank 0
         movlw    b'00000000' ;all outputs low
         movwf    portb
         bcf      porta,1     ;all outputs low
         bcf      porta,2
         bcf      porta,3
         bcf      porta,4
         call     blanks      ;fill display RAM with blanks
         call     hello       ;create message in display RAM
         call     del_5       ;allow lcd time to initialize itself
         call     initlcd     ;initialize display
         call     disp16      ;send 16 characters to display
enterm   clrf     rcvreg      ;yes
         call     rcv4800     ;to serial in subroutine
         movf     rcvreg,w    ;get byte received
         movwf    instr       ;store instruction
         clrf     rcvreg
         call     rcv4800     ;to serial in subroutine
         movf     rcvreg,w    ;get byte received
         movwf    char        ;store character or byte
         clrf     rcvreg
         call     rcv4800     ;to serial in subroutine
         movf     rcvreg,w    ;get byte received
         movwf    addr        ;store address
         movf     instr,w     ;get copy of instruction
         sublw    a'b'        ;compare with "b"
         btfsc    status,z    ;z flag set if bytes are equal
         goto     blnkram     ;bytes equal
         movf     instr,w     ;get copy of instruction
         sublw    a's'        ;compare with "s"
         btfsc    status,z    ;z flag set if bytes are equal
         goto     send16      ;bytes equal
         movf     instr,w     ;get copy of instruction
         sublw    a't'        ;compare with "t"
         btfsc    status,z    ;z flag set if bytes are equal
         goto     sndtst      ;bytes equal
         goto     enterm      ;wait for next transmission
;-----------------------------------------------------------
blnkram  call     blanks      ;fill display ram with blanks
         goto     enterm      ;back to main
;-----------------------------------------------------------
send16   call     disp16      ;send display RAM contents to LCD
         goto     enterm      ;back to main
;-----------------------------------------------------------
sndtst   call     test        ;load display RAM with msg "TEST"
         call     disp16      ;send display RAM contents to LCD
         goto     enterm      ;back to main
;-----------------------------------------------------------
chr_ram  movf     addr,w      ;get copy of display RAM address
```

```
        movwf    fsr           ;store in file select register
        movf     char,w        ;get copy of character to be display
        movwf    indf          ;to RAM address pointed to by FSR
        goto     enterm        ;back to main
;-------------------------------------------------------------
blanks  movlw    0x10          ;count=16
        movwf    count1
        movlw    0x20          ;first display RAM address
        movwf    fsr           ;indexed addressing
        movlw    0x20          ;ascii blank
store   movwf    indf          ;store in display RAM location
;                                  pointed to by file select register
        decfsz   count1,f      ;16?
        goto     incfsr        ;no
        return                 ;yes, done
incfsr  incf     fsr,f         ;increment file select register
        goto     store
;-------------------------------------------------------------
hello   movlw    'H'
        movwf    0x20
        movlw    'E'
        movwf    0x21
        movlw    'L'
        movwf    0x22
        movwf    0x23
        movlw    'O'
        movwf    0x24
        return
;-------------------------------------------------------------
test    movlw    'T'
        movwf    0x20
        movwf    0x23
        movlw    'E'
        movwf    0x21
        movlw    'S'
        movwf    0x22
        movlw    ' '
        movwf    0x24
        return
;-------------------------------------------------------------
initlcd bcf      porta,1       ;E line low
        bcf      porta,2       ;RS line low, set up for control
        call     del_125       ;delay 125 microseconds
        movlw    0x38          ;8-bit, 5X7
        movwf    portb         ;0011 1000
        call     pulse         ;pulse and delay
        movlw    0x0c          ;display on, cursor off
        movwf    portb         ;0000 1100
        call     pulse
        movlw    0x06          ;increment mode, no display shift
        movwf    portb         ;0000 0110
        call     pulse
        call     del_5         ;delay 5 milliseconds - required
;                                  before sending data
```

```
        return
;-------------------------------------------------------------
disp16  bcf     porta,1     ;E line low
        bcf     porta,2     ;RS line low, set up for control
        call    del_125     ;delay 125 microseconds
        movlw   0x80        ;control word = address first half
        movwf   portb
        call    pulse       ;pulse and delay
        bsf     porta,2     ;RS=1, set up for data
        call    del_125     ;delay 125 microseconds
        movlw   0x20        ;initialze file select register
        movwf   fsr
getchar movf    0x00,w      ;get character from display RAM
;                               location pointed to by file select
;                               register
        movwf   portb
        call    pulse       ;send data to display
        movlw   0x27        ;8th character sent?
        subwf   fsr,w       ;subtract w from fsr
        btfsc   status,z    ;test z flag
        goto    half        ;set up for last 8 characters
        movlw   2f          ;test number
        subwf   fsr,w
        btfsc   status,z    ;test z flag
        return              ;16 characters sent to lcd
        incf    fsr,f       ;move to next character location
        goto    getchar
half    bcf     porta,2     ;RS=0, set up for control
        call    del_125     ;delay 125 microseconds
        movlw   0xc0        ;control word = address second half
        movwf   portb
        call    pulse       ;pulse and delay
        bsf     porta,2     ;RS=1, set up for data
        incf    fsr,f       ;increment file select register to
;                               select next character
        call    del_125     ;delay 125 microseconds
        goto    getchar
;-------------------------------------------------------------
del_125 movlw   0x2a        ;approx 42x3 cycles (decimal)
        movwf   count1      ;load counter
repeat  decfsz  count1,f    ;decrement counter
        goto    repeat      ;not 0
        return              ;counter 0, ends delay
;-------------------------------------------------------------
del_5   movlw   0x29        ;decimal 40
        movwf   count2      ;to counter
delay   call    del_125     ;delay 125 microseconds
        decfsz  count2,f    ;do it 40 times = 5 milliseconds
        goto    delay
        return              ;counter 0, ends delay
;-------------------------------------------------------------
pulse   bsf     porta,1     ;pulse E line
        nop                 ;delay
        bcf     porta,1
```

```
        call    del_125     ;delay 125 microseconds
        return
;-----------------------------------------------------------
rcv4800 bcf     intcon,5    ;disable tmr0 interrupts
        bcf     intcon,7    ;disable global interrupts
        clrf    tmr0        ;clear timer/counter
        clrwdt              ;clear wdt prep prescaler assign
        bsf     status,rp0  ;to page 1
        movlw   b'11011000' ;set up timer/counter
        movwf   optreg
        bcf     status,rp0  ;back to page 0
        movlw   0x08        ;init shift counter
        movwf   count
sbit    btfsc   porta,0     ;look for start bit
        goto    sbit        ;mark
        movlw   0x98        ;start bit received, half bit time
        movwf   tmr0        ;load and start timer/counter
        bcf     intcon,2    ;clear tmr0 overflow flag
time1   btfss   intcon,2    ;timer overflow?
        goto    time1       ;no
        btfsc   porta,0     ;start bit still low?
        goto    sbit        ;false start, go back
        movlw   0x30        ;real, define N for timer
        movwf   tmr0        ;start timer/ctr - bit time
        bcf     intcon,2    ;clear tmr0 overflow flag
time2   btfss   intcon,2    ;timer overflow?
        goto    time2       ;no
        movlw   0x30        ;yes, define N for timer
        movwf   tmr0        ;start timer/ctr
        bcf     intcon,2    ;clear tmr0 overflow flag
        movf    porta,w     ;read port A
        movwf   temp        ;store
        rrf     temp,f      ;rotate bit 0 into carry flag
        rrf     rcvreg,f    ;rotate carry into rcvreg bit 7
        decfsz  count,f     ;shifted 8?
        goto    time2       ;no
time3   btfss   intcon,2    ;timer overflow?
        goto    time3       ;no
        return              ;yes, byte received
;-----------------------------------------------------------
        end
;-----------------------------------------------------------
;at blast time, select:
;       memory unprotected
;       watchdog timer disabled (default is enabled)
;       standard crystal (using 4 MHz osc for test)
;       power-up timer on
;===========================================================
```

Connect the PC, RS-232 converter and PIC/LCD. Turn on the PC and power-up the converter and PIC/LCD. The LCD should display "HELLO". The terminal program should be set up as usual with the baud rate 4800 selected.

Let's try sending a single ASCII character to the display PIC16 to tell it to display the word "TEST". Using the terminal program, type the letter "t" followed by any two letters. If all goes well, the word "TEST" will be displayed. Why type three characters? The PIC/LCD is expecting packets of three characters. When the "t" instruction is received, the program does not look at the second and third characters, so they may be garbage. The easiest thing for me to remember is to type "t" three times.

Clearing the display requires sending two instructions. First, the display RAM must be filled with blanks ("b" instruction character). Second, the blanks in the display RAM must be sent to the LCD ("s" instruction character). Typing "b" three times followed by typing "s" three times should do the trick.

Sending the letter "A" to be displayed in the left-most position of the LCD may be accomplished by typing "aA sss". This is the "a" instruction followed by the letter "A" followed by the display RAM address (ASCII space for address 0x20) followed by the "s" instruction three times.

Sending A Text File

I like to start by doing something simple. Let's send the following text file to the display:

ttt

We will create the text file in Notepad, name the file "ttt.txt" and save it.

Press the reset button on your display module. The display will read "HELLO".

Using Terminal, select "Transfers" from the menu. Select the file "ttt.txt" by highlighting it in the list. Click "OK" which sends the file. As you have probably already guessed, the LCD should display the word "TEST".

Next, we will display the words "TEXT FILE". We will need to send the characters to the display RAM and then cause the 16 characters in the display RAM to be sent to the LCD.

Letter	Address Hex	ASCII Character
T	0x20	space
E	0x21	!
X	0x22	"
T	0x23	#
F	0x25	%
I	0x26	$
L	0x27	'
E	0x28	(

The text file contains:

```
aT aE!aX"aT#aF%aI&aL'aE(sss
```

Manually clear the LCD first by typing "b" three times followed by typing "s" three times prior to sending the text file.

When creating your own text files, it is important to remember that a delay of 125 microseconds must occur between successive writes to the LCD. This means that a series of operations involving writes to the LCD cannot be transmitted as one file for execution on-the-fly because there is no way to build in the necessary time delays. This is why one text file can't clear the LCD followed immediately by sending characters to it.

SUMMARY

Using the information contained in this chapter, you will be able to design and build your own PIC16-controlled black boxes which can report to or be supervised by a PC which can:

- Send data or a command.
- Receive status information.
- Receive data - display data on-screen, print data, save data file, massage data with a spreadsheet program, graph data, do math manipulation, etc.

SIMPLE DIGITAL VOLTMETER EXPERIMENT

A simple digital voltmeter (DVM) may be built using two circuits and a few of the programs from PIC'n Up The Pace. This DVM is based on the PIC16C71, which has A/D capability, and the PIC/LCD module. The PIC16C71 does the A/D conversion, performs the math and some conversions, and sends the digits and decimal point to the PIC/LCD board to be displayed.

First, the hardware:

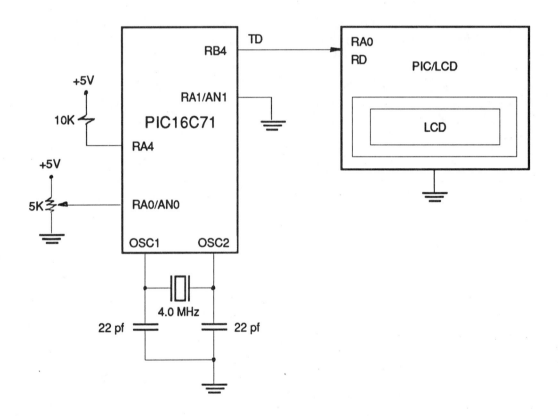

A clock oscillator circuit using a crystal and capacitors is shown this time for the sake of variety.

The display RAM locations are:

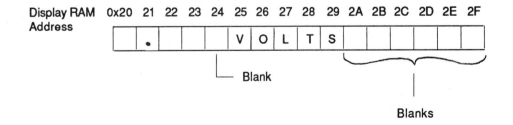

The programs modified and combined for this application are:

- A/D conversion   `ad16c71.asm`
- Multiplication - 8-bit x 8-bit, 16-bit result   `picm8.asm`
- 16-bit binary to 5-digit BCD conversion   `dblb2dy.asm`
- Round off two least significant decimal digits   `decrnd.asm`
- Display result with decimal point via serial   `templcd.asm`
  communication with PIC/LCD board

This project will be used as the basis for the data logging experiment which follows. The serial output to the LCD is on port B, pin 4 (which seems odd now) because it minimizes changes in the software modules used in the next experiment.

The A/D converter in the PIC16C71 counts up as it performs the conversion. A complete explanation may be found in PIC'n Up The Pace.

```
0.00-5.00 volts DC

0x00 = 0.00 volts        5 volts     = 0.0196 volts
0xFF = 4.998 volts      255 counts            count
```

It would be nice to be able to multiply the A/D conversion result by 0.0196 volts/count, but we can't. We can multiply the result by 196 and take care of the decimal point problem merely by placing it in the correct position when it is displayed by the LCD.

Multiplying by 196 produces a big number. Only the three most significant digits are meaningful in this application. They are held in the registers named tenk, onek and hund at the completion of the 16-bit binary to 5-digit BCD conversion process. A subroutine is used to round off the two least significant digits.

The rounded off result is converted to ASCII and sent serially, including the decimal point, to the PIC/LCD board. The process is repeated on a continuous basis.

Indexed addressing is used in conjunction with the file registers labeled tenk, onek, hund, ten and one, so they must be located consecutively at file register addresses 0x20, 0x21, etc.

Operation of the DVM is simple. Power it up, turn the shaft on the pot and observe the voltage reading.

This is not the most useful instrument you will ever own, but it serves to illustrate some PIC'n techniques which you may find useful in designing your own instrumentation and as the basis for the data logger described in the next experiment.

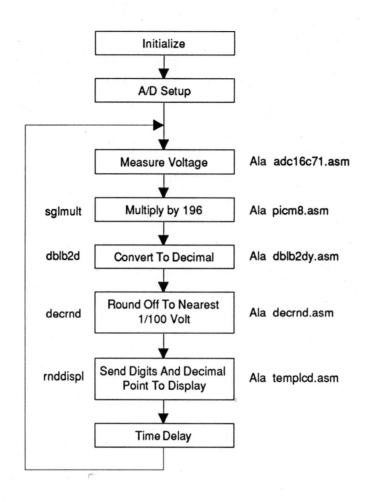

```
;======DVM.ASM=====================================10/16/98==
        list    p=16c71
        radix   hex
;------------------------------------------------------------
;       cpu equates (memory map)
indf    equ     0x00
tmr0    equ     0x01
pc      equ     0x02
status  equ     0x03
fsr     equ     0x04
porta   equ     0x05
portb   equ     0x06
adcon0  equ     0x08
adres   equ     0x09
intcon  equ     0x0b
;
count   equ     0x0c
ncount  equ     0x0d
mcount  equ     0x0e
;
number  equ     0x0f
multby  equ     0x10
data_lo equ     0x11
data_hi equ     0x12
```

244

```
;
index   equ     0x13
dig_ctr equ     0x14
lsb1    equ     0x15
msb1    equ     0x16
lsb2    equ     0x17
msb2    equ     0x18
flags   equ     0x19
;
sendreg equ     0x1a
instr   equ     0x1b
char    equ     0x1c
addr    equ     0x1d
hold    equ     0x1e
;
tenk    equ     0x20            ;must be at this location
onek    equ     0x21            ;  "    "   "     "       "
hund    equ     0x22            ;  "    "   "     "       "
ten     equ     0x23            ;  "    "   "     "       "
one     equ     0x24            ;  "    "   "     "       "
;
ones    equ     0x25
tenths  equ     0x26
hundths equ     0x27
;
optreg  equ     0x81
trisa   equ     0x85
trisb   equ     0x86
adcon1  equ     0x88
;--------------------------------------------------------------
;       bit equates
c       equ     0
ovflw   equ     0
z       equ     2
rp0     equ     5
;--------------------------------------------------------------
        org     0x000
        goto    start           ;skip over tables
;--------------------------------------------------------------
;tables for dblb2d
;
tbl_lo  addwf   pc,f            ;add index to program counter
        retlw   0x10            ;10,000 decimal
        retlw   0xe8            ;1,000 decimal
        retlw   0x64            ;100 decimal
        retlw   0x0a            ;10 decimal
;
tbl_hi  addwf   pc,f            ;add index to program counter
        retlw   0x27            ;10,000 decimal
        retlw   0x03            ;1,000 decimal
        retlw   0x00            ;100 decimal
        retlw   0x00            ;10 decimal
;--------------------------------------------------------------
start   bsf     status,rp0      ;switch to bank 1
```

```
        movlw   b'00000011'  ;port A inputs/outputs
        movwf   trisa
        clrf    trisb        ;port B outputs
        bcf     status,rp0   ;switch back to bank 0
        movlw   b'00010000'  ;output mark, bit 4 (serial - LCD)
                             ;    only bit 4 of port B used
        movwf   portb
        bcf     porta,2      ;initialize
        bcf     porta,3      ;      "
        bcf     porta,4      ;      "
        call    debounce
        call    debounce
        movlw   0x00         ;blanks to display RAM
        movwf   instr
        call    sndstf       ;send instruction to LCD module
decpt   movlw   0x03         ;ascii character follows
        movwf   instr
        movlw   0x2e         ;define ascii period
        movwf   char
        movlw   0x21         ;display RAM address
        movwf   addr
        call    sndstf       ;call send stuff
v       movlw   0x03         ;ascii character follows
        movwf   instr
        movlw   'V'          ;define ascii "V"
        movwf   char
        movlw   0x25         ;display RAM address
        movwf   addr
        call    sndstf       ;call send stuff
o       movlw   0x03         ;ascii character follows
        movwf   instr
        movlw   'O'          ;define ascii "O"
        movwf   char
        movlw   0x26         ;display RAM address
        movwf   addr
        call    sndstf       ;call send stuff
l       movlw   0x03         ;ascii character follows
        movwf   instr
        movlw   'L'          ;define ascii "L"
        movwf   char
        movlw   0x27         ;display RAM address
        movwf   addr
        call    sndstf       ;call send stuff
t       movlw   0x03         ;ascii character follows
        movwf   instr
        movlw   'T'          ;define ascii "T"
        movwf   char
        movlw   0x28         ;display RAM address
        movwf   addr
        call    sndstf       ;call send stuff
s       movlw   0x03         ;ascii character follows
        movwf   instr
        movlw   'S'          ;define ascii "S"
        movwf   char
```

```
            movlw    0x29           ;display RAM address
            movwf    addr
            call     sndstf         ;call send stuff
            movlw    0x01           ;send 16 characters to display
            movwf    instr
            call     sndstf         ;call send stuff
            call     debounce
            bsf      status,rp0     ;bank 1
            movlw    b'00000010'    ;port A, bits 1,0 analog input
            movwf    adcon1         ;   bits 3,2 digital I/O
            bcf      status,rp0     ;bank 0
            bcf      intcon,7       ;global interrupt disable
meas        movlw    b'10000001'    ;configure A/D - select AN0
            movwf    adcon0         ;   select conv clock, AN0 on
            call     del_20         ;delay 20 microseconds
            bsf      adcon0,2       ;start conversion
test        btfsc    adcon0,2       ;test go/done bit
            goto     test
            movf     adres,w        ;conv complete, get A/D result
            movwf    number         ;prep for multiply by 196
            movlw    0xc4           ;decimal 196
            movwf    multby
            call     sglmult        ;to 8x8 multiply
;prep for calling conversion subroutine
            movf     data_hi,w      ;get MS byte
            movwf    msb2
            movf     data_lo,w      ;get LS byte
            movwf    lsb2
            call     dblb2d         ;call conversion subroutine
            call     decrnd         ;call round off subroutine
            call     rnddispl       ;send rounded result to display
            call     debounce       ;wait a while (200 milliseconds)
            goto     meas           ;look at voltage again
;------------------------------------------------------------
del_20      movlw    0x07           ;delay 20 microseconds
            movwf    count
repeat      decfsz   count,f
            goto     repeat
            return
;------------------------------------------------------------
;200 millisecond delay
;
debounce    movlw    0xff           ;M
            movwf    mcount         ;to M counter
loadn       movlw    0xff           ;N
            movwf    ncount         ;to N counter
decn        decfsz   ncount,f       ;decrement N
            goto     decn           ;again
            decfsz   mcount,f       ;decrement M
            goto     loadn          ;again
            return                  ;done
;------------------------------------------------------------
;8-bit multiplication, 2-byte result
;       result in data_hi and data_lo
```

```
;
sglmult clrf     data_lo
        clrf     data_hi
        movf     number,w    ;get number to be multiplied into W
        bcf      status,c    ;clear carry flag
        btfsc    multby,0    ;bit 0
        addwf    data_hi,f
        rrf      data_hi,f
        rrf      data_lo,f
        btfsc    multby,1    ;bit 1
        addwf    data_hi,f
        rrf      data_hi,f
        rrf      data_lo,f
        btfsc    multby,2    ;bit 2
        addwf    data_hi,f
        rrf      data_hi,f
        rrf      data_lo,f
        btfsc    multby,3    ;bit 3
        addwf    data_hi,f
        rrf      data_hi,f
        rrf      data_lo,f
        btfsc    multby,4    ;bit 4
        addwf    data_hi,f
        rrf      data_hi,f
        rrf      data_lo,f
        btfsc    multby,5    ;bit 5
        addwf    data_hi,f
        rrf      data_hi,f
        rrf      data_lo,f
        btfsc    multby,6    ;bit 6
        addwf    data_hi,f
        rrf      data_hi,f
        rrf      data_lo,f
        btfsc    multby,7    ;bit 7
        addwf    data_hi,f
        rrf      data_hi,f
        rrf      data_lo,f
        return
;-------------------------------------------------------------
;double binary to decimal conversion
;accepts 0x0000 through ffff - 0 through 65535
;dblsub uses 2's comp plus flag
;result in tenk, onek, hund, one
;
dblb2d  clrf     tenk
        clrf     onek
        clrf     hund
        clrf     ten
        clrf     one
        clrf     index
        clrf     dig_ctr
        bcf      flags,ovflw
subtr   movf     index,w     ;get current index into W
        call     tbl_lo      ;get ls chunk for subtraction
```

```
        movwf   lsb1
        movf    index,w     ;get current index into W
        call    tbl_hi      ;get ms chunk for subtraction
        movwf   msb1
        call    dblsub      ;to double precision subtraction
        btfsc   status,c    ;test carry flag
        goto    incdig
        movlw   0x20        ;load base address of table
        movwf   fsr
        movf    index,w     ;get index
        addwf   fsr,f       ;add offset
        movf    dig_ctr,w   ;get digit counter contents
        movwf   indf        ;store at digit loc (indexed)
        movf    index,w     ;get index
        call    tbl_lo      ;get ls chunk for addition
        movwf   lsb1
        movf    index,w     ;get index
        call    tbl_hi      ;get ms chunk for addition
        movwf   msb1
        bcf     flags,ovflw
        call    dblplus     ;to double precision addition
        movf    index,w     ;get index
        sublw   0x03        ;index=3?
        btfsc   status,z
        goto    finish
        incf    index,f     ;increment digit index
        clrf    dig_ctr
        goto    subtr
;-------------------------------------------------------
incdig  incf    dig_ctr,f ;increment digit counter
        goto    subtr
;-------------------------------------------------------
finish  movf    lsb2,w      ;get 1's=remainder
        movwf   one
        return              ;done
;-------------------------------------------------------
dblsub  bcf     flags,ovflw ;clear overflow flag
        comf    lsb1,f      ;2's complement stuff
        comf    msb1,f
        movf    lsb1,w
        addlw   0x01
        movwf   lsb1
        btfsc   status,c
        incf    msb1,f
dblplus movf    lsb1,w
        addwf   lsb2,f      ;add low bytes
        btfsc   status,c
        bsf     flags,ovflw ;indicate overflow occured
        movf    msb1,w
        addwf   msb2,f      ;add high bytes
        btfss   flags,ovflw
        goto    dblx
        btfsc   status,c
        goto    dbl1
```

```
        movlw    0x01
        addwf    msb2,f
        goto     dblx
dbl1    incf     msb2,f
dblx    return
;----------------------------------------------------
;decimal round-off routine
;rounds off two least significant digits of a
;5-digit decimal number
;use only hund, onek and tenk in subsequent program as
;one and ten are left as trash
;
decrnd  movf     one,w         ;get one into W
        sublw    0x04          ;subtract W from 4, result in W
        btfss    status,c
        call     rnd1          ;if carry clear, round
        movf     ten,w         ;get ten into W
        sublw    0x04          ;subtract W from 4, result in W
        btfss    status,c
        call     rnd10         ;if carry clear, round
        return
;----------------------------------------------------
rnd1    incf     ten,f
        movf     ten,w         ;compare
        sublw    0x0a          ;result 10 decimal?
        btfss    status,z
        return                 ;not 10
        clrf     ten
rnd10   incf     hund,f
        movf     hund,w        ;compare
        sublw    0x0a          ;result 10 decimal?
        btfss    status,z
        return                 ;not 10
        clrf     hund
        incf     onek,f
        movf     onek,w        ;compare
        sublw    0x0a          ;result 10 decimal?
        btfss    status,z
        return                 ;not 10
        clrf     onek
        incf     tenk,f
        return
;--------------------------------------------------------
;send rounded result to LCD
;
rnddispl movf    tenk,w        ;rename for easier comprehension
        movwf    ones          ;from round off to display
        movf     onek,w
        movwf    tenths
        movf     hund,w
        movwf    hundths
do1s    movf     ones,w        ;get 1's digit
        call     hex2asc       ;convert binary digit to ascii
        movwf    char
```

```
              movlw    0x20            ;display RAM address
              movwf    addr
              movlw    0x03            ;ascii char follows, send to display RAM
              movwf    instr
              call     sndstf          ;send 1's digit to display RAM
              call     debounce        ;time delay
do10ths  movf    tenths,w        ;get 10ths digit
              call     hex2asc         ;convert binary digit to ascii
              movwf    char
              movlw    0x22            ;display RAM address
              movwf    addr
              movlw    0x03            ;ascii char follows, send to display RAM
              movwf    instr
              call     sndstf          ;send 10ths digit to display RAM
              call     debounce        ;time delay
do100ths  movf    hundths,w       ;get 100ths digit
              call     hex2asc         ;convert binary digit to ascii
              movwf    char
              movlw    0x23            ;display RAM address
              movwf    addr
              movlw    0x03            ;ascii char follows, send to display RAM
              movwf    instr
              call     sndstf          ;send 100ths digit to display RAM
              call     debounce        ;time delay
send     movlw    0x01            ;send 16 characters to display
              movwf    instr
              call     sndstf          ;to LCD module
              return
;-------------------------------------------------------------
sndstf   movf    instr,w         ;get instruction
              movwf    sendreg         ;to be sent
              call     ser_out         ;to serial out subroutine
              movf     char,w          ;get character or hex byte
              movwf    sendreg         ;to be sent
              call     ser_out         ;to serial out subroutine
              movf     addr,w          ;get address
              movwf    sendreg         ;to be sent
              call     ser_out         ;to serial out subroutine
              return
;-------------------------------------------------------------
ser_out  bcf     intcon,5        ;disable tmr0 interrupts
              bcf      intcon,7        ;disable global interrupts
              clrf     tmr0            ;clear timer/counter
              clrwdt                   ;clear wdt prep prescaler assign
              bsf      status,rp0      ;to page 1
              movlw    b'11011000'     ;set up timer/counter
              movwf    optreg
              bcf      status,rp0      ;back to page 0
              movlw    0x08            ;init shift counter
              movwf    count
              bcf      portb,4         ;start bit
              clrf     tmr0            ;start timer/counter
              bcf      intcon,2        ;clear tmr0 overflow flag
time1    btfss   intcon,2        ;timer overflow?
```

```
               goto    time1           ;no
               bcf     intcon,2        ;yes, clear overflow flag
nxtbit  rlf     sendreg,f              ;rotate msb into carry flag
               bcf     portb,4         ;clear port A, bit 1
               btfsc   status,c        ;test carry flag
               bsf     portb,4         ;bit is set
time2   btfss   intcon,2               ;timer overflow?
               goto    time2           ;no
               bcf     intcon,2        ;clear overflow flag
               decfsz  count,f         ;shifted 8?
               goto    nxtbit          ;no
               bsf     portb,4         ;yes, output mark
time3   btfss   intcon,2               ;timer overflow?
               goto    time3           ;no
               return                  ;done
;-------------------------------------------------------------
;enter with hex digit in w
;
hex2asc movwf   hold            ;store copy of hex digit
               sublw   0x09            ;subtract w from 1 less than 0x0a
               btfss   status,c        ;carry flag set if w < 0x0a
               goto    add37
               goto    add30
add37   movf    hold,w          ;get hex digit
               addlw   0x37
               return                  ;return with ascii in w
add30   movf    hold,w          ;get hex digit
               addlw   0x30
               return                  ;return with ascii in w
;-------------------------------------------------------------
               end
;-------------------------------------------------------------
;at blast time, select:
;       memory unprotected
;       watchdog timer disabled (default is enabled)
;       standard crystal (using 4 MHz osc for test) XT
;       power-up timer on
;=============================================================
```

SIMPLE DATA LOGGER EXPERIMENT

A simple data logger may be built using the PIC16C71-based DVM presented in the previous chapter plus two more programs from PIC'n Up The Pace plus a PIC-to-PC serial communication subroutine presented earlier in this book. The idea is to take a bunch of work we have already done and combine it into a device which will:

- Log voltage data measured once a second from the time the "ready" switch is opened until a total of 60 measurements have been made and the data stored.
- Display the data one reading at a time at 4 second intervals on a LCD beginning when the "start" switch is opened.
- Upload the data to a PC serially on command via a serial cable in proper format for display, graphing, and printing.

The hardware consists of the items used in the DVM experiment connected in the same way plus some control switches, a serial EEPROM for storing the data and a RS-232 converter module for communicating with the PC. An LED indicates that data is being logged, that logging is complete, or that uploading to a PC is complete.

The LCD is not used while logging data. Timer 0 is needed for generating the 1 second ticks, so it is not available for timing the serial communication with the PIC/LCD module. I have chosen to stay with the PIC16C71 for this experiment instead of going to a larger part with two or more timer/counters which would make it possible to log and display data simultaneously.

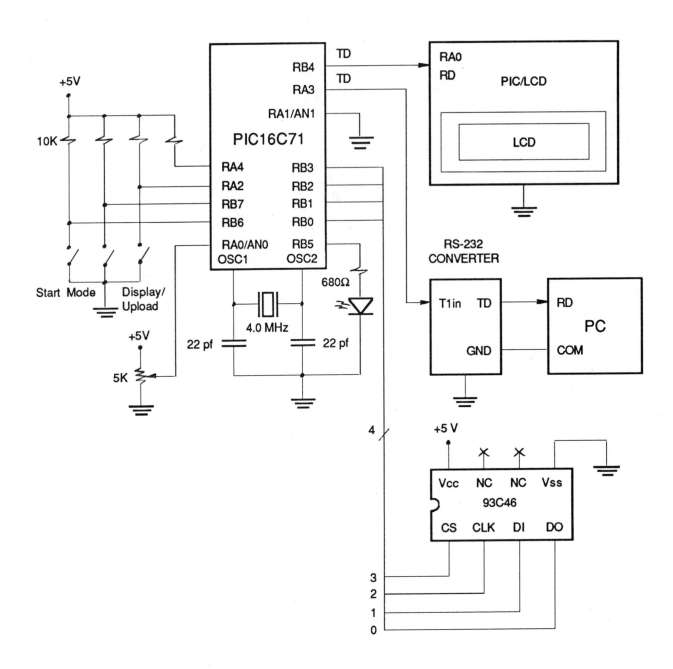

The display RAM locations are:

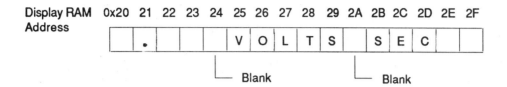

The additional software to be modified and incorporated includes:

- Serial EEPROM interface   `93C46.asm`
- 8-bit binary to 3-digit BCD conversion   `binlcd.asm`
- Serial communication - PIC-to PC   `snd4800.asm`
- Format for sending text to PC screen   `format2.asm`

The program first looks at a mode select switch to see whether the PIC16 is supposed to log data or display/upload data. If logging is selected, voltage measurements are made at one second intervals until 60 data points are logged and stored as 8-bit binary values. The PIC16 goes into a loop after that to wait until someone comes along and turns off the power. Assuming data has been logged, the user turns the mode select switch to the display/upload position and selects either display via LCD or upload to a PC using a second switch. On power-up, the PIC16 will begin displaying data via the PIC/LCD module or will send data to the PC according to the selection. The data is converted from binary to BCD, rounded off, and converted to ASCII in the process of displaying or uploading it.

Following are flow charts which illustrate the main program for initialization, the interrupt service routine for logging data at 1-second intervals, the display data sequentially via a LCD routine, and the upload data to a PC routine. Flow charts and explanations for the serial EEPROM subroutines and the 8-bit binary to 3-digit BCD conversion routine are presented in **PIC'n Up The Pace**. The flow chart for the PIC-to-PC serial routine is presented in the chapter on PIC-to PC serial interface in this book.

The code modules developed previously for other applications have been modified slightly to take care of things like changes in pin assignments and to eliminate duplicate labels in the code. Little effort has been made to minimize the number of file registers required by renaming and combining. The objective is to maximize your understanding by making it easy to go back to where the code was developed originally to read about details or philosophy.

The base address of a table used with indexed addressing must be 0x20 as noted in the source code listing.

MAIN PROGRAM

The main program initializes the ports, determines mode and function selection and directs program execution to subroutines which do the work.

Tables are located up front so as to be located on page zero by the assembler.

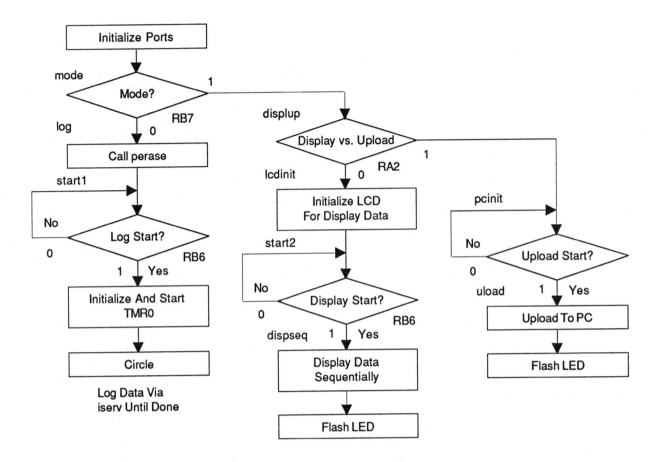

DATA LOGGING

The first 60 EEPROM locations are erased via a subroutine prior to recording data.

An LED is toggled at the end of each 1 second interval to indicate data is being logged. At the completion of logging the 60 data points, the LED flashes to indicate that logging has been completed.

As the first step in generating the 1 second time intervals, the internal instruction cycle clock (1 MHz) is multiplied by 256 via the timer 0 prescaler.

$$\frac{1\ \mu sec}{256\ \mu sec} = 3906$$

Each timer 0 overflow triggers incrementing a file register labeled "time". Each overflow of the time register multiplies by 256.

$$\frac{3906}{256} = 15.2578$$

The time register overflows 15 times and then the register is loaded with the value 0xBD (decimal 189). The time register will overflow after 66 counts.

```
(0.2578)(256) = 66

    255
  -  66
    189 = 0xBD
```

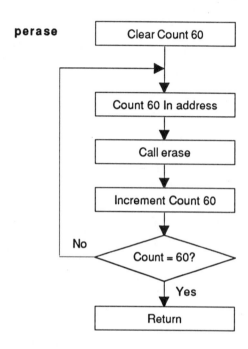

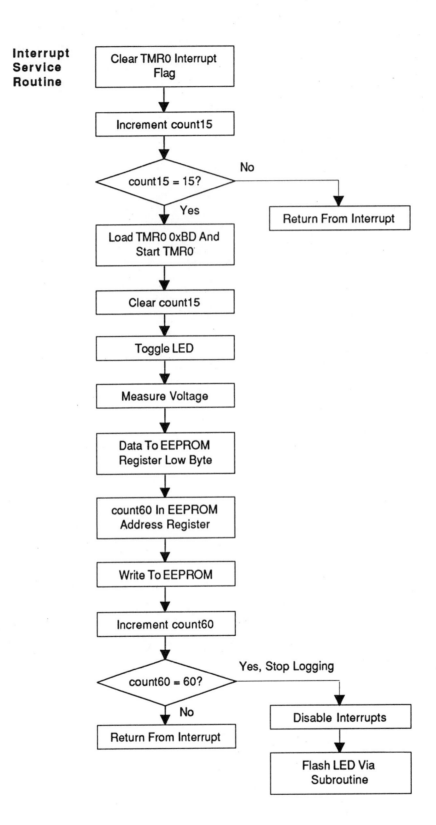

Interrupt Service Routine

Clear TMR0 Interrupt Flag

Increment count15

count15 = 15? — No → Return From Interrupt

Yes

Load TMR0 0xBD And Start TMR0

Clear count15

Toggle LED

Measure Voltage

Data To EEPROM Register Low Byte

count60 In EEPROM Address Register

Write To EEPROM

Increment count60

count60 = 60? — Yes, Stop Logging → Disable Interrupts → Flash LED Via Subroutine

No

Return From Interrupt

DISPLAY DATA SEQUENTIALLY VIA LCD

The flow chart follows:

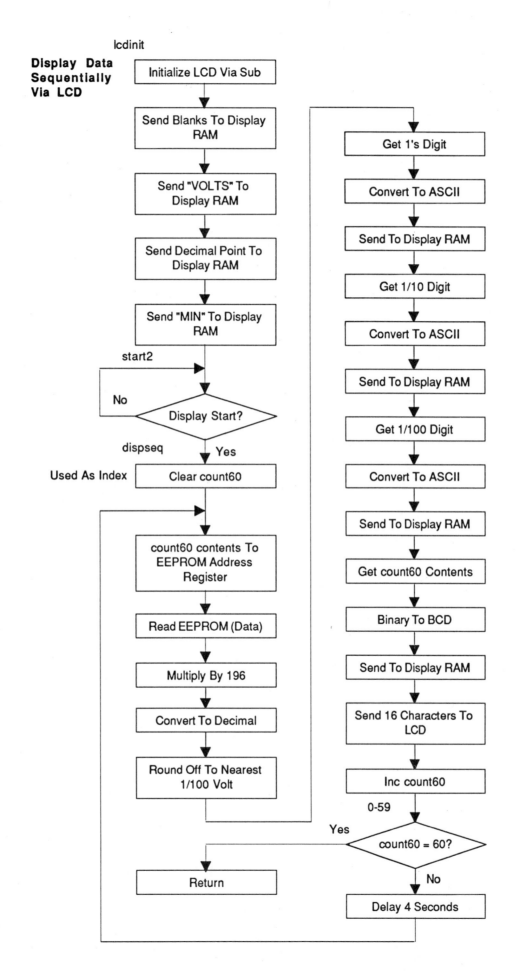

Display Data Sequentially Via LCD

lcdinit

Initialize LCD Via Sub

Send Blanks To Display RAM

Send "VOLTS" To Display RAM

Send Decimal Point To Display RAM

Send "MIN" To Display RAM

start2

Display Start? — No

dispseq — Yes

Used As Index — Clear count60

count60 contents To EEPROM Address Register

Read EEPROM (Data)

Multiply By 196

Convert To Decimal

Round Off To Nearest 1/100 Volt

Get 1's Digit

Convert To ASCII

Send To Display RAM

Get 1/10 Digit

Convert To ASCII

Send To Display RAM

Get 1/100 Digit

Convert To ASCII

Send To Display RAM

Get count60 Contents

Binary To BCD

Send To Display RAM

Send 16 Characters To LCD

Inc count60

0-59

count60 = 60? — Yes / No

Delay 4 Seconds

Return

259

UPLOADING DATA TO A PC

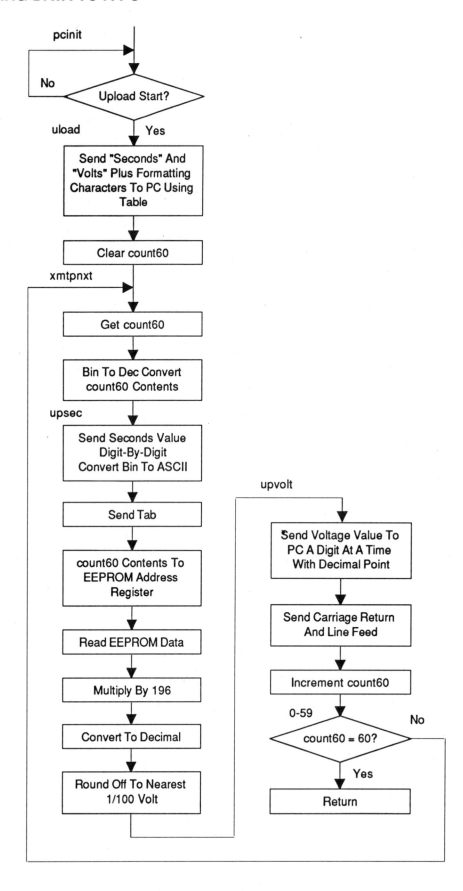

```
;======LOG.ASM===================================10/29/98==
        list    p=16c71
        radix   hex
;--------------------------------------------------------------
;       cpu equates (memory map)
indf    equ     0x00
tmr0    equ     0x01
pc      equ     0x02
status  equ     0x03
fsr     equ     0x04
porta   equ     0x05
portb   equ     0x06
adcon0  equ     0x08
adres   equ     0x09
intcon  equ     0x0b
;
count   equ     0x0c
ncount  equ     0x0d
mcount  equ     0x0e
;
number  equ     0x0f
multby  equ     0x10
data_lo equ     0x11
data_hi equ     0x12
;
index   equ     0x13
dig_ctr equ     0x14
lsb1    equ     0x15
msb1    equ     0x16
lsb2    equ     0x17
msb2    equ     0x18
flags   equ     0x19
;
sendreg equ     0x1a
instr   equ     0x1b
char    equ     0x1c
addr    equ     0x1d
hold    equ     0x1e
;
count60 equ     0x1f
;
tenk    equ     0x20            ;must be at this location
onek    equ     0x21            ;  "   "  "    "       "
hund    equ     0x22            ;  "   "  "    "       "
ten     equ     0x23            ;  "   "  "    "       "
one     equ     0x24            ;  "   "  "    "       "
;
ones    equ     0x25
tenths  equ     0x26
hundths equ     0x27
;
cook    equ     0x28
hibyte  equ     0x29
```

```
address equ      0x2a
temp    equ      0x2b
count15 equ      0x2c
ctr     equ      0x2d
;
optreg  equ      0x81
trisa   equ      0x85
trisb   equ      0x86
adcon1  equ      0x88
;------------------------------------------------------------
;       bit equates
c       equ      0
ovflw   equ      0
z       equ      2
rp0     equ      5
;------------------------------------------------------------
        org      0x000
        goto     start       ;skip over location pointed to by
                             ;  interrupt vector and tables
;
        org      0x004
        goto     iserv       ;to start of interrupt service routine
;------------------------------------------------------------
;tables for dblb2d
;
tbl_lo  addwf    pc,f        ;add index to program counter
        retlw    0x10        ;10,000 decimal
        retlw    0xe8        ;1,000 decimal
        retlw    0x64        ;100 decimal
        retlw    0x0a        ;10 decimal
;
tbl_hi  addwf    pc,f        ;add index to program counter
        retlw    0x27        ;10,000 decimal
        retlw    0x03        ;1,000 decimal
        retlw    0x00        ;100 decimal
        retlw    0x00        ;10 decimal
;------------------------------------------------------------
;table for binlcd
;
table   addwf    pc,f        ;add index to program counter
        retlw    0x64        ;100 decimal
        retlw    0x0a        ;10 decimal
;------------------------------------------------------------
;table for uload
;
getchar addwf    pc,f        ;add offset to program counter
        retlw    a'S'        ;ASCII "S" to be sent
        retlw    a'e'        ;ASCII "e" to be sent
        retlw    a'c'        ;ASCII "c" to be sent
        retlw    a'o'        ;ASCII "o" to be sent
        retlw    a'n'        ;ASCII "n" to be sent
        retlw    a'd'        ;ASCII "d" to be sent
        retlw    a's'        ;ASCII "s" to be sent
        retlw    b'00001001' ;tab
```

262

```
        retlw    a'V'           ;ASCII "V" to be sent
        retlw    a'o'           ;ASCII "o" to be sent
        retlw    a'l'           ;ASCII "l" to be sent
        retlw    a't'           ;ASCII "t" to be sent
        retlw    a's'           ;ASCII "s" to be sent
        retlw    b'00001101'    ;carriage return
        retlw    b'00001010'    ;line feed
        retlw    b'00001010'    ;line feed
;-------------------------------------------------------------
start   bsf      status,rp0     ;switch to bank 1
        movlw    b'00000010'    ;port A, bits 1,0 analog input
        movwf    adcon1         ;   bits 3,2 digital I/O
        movlw    b'00000111'    ;port A inputs/outputs
        movwf    trisa
        movlw    b'11000001'    ;port B inputs/outputs
        movwf    trisb
        bcf      status,rp0     ;switch back to bank 0
        bsf      portb,4        ;output mark, bit 4 (serial - LCD)
        bsf      porta,3        ;output mark, bit 3 (serial - PC)
        bcf      porta,4        ;initialize, not used
        bcf      portb,1        ;initialize
        bcf      portb,2        ;initialize
        bcf      portb,3        ;initialize
        bcf      portb,5        ;LED off
;-------------------------------------------------------------
mode    btfsc    portb,7        ;test mode switch
        goto     displup
log     bcf      intcon,7       ;global interrupt disable
        call     perase         ;erase eeprom
start1  btfss    portb,6        ;start?
        goto     start1         ;not yet
        clrwdt                  ;clear WDT and prescaler
        bsf      status,rp0     ;bank 1
        movlw    b'11010111'    ;select tmr0, prescale value
        movwf    optreg         ;   and clock source
        bcf      status,rp0     ;bank 0
        clrf     tmr0           ;start timer 0
        clrf     count15
        clrf     count60
        bcf      intcon,2       ;clear timer 0 interrupt flag
        bsf      intcon,7       ;enable global interrupts
        bsf      intcon,5       ;enable timer 0 interrupts
circle1 goto     circle1        ;log data via iserv routine 'til done
;-------------------------------------------------------------
displup btfsc    porta,2        ;test display vs. upload switch
        goto     pcinit         ;upload data to PC
        call     lcdinit        ;display data via PIC/LCD module
start2  btfss    portb,6        ;start?
        goto     start2         ;not yet
        call     dispseq
        goto     flash          ;done
;-------------------------------------------------------------
pcinit  btfss    portb,6        ;start?
        goto     pcinit         ;not yet
```

```
        call    uload
        goto    flash           ;done
;------------------------------------------------------------
iserv   bcf     intcon,2        ;clear timer 0 interrupt flag
        incf    count15,f
        movf    count15,w       ;get 15 counter contents
        sublw   d'15'           ;compare with decimal 15
        btfss   status,z        ;equal?
        retfie                  ;no
        movlw   0xbd            ;time interval
        movwf   tmr0            ;load and start timer 0
        clrf    count15
        btfss   portb,5         ;test LED status
        goto    setbit
        bcf     portb,5         ;LED off
        goto    contin
setbit  bsf     portb,5         ;LED on
contin  call    meas            ;measure voltage
        movwf   data_lo         ;ready for write to eeprom
        movf    count60,w       ;get eeprom address
        movwf   address
        call    write
        incf    count60,f
        movf    count60,w       ;get 60 counter contents
        sublw   d'60'           ;compare
        btfss   status,z
        retfie                  ;not done
        bcf     intcon,5        ;disable timer 0 interrupts
        bcf     intcon,7        ;disable global interrupts
        goto    flash           ;done
;------------------------------------------------------------
dispseq clrf    count60         ;clear 60 counter
dispnxt movf    count60,w       ;get 60 counter contents
        movwf   address         ;address for eeprom read
        call    read            ;get data
        movf    cook,w
        call    mult196         ;multiply by 196
;prep for calling conversion subroutine
        movf    data_hi,w       ;get MS byte
        movwf   msb2
        movf    data_lo,w       ;get LS byte
        movwf   lsb2
        call    dblb2d          ;call conversion subroutine
        call    decrnd          ;call round off subroutine
        call    rnddispl        ;send rounded result to display RAM
        movf    count60,w       ;get 60 counter contents
        call    bin2dec         ;call 8-bit binary to 3-digit bcd
                                ;   conversion routine
        call    zcheck          ;time to display RAM
        call    send            ;send 16 characters to display
        call    debounce        ;wait a while (200 milliseconds)
        incf    count60,f       ;do 0 to 59
        movf    count60,w       ;get 60 counter contents
        sublw   d'60'           ;compare
```

264

```
          btfsc    status,z
          return                ;done
          call     delay4       ;delay 4 seconds
          goto     dispnxt      ;display next data
;----------------------------------------------------------
flash     bsf      portb,5      ;LED on
          call     debounce     ;delay
          call     debounce
          bcf      portb,5      ;LED off
          call     debounce     ;delay
          call     debounce
          goto     flash
;----------------------------------------------------------
uload     clrf     ctr          ;zero counter
charout   movf     ctr,w        ;get count = offest
          call     getchar      ;get character from table
          movwf    sendreg      ;store
          call     snd4800      ;to serial out subroutine
          incf     ctr,f        ;increment counter
          movf     ctr,w        ;contents of counter into w
          sublw    d'16'        ;subtract decimal 16 from w - compare
          btfss    status,2     ;test z-flag, skip next instruction
                                ;      if result 1 meaning counter=16
          goto     charout      ;not done yet
          clrf     count60      ;clear 60 counter
xmtpnxt   movf     count60,w    ;get 60 counter contents
          call     bin2dec      ;call 8-bit binary to 3-digit bcd
                                ;    conversion routine
          call     upsec        ;send seconds to PC
          movf     count60,w    ;get 60 counter contents
          movwf    address      ;address for eeprom read
          call     read         ;get data
          movf     cook,w
          call     mult196      ;multiply by 196
;prep for calling conversion subroutine
          movf     data_hi,w    ;get MS byte
          movwf    msb2
          movf     data_lo,w    ;get LS byte
          movwf    lsb2
          call     dblb2d       ;call conversion subroutine
          call     decrnd       ;call round off subroutine
          call     upvolt       ;sent volts to PC
          incf     count60,f    ;do 0 to 59
          movf     count60,w    ;get 60 counter contents
          sublw    d'60'        ;compare
          btfsc    status,z
          return                ;done
          goto     xmtpnxt      ;transmit next data
;----------------------------------------------------------
perase    clrf     count60
clean     movf     count60,w    ;get contents of 60 counter
          movwf    address      ;address for eeprom erase
          call     erase        ;erase via subroutine
          incf     count60,f
```

```
        movf    count60,w   ;get 60 counter contents in W
        sublw   d'60'       ;compare with 60
        btfss   status,z
        goto    clean       ;not done yet
        return
;-----------------------------------------------------------
delay4  clrf    ctr         ;delay 4 seconds
sec4    call    debounce
        incf    ctr,f
        movf    ctr,w       ;get counter contents
        sublw   d'20'
        btfss   status,z
        goto    sec4
        return
;-----------------------------------------------------------
upsec   movf    ten,w       ;seconds, tens digit
        call    hex2asc     ;convert binary digit to ascii
        movwf   sendreg
        call    snd4800     ;to serial out routine
        movf    one,w       ;seconds, ones digit
        call    hex2asc     ;convert binary digit to ascii
        movwf   sendreg
        call    snd4800     ;to serial out routine
        movlw   b'00001001' ;tab
        movwf   sendreg
        call    snd4800     ;to serial out routine
        return
;-----------------------------------------------------------
upvolt  movf    tenk,w      ;voltage, ones digit
        call    hex2asc     ;convert binary digit to ascii
        movwf   sendreg
        call    snd4800     ;to serial out routine
        movlw   0x2e        ;ascii period
        movwf   sendreg
        call    snd4800     ;to serial out routine
        movf    onek,w      ;voltage, tenths digit
        call    hex2asc     ;convert binary digit to ascii
        movwf   sendreg
        call    snd4800     ;to serial out routine
        movf    hund,w      ;voltage, hundredths digit
        call    hex2asc     ;convert binary digit to ascii
        movwf   sendreg
        call    snd4800     ;to serial out routine
        movlw   b'00001101' ;carriage return
        movwf   sendreg
        call    snd4800     ;to serial out routine
        movlw   b'00001010' ;line feed
        movwf   sendreg
        call    snd4800     ;to serial out routine
        return              ;done
;-----------------------------------------------------------
lcdinit call    debounce    ;be sure LCD has time to initialize
        call    debounce
        movlw   0x00        ;blanks to display RAM
```

```
          movwf    instr
          call     sndstf        ;send instruction to LCD module
decpt     movlw    0x03          ;ascii character follows
          movwf    instr
          movlw    0x2e          ;define ascii period
          movwf    char
          movlw    0x21          ;display RAM address
          movwf    addr
          call     sndstf        ;call send stuff
v         movlw    0x03          ;ascii character follows
          movwf    instr
          movlw    'V'           ;define ascii "V"
          movwf    char
          movlw    0x25          ;display RAM address
          movwf    addr
          call     sndstf        ;call send stuff
o         movlw    0x03          ;ascii character follows
          movwf    instr
          movlw    'O'           ;define ascii "O"
          movwf    char
          movlw    0x26          ;display RAM address
          movwf    addr
          call     sndstf        ;call send stuff
l         movlw    0x03          ;ascii character follows
          movwf    instr
          movlw    'L'           ;define ascii "L"
          movwf    char
          movlw    0x27          ;display RAM address
          movwf    addr
          call     sndstf        ;call send stuff
t         movlw    0x03          ;ascii character follows
          movwf    instr
          movlw    'T'           ;define ascii "T"
          movwf    char
          movlw    0x28          ;display RAM address
          movwf    addr
          call     sndstf        ;call send stuff
s         movlw    0x03          ;ascii character follows
          movwf    instr
          movlw    'S'           ;define ascii "S"
          movwf    char
          movlw    0x29          ;display RAM address
          movwf    addr
          call     sndstf        ;call send stuff
          movlw    0x2b          ;display RAM address
          movwf    addr
          call     sndstf        ;call send stuff
e         movlw    0x03          ;ascii character follows
          movwf    instr
          movlw    'E'           ;define ascii "E"
          movwf    char
          movlw    0x2c          ;display RAM address
          movwf    addr
          call     sndstf        ;call send stuff
```

```
C          movlw    0x03         ;ascii character follows
           movwf    instr
           movlw    'C'          ;define ascii "C"
           movwf    char
           movlw    0x2d         ;display RAM address
           movwf    addr
           call     sndstf       ;call send stuff
           movlw    0x01         ;send 16 characters to display
           movwf    instr
           call     sndstf       ;call send stuff
           call     debounce
           return
;--------------------------------------------------------------
;a/d conversion
;          exit with a/d result in W register
meas       movlw    b'10000001' ;configure A/D - select AN0
           movwf    adcon0       ;    select conv clock, AN0 on
           call     del_20       ;delay 20 microseconds
           bsf      adcon0,2     ;start conversion
test       btfsc    adcon0,2     ;test go/done bit
           goto     test
           movf     adres,w      ;conv complete, get A/D result
           return
;--------------------------------------------------------------
mult196    movwf    number       ;prep for multiply by 196
           movlw    0xc4         ;decimal 196
           movwf    multby
           call     sglmult      ;to 8x8 multiply
           return
;--------------------------------------------------------------
del_20     movlw    0x07         ;delay 20 microseconds
           movwf    count
repeat     decfsz   count,f
           goto     repeat
           return
;--------------------------------------------------------------
;200 millisecond delay
;
debounce   movlw    0xff         ;M
           movwf    mcount       ;to M counter
loadn      movlw    0xff         ;N
           movwf    ncount       ;to N counter
decn       decfsz   ncount,f     ;decrement N
           goto     decn         ;again
           decfsz   mcount,f     ;decrement M
           goto     loadn        ;again
           return                ;done
;--------------------------------------------------------------
;8-bit multiplication, 2-byte result
;       result in data_hi and data_lo
;
sglmult    clrf     data_lo
           clrf     data_hi
           movf     number,w     ;get number to be multiplied into W
```

```
        bcf      status,c      ;clear carry flag
        btfsc    multby,0      ;bit 0
        addwf    data_hi,f
        rrf      data_hi,f
        rrf      data_lo,f
        btfsc    multby,1      ;bit 1
        addwf    data_hi,f
        rrf      data_hi,f
        rrf      data_lo,f
        btfsc    multby,2      ;bit 2
        addwf    data_hi,f
        rrf      data_hi,f
        rrf      data_lo,f
        btfsc    multby,3      ;bit 3
        addwf    data_hi,f
        rrf      data_hi,f
        rrf      data_lo,f
        btfsc    multby,4      ;bit 4
        addwf    data_hi,f
        rrf      data_hi,f
        rrf      data_lo,f
        btfsc    multby,5      ;bit 5
        addwf    data_hi,f
        rrf      data_hi,f
        rrf      data_lo,f
        btfsc    multby,6      ;bit 6
        addwf    data_hi,f
        rrf      data_hi,f
        rrf      data_lo,f
        btfsc    multby,7      ;bit 7
        addwf    data_hi,f
        rrf      data_hi,f
        rrf      data_lo,f
        return
;------------------------------------------------------------
;double binary to decimal conversion
;accepts 0x0000 through ffff - 0 through 65535
;dblsub uses 2's comp plus flag
;result in tenk, onek, hund, one
;
dblb2d  clrf     tenk
        clrf     onek
        clrf     hund
        clrf     ten
        clrf     one
        clrf     index
        clrf     dig_ctr
        bcf      flags,ovflw
subtr   movf     index,w       ;get current index into W
        call     tbl_lo        ;get ls chunk for subtraction
        movwf    lsb1
        movf     index,w       ;get current index into W
        call     tbl_hi        ;get ms chunk for subtraction
        movwf    msb1
```

```
        call    dblsub      ;to double precision subtraction
        btfsc   status,c    ;test carry flag
        goto    incdig
        movlw   0x20        ;load base address of table
        movwf   fsr
        movf    index,w     ;get index
        addwf   fsr,f       ;add offset
        movf    dig_ctr,w   ;get digit counter contents
        movwf   indf        ;store at digit loc (indexed)
        movf    index,w     ;get index
        call    tbl_lo      ;get ls chunk for addition
        movwf   lsb1
        movf    index,w     ;get index
        call    tbl_hi      ;get ms chunk for addition
        movwf   msb1
        bcf     flags,ovflw
        call    dblplus     ;to double precision addition
        movf    index,w     ;get index
        sublw   0x03        ;index=3?
        btfsc   status,z
        goto    finish
        incf    index,f     ;increment digit index
        clrf    dig_ctr
        goto    subtr
;-------------------------------------------------
incdig  incf    dig_ctr,f   ;increment digit counter
        goto    subtr
;-------------------------------------------------
finish  movf    lsb2,w      ;get 1's=remainder
        movwf   one
        return              ;done
;-------------------------------------------------
dblsub  bcf     flags,ovflw ;clear overflow flag
        comf    lsb1,f      ;2's complement stuff
        comf    msb1,f
        movf    lsb1,w
        addlw   0x01
        movwf   lsb1
        btfsc   status,c
        incf    msb1,f
dblplus movf    lsb1,w
        addwf   lsb2,f      ;add low bytes
        btfsc   status,c
        bsf     flags,ovflw ;indicate overflow occured
        movf    msb1,w
        addwf   msb2,f      ;add high bytes
        btfss   flags,ovflw
        goto    dblx
        btfsc   status,c
        goto    dbl1
        movlw   0x01
        addwf   msb2,f
        goto    dblx
dbl1    incf    msb2,f
```

270

```
dblx      return
;------------------------------------------------------
;decimal round-off routine
;rounds off two least significant digits of a
;5-digit decimal number
;use only hund, onek and tenk in subsequent program as
;one and ten are left as trash
;
decrnd    movf     one,w         ;get one into W
          sublw    0x04          ;subtract W from 4, result in W
          btfss    status,c
          call     rnd1          ;if carry clear, round
          movf     ten,w         ;get ten into W
          sublw    0x04          ;subtract W from 4, result in W
          btfss    status,c
          call     rnd10         ;if carry clear, round
          return
;------------------------------------------------------
rnd1      incf     ten,f
          movf     ten,w         ;compare
          sublw    0x0a          ;result 10 decimal?
          btfss    status,z
          return                 ;not 10
          clrf     ten
rnd10     incf     hund,f
          movf     hund,w        ;compare
          sublw    0x0a          ;result 10 decimal?
          btfss    status,z
          return                 ;not 10
          clrf     hund
          incf     onek,f
          movf     onek,w        ;compare
          sublw    0x0a          ;result 10 decimal?
          btfss    status,z
          return                 ;not 10
          clrf     onek
          incf     tenk,f
          return
;----------------------------------------------------------
;send rounded result to display RAM
;
rnddispl  movf     tenk,w        ;rename for easier comprehension
          movwf    ones          ;from round off to display
          movf     onek,w
          movwf    tenths
          movf     hund,w
          movwf    hundths
do1s      movf     ones,w        ;get 1's digit
          call     hex2asc       ;convert binary digit to ascii
          movwf    char
          movlw    0x20          ;display RAM address
          movwf    addr
          movlw    0x03          ;ascii char follows, send to display RAM
          movwf    instr
```

```
          call     sndstf      ;send 1's digit to display RAM
          call     debounce    ;time delay
do10ths   movf     tenths,w    ;get 10ths digit
          call     hex2asc     ;convert binary digit to ascii
          movwf    char
          movlw    0x22        ;display RAM address
          movwf    addr
          movlw    0x03        ;ascii char follows, send to display RAM
          movwf    instr
          call     sndstf      ;send 10ths digit to display RAM
          call     debounce    ;time delay
do100ths  movf     hundths,w   ;get 100ths digit
          call     hex2asc     ;convert binary digit to ascii
          movwf    char
          movlw    0x23        ;display RAM address
          movwf    addr
          movlw    0x03        ;ascii char follows, send to display RAM
          movwf    instr
          call     sndstf      ;send 100ths digit to display RAM
          call     debounce    ;time delay
          return
;-----------------------------------------------------------
send      movlw    0x01        ;send 16 characters to display
          movwf    instr
          call     sndstf      ;to LCD module
          return
;-----------------------------------------------------------
sndstf    movf     instr,w     ;get instruction
          movwf    sendreg     ;to be sent
          call     ser_out     ;to serial out subroutine
          movf     char,w      ;get character or hex byte
          movwf    sendreg     ;to be sent
          call     ser_out     ;to serial out subroutine
          movf     addr,w      ;get address
          movwf    sendreg     ;to be sent
          call     ser_out     ;to serial out subroutine
          return
;-----------------------------------------------------------
ser_out   bcf      intcon,5    ;disable tmr0 interrupts
          bcf      intcon,7    ;disable global interrupts
          clrf     tmr0        ;clear timer/counter
          clrwdt               ;clear wdt prep prescaler assign
          bsf      status,rp0  ;to page 1
          movlw    b'11011000' ;set up timer/counter
          movwf    optreg
          bcf      status,rp0  ;back to page 0
          movlw    0x08        ;init shift counter
          movwf    count
          bcf      portb,4     ;start bit
          clrf     tmr0        ;start timer/counter
          bcf      intcon,2    ;clear tmr0 overflow flag
time1     btfss    intcon,2    ;timer overflow?
          goto     time1       ;no
          bcf      intcon,2    ;yes, clear overflow flag
```

272

```
nxtbit   rlf     sendreg,f     ;rotate msb into carry flag
         bcf     portb,4       ;clear port A, bit 1
         btfsc   status,c      ;test carry flag
         bsf     portb,4       ;bit is set
time2    btfss   intcon,2      ;timer overflow?
         goto    time2         ;no
         bcf     intcon,2      ;clear overflow flag
         decfsz  count,f       ;shifted 8?
         goto    nxtbit        ;no
         bsf     portb,4       ;yes, output mark
time3    btfss   intcon,2      ;timer overflow?
         goto    time3         ;no
         return                ;done
;--------------------------------------------------------------
;enter with hex digit in w
;
hex2asc  movwf   hold          ;store copy of hex digit
         sublw   0x09          ;subtract w from 1 less than 0x0a
         btfss   status,c      ;carry flag set if w < 0x0a
         goto    add37
         goto    add30
add37    movf    hold,w        ;get hex digit
         addlw   0x37
         return                ;return with ascii in w
add30    movf    hold,w        ;get hex digit
         addlw   0x30
         return                ;return with ascii in w
;--------------------------------------------------------------
;eeprom subroutines
;to write, call write subroutine
;    expects:
;        address in address register
;        hi data in data_hi
;        lo data in data_lo
;to read, call read subroutine
;    expects:
;        address in address register
;    result of read:
;        lo byte in cook register
;        hi byte in hibyte register (not used in this application)
;to erase, call erase subroutine
;    expects:
;        address in address register
;
ewen     movlw   0x30          ;ewen op code
         movwf   cook          ;to cook
         bsf     portb,1       ;send start bit
         bsf     portb,2       ;shift
         bcf     portb,2
         call    sendbits      ;send ewen op code
         return
;--------------------------------------------------------------
ewds     movlw   0x00          ;ewds op code
         movwf   cook          ;to cook
```

```
        bsf     portb,1     ;send start bit
        bsf     portb,2     ;shift
        bcf     portb,2
        call    sendbits    ;send ewds op code
        return
;-----------------------------------------------------------
write   bsf     portb,3     ;cs high
        call    ewen        ;erase/write enable
        bcf     portb,3     ;cs low
        nop                 ;1 microsecond min
        bsf     portb,3     ;cs high
        movf    address,w   ;get address
        movwf   cook        ;store in cook
        bcf     cook,7      ;op code
        bsf     cook,6      ;ms 2 bits
        bsf     portb,1     ;send start bit
        bsf     portb,2     ;shift
        bcf     portb,2
        call    sendbits    ;send address
        movf    data_hi,w   ;get data hi
        movwf   cook
        call    sendbits    ;send data hi
        movf    data_lo,w   ;get data lo
        movwf   cook
        call    sendbits    ;send data lo
        bcf     portb,3     ;cs low
        nop                 ;1 microsecond min
        bsf     portb,3     ;cs high
ecycle2 btfss   portb,0     ;erase cycle complete?
        goto    ecycle2     ;not yet
        bcf     portb,3     ;cs low
        nop                 ;1 microsecond min
        call    ewds        ;yes, erase/write disable
        bcf     portb,3     ;cs low
        nop                 ;1 microsecond min
        return
;-----------------------------------------------------------
read    bsf     portb,3     ;cs high
        movf    address,w   ;get address
        movwf   cook
        bsf     cook,7      ;op code
        bcf     cook,6      ;ms 2 bits
        bsf     portb,1     ;send start bit
        bsf     portb,2     ;shift
        bcf     portb,2
        call    sendbits    ;send address
        call    getprom     ;shift hi 8 bits out of eeprom
        movf    cook,w      ;hi byte result in hibyte
        movwf   hibyte
        call    getprom     ;shift lo 8 bits out of eeprom
        bcf     portb,3     ;cs low
        nop                 ;1microsecond min
        return              ;exit sub with lo byte in cook
;-----------------------------------------------------------
```

```
sendbits movlw    0x08          ;count=8
         movwf    count
sbit     call     sendbit       ;send 1 bit
         decfsz   count,f       ;done?
         goto     sftcook       ;no
         return                 ;yes
sftcook rlf       cook,f        ;shift cook left
         goto     sbit          ;again
;-----------------------------------------------------------
sendbit bcf       portb,1       ;default
         btfsc    cook,7        ;test cook bit 7
         bsf      portb,1       ;bit is set
shift1   bsf      portb,2       ;shift
         bcf      portb,2
         return
;-----------------------------------------------------------
getprom movlw     0x08          ;count=8
         movwf    count
shift2   bsf      portb,2       ;shift
         bcf      portb,2
         movf     portb,w       ;read port B
         movwf    temp          ;store copy
         rrf      temp,f        ;rotate bit into carry flag
         rlf      cook,f        ;rotate carry flag into cook
         decfsz   count,f       ;decrement counter
         goto     shift2
         return                 ;done
;-----------------------------------------------------------
erase    bsf      portb,3       ;cs high
         call     ewen          ;erase/write enable
         bcf      portb,3       ;cs low
         nop                    ;1 microsecond min
         bsf      portb,3       ;cs high
         movf     address,w     ;get address
         movwf    cook          ;store in cook
         bsf      cook,7        ;op code
         bsf      cook,6        ;ms 2 bits
         bsf      portb,1       ;send start bit
         bsf      portb,2       ;shift
         bcf      portb,2
         call     sendbits      ;send address
         bcf      portb,3       ;cs low
         nop                    ;1 microsecond min
         bsf      portb,3       ;cs high
ecycle1 btfss     portb,0       ;erase cycle complete?
         goto     ecycle1       ;not yet
         bcf      portb,3       ;cs low
         nop                    ;1microsecond min
         call     ewds          ;yes, erase/write disable
         bcf      portb,3       ;cs low
         nop                    ;1microsecond min
         return
;-----------------------------------------------------------
;display seconds
```

```
;     throw away 100's digit
zcheck  movf    ten,w       ;get 10's digit
        sublw   0x00        ;compare - digit=0?
        btfsc   status,z
        goto    tzero       ;yes
do10z   movf    ten,w       ;get 10's digit
        call    hex2asc     ;convert binary digit to ascii
        movwf   char
        movlw   0x2e        ;display RAM address
        movwf   addr
        movlw   0x03        ;ascii char follows, send to display RAM
        movwf   instr
        call    sndstf      ;send 10's digit to display RAM
        call    debounce    ;time delay
do1z    movf    one,w       ;get 1's digit
        call    hex2asc     ;convert binary digit to ascii
        movwf   char
        movlw   0x2f        ;display RAM address
        movwf   addr
        movlw   0x03        ;ascii char follows, send to display RAM
        movwf   instr
        call    sndstf      ;send 1's digit to display RAM
        call    debounce    ;time delay
        return
;----------------------------------------------------------
tzero   movlw   0x20        ;ascii blank
        movwf   char
        movlw   0x2e        ;display RAM address
        movwf   addr
        movlw   0x03        ;ascii character to display RAM
        movwf   instr
        call    sndstf
        call    debounce
        goto    do1z
;----------------------------------------------------------
;enter with 8-bit binary number in W
;note that base address of table is 0x22
;
bin2dec movwf   number      ;store copy of number
        clrf    hund
        clrf    ten
        clrf    one
        clrf    index
        clrf    dig_ctr
subtrz  movf    index,w     ;get current index into W
        call    table       ;get chunk for subtraction
        subwf   number,f    ;test
        btfsc   status,c    ;test carry flag
        goto    incdigz
        movlw   0x22        ;load base address of table
        movwf   fsr
        movf    index,w     ;get index
        addwf   fsr,f       ;add offset
        movf    dig_ctr,w   ;get digit counter contents
```

276

```
        movwf   indf            ;store at digit loc (indexed)
        movf    index,w         ;get index
        call    table           ;get chunk for addition
        addwf   number,f        ;add back
        movf    index,w         ;get index
        sublw   0x01            ;index=1?
        btfsc   status,z
        goto    finishz
        incf    index,f         ;increment digit index
        clrf    dig_ctr
        goto    subtrz
;-------------------------------------------------------------
incdigz incf    dig_ctr,f       ;increment digit counter
        goto    subtrz
;-------------------------------------------------------------
finishz movf    number,w        ;get 1's=remainder
        movwf   one
        return
;-------------------------------------------------------------
;serial output to PC
;       expects ascii character in sendreg
;
snd4800 bcf     intcon,5        ;disable tmr0 interrupts
        bcf     intcon,7        ;disable global interrupts
        clrf    tmr0            ;clear timer/counter
        clrwdt                  ;clear wdt prep prescaler assign
        bsf     status,rp0      ;to page 1
        movlw   b'11011000'     ;set up timer/counter
        movwf   optreg
        bcf     status,rp0      ;back to page 0
        movlw   0x08            ;init shift counter
        movwf   count
        bcf     porta,3         ;start bit
        movlw   0x30            ;define N for timer
        movwf   tmr0            ;start timer/counter
        bcf     intcon,2        ;clear tmr0 overflow flag
time1pc btfss   intcon,2        ;timer overflow?
        goto    time1pc         ;no
        movlw   0x30            ;yes, define N for timer
        movwf   tmr0            ;start timer/counter
        bcf     intcon,2        ;clear overflow flag
nxtbitpc rrf    sendreg,f       ;rotate lsb into carry flag
        bcf     porta,3         ;clear port A, bit 1
        btfsc   status,c        ;test carry flag
        bsf     porta,3         ;bit is set
time2pc btfss   intcon,2        ;timer overflow?
        goto    time2pc         ;no
        movlw   0x30            ;yes, define N for timer
        movwf   tmr0            ;start timer/counter
        bcf     intcon,2        ;clear overflow flag
        decfsz  count,f         ;shifted 8?
        goto    nxtbitpc        ;no
        bsf     porta,3         ;yes, output mark
time3pc btfss   intcon,2        ;timer overflow?
```

```
        goto   time3pc     ;no
        return             ;yes, done
;------------------------------------------------------------
        end
;------------------------------------------------------------
;at blast time, select:
;       memory unprotected
;       watchdog timer disabled (default is enabled)
;       standard crystal (using 4 MHz osc for test) XT
;       power-up timer on
;============================================================
```

OPERATING PROCEDURE

Switch Functions:

```
           ------------------------------------------------
           |   Closed      |      Open      | Port
           ------------------------------------------------
Mode Select    | Log data      | Display/Upload | RB7
           ------------------------------------------------
Start          | Wait          | Start          | RB6
           ------------------------------------------------
Display/Upload | Display - LCD | Upload - PC    | RA2
           ------------------------------------------------
```

To Log Data:

Power-up or reset with -
        Mode select switch closed.
        Start switch closed.
        Display/upload switch closed.
Open start switch to start logging.
LED toggled once/second as data is logged - flashes on completion.

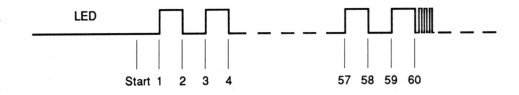

278

To Display Data Via LCD:

Power-up or reset with -
        Mode select switch open.
        Start switch closed.
        Display/upload switch closed.
Open start switch to start display sequence.
Voltage and seconds displayed for 4 seconds per logged data point.
LED flashes on completion

To Upload Data To A PC:

Power-up or reset with -
        Mode select switch open.
        Start switch closed.
        Display/upload switch open.
Open terminal program and, if desired, enter name of incoming file on PC.
Note that the settings for baud rate, etc. must be as per previous examples.
Open start switch to send file to PC.
Headings and data will appear on-screen.
LED flashes on completion

SPREADSHEET AND GRAPHING DATA - WINDOWS 3.x

The data must be received by the PC by assigning a file name prior to transferring the data. When the data file has been received, open the file in Notepad. Highlight the two columns of data (minus headings) and copy them (Edit>Copy). Open Microsoft Works and:

- 1) Select "spreadsheet". Paste the data (Edit>Paste) in cell A-1. The seconds data will appear in column A and the voltage data will appear in column B.
- 2) Charts>Create New Chart. The result will be a meaningless bar chart.
- 3) Edit>Series. In the dialog box:

```
┌─────────────────────────────────────────────────────┐
│ Value [Y] Series                                      │
│                                                       │
│     1st :  │ B1:B60        │                          │
│                                                       │
│     2nd :  │               │                          │
│                                                       │
│  Category [X] Series :  │                          │   │
│                                                       │
└─────────────────────────────────────────────────────┘
```

Click OK.
A meaningful bar chart will appear.
- 4) Gallery>Line. In the dialog box:
     Select number 2.
     Click OK.
     A meaningful line graph will appear!
- 5) Edit>Titles. In the Dialog box:

```
┌─────────────────────────────────────────────────────┐
│       Chart Title :  │ VOLTAGE vs. TIME     │          │
│                                                       │
│          Subtitle :  │                      │          │
│                                                       │
│ Horizontal [X] Axis :  │ Seconds            │          │
│                                                       │
│   Vertical [Y] Axis :  │ Volts              │          │
│                                                       │
│ Right Vertical Axis :  │                    │          │
│                                                       │
└─────────────────────────────────────────────────────┘
```

- 6) Click OK.

Sample data and the resulting graph follow:

I was unable to label the horizontal [x] axis in a meaningful way using Works under Windows 3.1.

Note: If you don't bring the data into Terminal as a file (preassign file name) and open it in Notepad, the copy and paste operation will not work properly. If you copy the data from the Terminal screen, the full width of the screen becomes highlighted during the selection process instead of a block two columns wide. The copied result will not fit into the spreadsheet format.

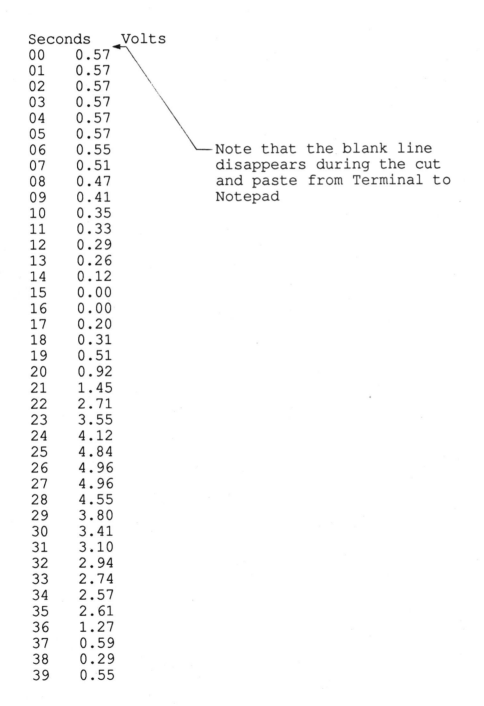

```
Seconds    Volts
00     0.57
01     0.57
02     0.57
03     0.57
04     0.57
05     0.57
06     0.55        ─Note that the blank line
07     0.51         disappears during the cut
08     0.47         and paste from Terminal to
09     0.41         Notepad
10     0.35
11     0.33
12     0.29
13     0.26
14     0.12
15     0.00
16     0.00
17     0.20
18     0.31
19     0.51
20     0.92
21     1.45
22     2.71
23     3.55
24     4.12
25     4.84
26     4.96
27     4.96
28     4.55
29     3.80
30     3.41
31     3.10
32     2.94
33     2.74
34     2.57
35     2.61
36     1.27
37     0.59
38     0.29
39     0.55
```

40	1.37
41	3.14
42	4.08
43	4.94
44	4.96
45	4.96
46	4.96
47	4.96
48	4.41
49	2.90
50	2.16
51	1.90
52	1.78
53	0.84
54	0.59
55	0.29
56	0.16
57	0.00
58	0.00
59	0.10

Voltage vs. Time

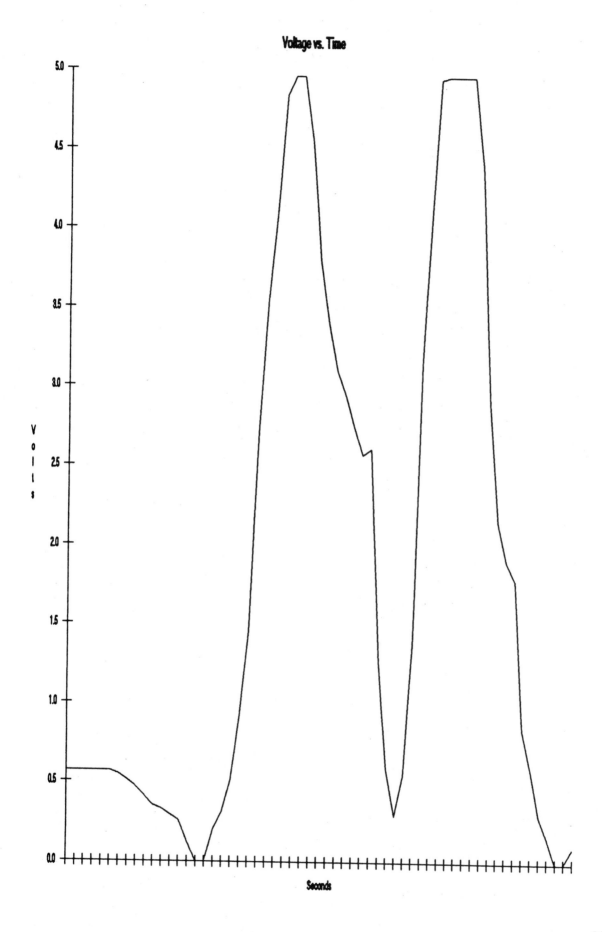

SPREADSHEET AND GRAPHING DATA - WINDOWS 95

The data must be received by the PC by assigning a file name prior to transferring the data. When the data file has been received, open the file in Notepad. Highlight the two columns of data (minus headings) and copy them (Edit>Copy). Open Microsoft Works and:

- 1) With the Works Tools tab selected, select "spreadsheet".
- 2) Paste the data (Edit>Paste) in cell A-1. The seconds data will appear in column A and the voltage data will appear in column **B**.
- 3) Tools>Create New Chart. The result will be a meaningless bar chart on the right side of a dialog box and a matrix of graph pictures on the left.
- 4) With the Basic Options tab selected (default), click on the line graph symbol with two lines (top row, second from the right in the matrix) in the dialog box. The result will be a meaningless line graph.
- 5) With the Advanced Options tab selected, a dialog box appears with your graph on the right side and three rows of buttons on the left under the heading "How is your spreadsheet data organized?".
  - 1) Which way does your series go? Select "down" (default).
  - 2) First row contains: Select "A category" (default).
  - 3) First column contains: Select "Category labels".
  - A meaningful line graph will appear!
- 6) Click "OK".
- 7) Format>Horizontal [X] Axis.
- 8) In the dialog box, change the label frequency to "10".
- 9) Click "OK".
- 10) Edit Titles

```
         Chart Title :  VOLTAGE vs. TIME

  Horizontal [X] Axis :  Seconds

    Vertical [Y] Axis :  Volts
```

- 11) Click "OK".

The sample data looks the same as for Windows 3.x and the resulting graph follows:

Note: If you don't bring the data into Terminal as a file (preassign file name) and open it in Notepad, the copy and paste operation will not work properly. If you copy the data from the Terminal screen, the full width of the screen becomes highlighted during the selection process instead of a block two columns wide. The copied result will not fit into the spreadsheet format.

Voltage vs. Time

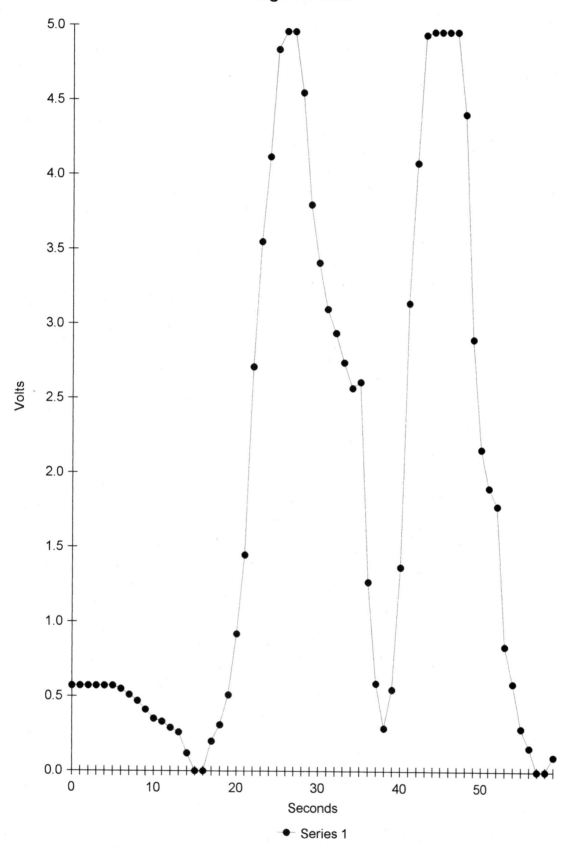

Series 1

285

SUMMARY

The data logger presented here is intended to serve as an example of how the techniques you have learned may be combined to create fun and useful projects. You may want to refine the data logger or modify it to suit your specific purposes. The sample time could be in the microseconds or hours range. The sensor employed could measure temperature, position, light level or .... Have fun!

APPENDIX A
PROGRAM LISTINGS vs. PAGE NUMBER

```
--------------------------------------------------------
    By Page Number                     Alphanumeric
--------------------------------------------------------
     8pin.asm       16              128.asm       22
     8pin2.asm      18             2000.asm       29
      128.asm       22               32.asm       26
   pgentst.asm      25            65280.asm       32
       32.asm       26             8pin.asm       16
     2000.asm       29            8pin2.asm       18
    65280.asm       32             capt.asm       71
   freqout.asm      34           ccppwm.asm      124
    tst63.asm       40          ccppwmx.asm      137
     tmr2.asm       46             cmpr.asm       75
   tsttmr2.asm      50         decent63.asm      144
     tmr1.asm       63              dvm.asm      244
     read.asm       68          format1.asm      228
     capt.asm       71          format2.asm      231
     cmpr.asm       75             free.asm       85
     sngl.asm       80          freeadd.asm       89
   one128.asm       82             freq.asm      107
     free.asm       85           freqck.asm      192
  freeadd.asm       89          freqgen.asm      166
   period.asm       95          freqout.asm       34
    pdccp.asm      100          hdwpwmx.asm      120
     freq.asm      107          hdwpwmy.asm      129
  seconds.asm      110              log.asm      261
     time.asm      114           one128.asm       82
  hdwpwmx.asm       120            pclcd.asm      235
   ccppwm.asm      124            pdccp.asm      100
  hdwpwmy.asm       129             pdck.asm      179
  ccppwmx.asm       137           period.asm       95
 decent63.asm       144          pgentst.asm       25
   pulsgen.asm      155          pulsgen.asm      155
   freqgen.asm      166          rcv4800.asm      219
     pdck.asm       179            read.asm       68
   freqck.asm       192          seconds.asm      110
   snd4800.asm      216          snd4800.asm      216
   rcv4800.asm      219             sngl.asm       80
   format1.asm      228             time.asm      114
   format2.asm      231             tmr1.asm       63
    pclcd.asm       235             tmr2.asm       46
      dvm.asm       244            tst63.asm       40
      log.asm       261          tsttmr2.asm       50
```

APPENDIX B
PIC16C63 CONTROL REGISTERS

T1CON

Controls Timer 1 (TMR1).

U	U	R/W	R/W	R/W	R/W	R/W	R/W	
		T1CKPS1	T1CKPS0	T1OSCEN	T1SYNC	TMR1CS	TMR1ON	0x10
7							0	

R = Readable bit
W = Writeable bit
U = Unimplemented bit, read as "0"
Power on reset 00000000

Bits 7,6   Unimplemented, read as "0"

Bits 5,4   **T1CKPS1:T1CKPS0:** Timer 1 Input Clock Prescale
            Select Bits
            00 = 1:1 Prescale value
            01 = 1:2 Prescale value
            10 = 1:4 Prescale value
            11 = 1:8 Prescale value

Bit 3   **T1OSCEN:** Timer 1 Oscillator Enable Bit
            1 = Oscillator Enabled
            0 = Oscillator Shut Off
            Note: The oscillator inverter and feedback
                  resistor may be turned off to eliminate
                  power drain.

Bit 2   **T1SYNC:** Timer 1 External Clock Input
                  Synchronization Control Bit
            When TMR1CS Bit = 1:
                1 = Do not synchronize external clock
                    input
                0 = Synchronize external clock input
            When TMR1CS Bit = 0:
                This bit is ignored. Timer 1 uses the
                    internal clock when TMR1CS = 0

Bit 1   **TMR1CS:** Timer 1 Clock Source Select Bit
            1 = External clock from T1OSCI (on rising edge)
                    (See pinouts for pin with T1OSCI function)
            0 = Internal clock ($F_{osc}/4$)

Bit 0   **TMR1ON:** Timer On Bit
            1 = Enables Timer 1
            0 = Stops Timer 1

T2CON

Controls Timer 2 (TMR2).

U	R/W	R/W	R/W	R/W	R/W	R/W	R/W	
	TOUTPS3	TOUTPS2	TOUTPS1	TOUTPS0	TMR2ON	T2CKPS1	T2CKPS0	0x12

7   0

R = Readable bit
W = Writeable bit
U = Unimplemented bit, read as "0"
Power on reset 00000000

Bit 7   Unimplemented, read as "0"

Bits 6,3   **T1OUTS3:TOUTPS0:** Timer 2 Output Postscale
                 Select Bits
                 0000 = 1:1 Postscale value
                 0001 = 1:2 Postscale value
                       •
                       •
                 1111 = 1:16 Postscale value

Bit 2   **TMR2ON:** Timer 2 On Bit
                 1 = TMR2 On
                 0 = TMR2 Off

Bits 1,0   **T2CKPS1:T2CKPS0:** Timer 2 Clock Prescale Select Bits
                 00 = 1:1 Prescale value
                 01 = 1:4 Prescale value
                 1x = 1:16 Prescale value

CCP1CON

Controls CCP1 Module.

U	U	R/W	R/W	R/W	R/W	R/W	R/W	
		CCP1X	CCP1Y	CCP1M3	CCP1M2	CCP1M1	CCP1M0	0x17

7   0

R = Readable bit
W = Writeable bit
U = Unimplemented bit, read as "0"
Power on reset 00000000

Bit 7,6   Unimplemented, read as "0"

Bits 5,4   **CCP1X:CCP1Y:** PWM Least Significant Bits
Capture Mode - Unused
Compare Mode - Unused
PWM Mode - 2 bits are least significant bits of the
    PWM duty cycle

Bits 3-0   **CCP1M3:CCP1M0:** CCP1 Mode Select Bits
0000 = CCP1 Module Off (Resets CCP1 Module)
0100 = Capture mode, every falling edge
0101 = Capture mode, every rising edge
0110 = Capture mode, every 4th rising edge
0111 = Capture mode, every 16th rising edge
1000 = Compare mode, set output pin on match
      and set CCP1 interrupt flag
1001 = Compare mode, clear pin output on match
      and set CCP1 interrupt flag
1010 = Software interrupt on match and set CCP1
      interrupt flag, CCP1 pin unaffected
1011 = Trigger special event on match, set CCP1
      interrupt flag and clear TMR1
11xx = PWM mode

291

INTCON

Interrupt Control Register.

R/W	R/W	R/W	R/W	R/W	R/W	R/W	R/W	
GIE	PEIE	T0IE	INTE	RBIE	T0IF	INTF	RBIF	0x0B

7   0

R = Readable bit
W = Writeable bit
Power on reset 0000000x

Bit 7   **GIE:** Global Interrupt Enable Bit
                  1 = Enables all unmasked interrupts
                  0 = Disables all interrupts

Bit 6   **PEIE:** Peripheral Interrupt Enable Bit
                  1 = Enables all unmasked peripheral interrupts
                  0 = Disables all peripheral interrupts

Bit 5   **T0IE:** TMR0 Overflow Interrupt Enable Bit
                  1 = Enables TMR0 overflow interrupts
                  0 = Disables TMR0 overflow interrupts

Bit 4   **INTE:** RB0/INT External Interrupt Enable Bit
                  1 = Enables RB0/INT external interrupts
                  0 = Disables RB0/INT external interrupts

Bit 3   **RBIE:** RB Port Change Enable Bit
                  1 = Enables RB port change interrupts
                  0 = Disables RB port change interrupts

Bit 2   **T0IF:** TMR0 Overflow Interrupt Flag
                  1 = TMR0 overflowed (must be cleared in software)
                  0 = TMR0 did not overflow

Bit 1   **INTF:** RB0/INT External Interrupt Flag
                  1 = RB0/INT external interrupt occured (must be
                            cleared in software)
                  0 = RB0/INT external interrupt did not occur

Bit 0   **RBIF:** RB Port Change Interrupt Flag
                  1 = At least one of the RB7:RB4 pins changed state
                  0 = None of the RB7:RB4 pins have changed state

PIE1

Peripheral Interrupt Enable Register.

Q	Q	R/W	R/W	R/W	R/W	R/W	R/W	
		RCIE	TXIE	SSPIE	CCP1IE	TMR2IE	TMR1IE	0x8C

7   0

R = Readable bit
W = Writeable bit
Q = Reserved, R/W, maintain as "0"
Power on reset 00000000

Bit 7,6   Reserved, always maintain these bits clear

Bit 5   **RCIE:** USART Receive Interrupt Enable Bit
                1 = Enables USART receive interrupts
                0 = Disables USART receive interrupts

Bit 4   **TXIE:** USART Transmit Interrupt Enable Bit
                1 = Enables USART transmit interrupts
                0 = Disables USART transmit interrupts

Bit 3   **SSPIE:** Synchronous Serial Port Interrupt Enable Bit
                1 = Enables SSP interrupts
                0 = Disables SSP interrupts

Bit 2   **CCP1IE:** CCP1 Interrupt Enable Bit
                1 = Enables CCP1 interrupts
                0 = Disables CCP1 interrupts

Bit 1   **TMR2IE:** TMR2 Interrupt Enable Bit
                1 = Enables TMR2 interrupts
                0 = Disables TMR2 interrupts

Bit 0   **TMR1IE:** TMR1 Overflow Interrupt Enable Bit
                1 = Enables TMR1 overflow interrupts
                0 = Disables TMR1 overflow interrupts

PIR1

Peripheral Interrupt Flag Register.

Q	Q	R	R	R/W	R/W	R/W	R/W	
		RCIF	TXIF	SSPIF	CCP1IF	TMR2IF	TMR1IF	0x0C

7   0

R = Readable bit
W = Writeable bit
Q = Reserved, R/W, maintain as "0"
Power on reset 00000000

Bit 7,6   Reserved, always maintain these bits clear

Bit 5   **RCIF**: USART Receive Interrupt Flag
             1 = USART receive buffer is full
             0 = USART receive buffer is empty

Bit 4   **TXIF**: USART Transmit Interrupt Flag
             1 = USART transmit buffer is full
             0 = USART transmit buffer is empty

Bit 3   **SSPIF**: Synchronous Serial Port Interrupt Flag
                    (must be cleared in software)
             1 = Transmission/reception complete
             0 = Waiting to transmit/receive

Bit 2   **CCP1IF**: CCP1 Interrupt Flag
             Capture Mode
                    1 = Capture occured (flag must be cleared in
                          software)
                    0 = Capture has not occured
             Compare Mode
                    1 = Compare match occured (flag must be cleared
                          in software)
                    0 = Compare match has not occured
             PWM Mode - Unused

Bit 1   **TMR2IF**: TMR2 Interrupt Flag
             1 = TMR2 interrupt occured (must be cleared in
                    software)
             0 = TMR2 interrupt has not occured

Bit 0   **TMR1IF**: TMR1 Overflow Interrupt Flag
             1 = TMR1 overflow occured (must be cleared in
                    software)
             0 = TMR1 overflow has not occured

APPENDIX C
'84 ON A BOARD

A simple circuit module may be assembled for use in experiments in this book. It includes an 18-pin socket for a PIC16F84 (or PIC16C71) with clock oscillator, reset, power supply decoupling capacitor, and port pullup resistors. The pullup resistors are used in the experiments primarily for the purpose of preventing unused inputs from floating. There are pullups on port B built into the PIC16F84. I decided not to use them because they just add confusion to the program examples and detract from explanation of the applications themselves. So...... if you use the circuit module, remember to activate (via DIP switches) pullup resistors on all unused port lines (input or output). You can save refinements for later.

I recommend connecting the port lines to a 16-pin DIP socket. A 16-conductor ribbon cable terminated with 16-pin DIP plugs may then be used to connect the '84 on a board to a solderless breadboard for many of the experiments. The wiring done on the solderless breadboard is minimal and chances are you won't want to preserve the specialized part of the circuit after you have done the experiment anyway (on to better things).

I would definitely use a ZIF socket for the '84 to avoid bending or damaging the pins.

The same circuit module may be used for the PIC16C71 DVM and data logger experiments by substituting a PIC16C71 in the microcontroller socket.

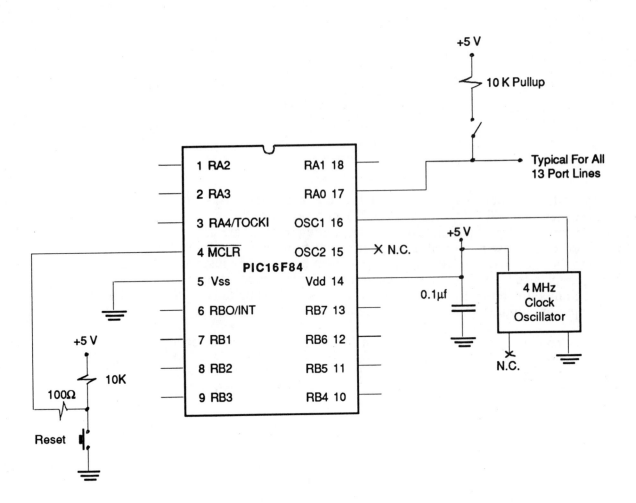

APPENDIX D
PIC/LCD

The PIC/LCD circuit presented in PIC'n Up The Pace is shown here along with code to test it after it is assembled as well as the code needed to use it as a serial slave LCD unit as part of the experiments in this book.

PIC/LCD Circuit

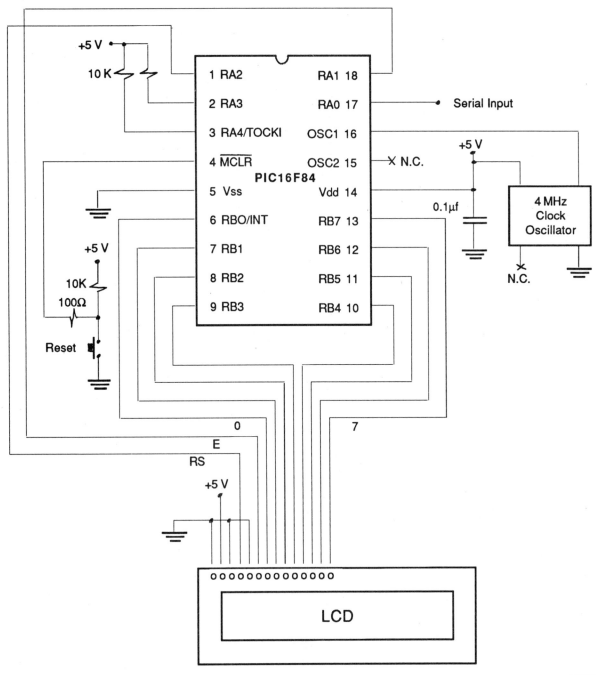

Testing The Circuit

The complete assembly source code for testing the display demo circuit follows. The display should have a blinking cursor at the left position and all other characters should be blank. This demonstrates that the circuit and LCD module are operating properly.

```
;======LCDTST.ASM==================================5/5/97==
        list    p=16f84
        radix   hex
;----------------------------------------------------------
;       cpu equates (memory map)
status  equ     0x03
porta   equ     0x05
portb   equ     0x06
count1  equ     0x0c
count2  equ     0c0d
trisa   equ     0x85
trisb   equ     0x86
;----------------------------------------------------------
;       bit equates
rp0     equ     5
;----------------------------------------------------------
        org     0x000
;
start   bsf     status,rp0  ;switch to bank 1
        movlw   b'00000000' ;outputs
        movwf   trisa
        movwf   trisb
        bcf     status,rp0  ;switch back to bank 0
        movlw   b'00000000' ;all outputs low
        movwf   porta
        movwf   portb
        call    del_5       ;allow lcd time to initialize itself
        call    initlcd     ;initialize display
circle  goto    circle      ;done
;----------------------------------------------------------
initlcd bcf     porta,1     ;E line low
        bcf     porta,2     ;RS line low, set up for control
        call    del_125     ;delay 125 microseconds
        movlw   0x38        ;8-bit, 5X7
        movwf   portb       ;0011 1000
        call    pulse       ;pulse and delay
        movlw   0x0f        ;display on, cursor blinking
        movwf   portb       ;0000 1111
        call    pulse
        movlw   0x01        ;clear display
        movwf   portb       ;0000 0001
        call    pulse
        call    del_5       ;delay 5 milliseconds after init
        return
;----------------------------------------------------------
del_125 movlw   0x2a        ;approx 42x3 cycles (decimal)
        movwf   count1      ;load counter
```

298

```
repeat  decfsz  count1,f     ;decrement counter
        goto    repeat       ;not 0
        return               ;counter 0, ends delay
;----------------------------------------------------------
del_5   movlw   0x29         ;decimal 40
        movwf   count2       ;to counter
delay   call    del_125      ;delay 125 microseconds
        decfsz  count2,f     ;do it 40 times = 5 milliseconds
        goto    delay
        return               ;counter 0, ends delay
;----------------------------------------------------------
pulse   bsf     porta,1      ;pulse E line
        nop                  ;delay
        bcf     porta,1
        call    del_125      ;delay 125 microseconds
        return
;----------------------------------------------------------
        end
;----------------------------------------------------------
;at blast time, select:
;       memory unprotected
;       watchdog timer disabled (default is enabled)
;       standard crystal (using 4 MHz osc for test) XT
;       power-up timer on
;==========================================================
```

LCD MODULE SERIAL INTERFACE

It is useful to employ the LCD module as part of a more complex system by connecting it to another PIC16 via a 1-wire serial interface. We can do it by combining techniques and boards we already have. The '63 on a board or '71 on a board will be the "master" and the PIC/LCD unit will be the slave.

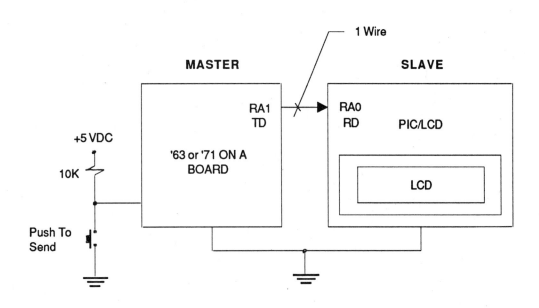

My list of functions the slave should perform under direction of the master is:

- Display "HELLO" at power-on
- Display "TEST" on command
- Blank display
- Place a single ASCII character in any one of 16 display RAM locations
- Send the contents of display RAM to the display
- Display a hex byte as 2 hex digits and as 8 bits

There are lots of ways to do this. My solution follows. You may want to modify mine for your own use or to do it a different way altogether. See PIC'n Up The Pace for details.

Any time something is sent to the display, an instruction must be included to tell the slave what to do. Sometimes there will be an ASCII character or hex byte to be sent. Sometimes an address (RAM location) must be specified. I decided the easiest way to do this is always send 3 bytes at a time even if only 1 or 2 are needed. This makes the software simpler at the flow chart level.

Packets - 3 bytes (2nd and 3rd may be garbage).

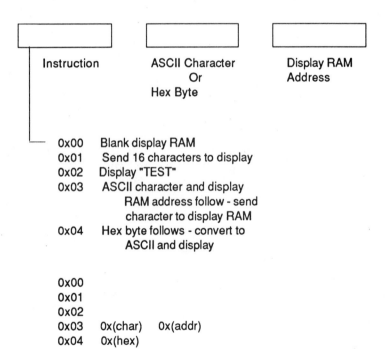

Instruction	ASCII Character Or Hex Byte	Display RAM Address

0x00 Blank display RAM
0x01 Send 16 characters to display
0x02 Display "TEST"
0x03 ASCII character and display
      RAM address follow - send
      character to display RAM
0x04 Hex byte follows - convert to
      ASCII and display

0x00
0x01
0x02
0x03 0x(char) 0x(addr)
0x04 0x(hex)

The PIC16F84 code for operating the PIC/LCD module as a slave follows. The code for the PIC16C63 or PIC16C71 used in the experiments in this book includes the code to perform the master function for communication between the two boards.

```
;======LCDSLV.ASM================================5/19/97==
        list    p=16f84
        radix   hex
;----------------------------------------------------------------
;       cpu equates (memory map)
indf    equ     0x00
tmr0    equ     0x01
pc      equ     0x02
status  equ     0x03
fsr     equ     0x04
porta   equ     0x05
portb   equ     0x06
intcon  equ     0x0b
hexbyte equ     0x0c
ms_dig  equ     0x0d
ls_dig  equ     0x0e
hold    equ     0x0f
sa      equ     0x10
sb      equ     0x11
sc      equ     0x12
sd      equ     0x13
count1  equ     0x14
count2  equ     0x15
rcvreg  equ     0x16
count   equ     0x17
temp    equ     0x18
instr   equ     0x19
char    equ     0x1a
addr    equ     0x1b
optreg  equ     0x81
trisa   equ     0x85
trisb   equ     0x86
;----------------------------------------------------------------
;       bit equates
c       equ     0
z       equ     2
rp0     equ     5
;----------------------------------------------------------------
        org     0x000
;
start   goto    main            ;leap over tables
;----------------------------------------------------------------
table   addwf   pc,f            ;add offset to program counter
        retlw   0x00            ;0
        retlw   0x01            ;1
        retlw   0x04            ;2
        retlw   0x07            ;3
        retlw   0x0b            ;4
        retlw   0x0e            ;5
        retlw   0x12            ;6
        retlw   0x16            ;7
        retlw   0x1a            ;8
        retlw   0x1d            ;9
        retlw   0x21            ;a
```

```
        retlw   0x25            ;b
        retlw   0x29            ;c
        retlw   0x2d            ;d
        retlw   0x31            ;e
        retlw   0x35            ;f
;------------------------------------------------------------
makbits addwf   pc,f            ;add offset to program counter
        return                  ;0x0    0000    leave as is
        movlw   0x31            ;0x1    0001
        movwf   sd
        return
        movlw   0x31            ;0x2    0010
        movwf   sc
        return
        movlw   0x31            ;0x3    0011
        movwf   sc
        movwf   sd
        return
        movlw   0x31            ;0x4    0100
        movwf   sb
        return
        movlw   0x31            ;0x5    0101
        movwf   sb
        movwf   sd
        return
        movlw   0x31            ;0x6    0110
        movwf   sb
        movwf   sc
        return
        call    fill1s          ;0x7    0111    fill with 1,s
        movlw   0x30
        movwf   sa
        return
        movlw   0x31            ;0x8    1000
        movwf   sa
        return
        movlw   0x31            ;0x9    1001
        movwf   sa
        movwf   sd
        return
        movlw   0x31            ;0xa    1010
        movwf   sa
        movwf   sc
        return
        call    fill1s          ;0xb    1011    fill with 1,s
        movlw   0x30
        movwf   sb
        return
        movlw   0x31            ;0xc    1100
        movwf   sa
        movwf   sb
        return
        call    fill1s          ;0xd    1101    fill with 1,s
        movlw   0x30
```

```
        movwf   sc
        return
        call    fill1s      ;0xe    1110    fill with 1,s
        movlw   0x30
        movwf   sd
        return
        goto    fill1s      ;0xf    1111    fill with 1,s
        return
;----------------------------------------------------------
main    bsf     status,rp0  ;switch to bank 1
        movlw   b'00000001' ;port A inputs/outputs
        movwf   trisa
        movlw   b'00000000' ;port B outputs
        movwf   trisb
        bcf     status,rp0  ;back to bank 0
        movlw   b'00000000' ;all outputs low
        movwf   portb
        bcf     porta,1     ;all outputs low
        bcf     porta,2
        bcf     porta,3
        bcf     porta,4
        call    blanks      ;fill display RAM with blanks
        call    hello       ;create message in display RAM
        call    del_5       ;allow lcd time to initialize itself
        call    initlcd     ;initialize display
        call    disp16      ;send 16 characters to display
enterm  clrf    rcvreg      ;yes
        call    ser_in      ;to serial in subroutine
        movf    rcvreg,w    ;get byte received
        movwf   instr       ;store instruction
        clrf    rcvreg
        call    ser_in      ;to serial in subroutine
        movf    rcvreg,w    ;get byte received
        movwf   char        ;store character or byte
        clrf    rcvreg
        call    ser_in      ;to serial in subroutine
        movf    rcvreg,w    ;get byte received
        movwf   addr        ;store address
        movf    instr,w     ;get copy of instruction
        sublw   0x00        ;compare with 0x00
        btfsc   status,z    ;z flag set if bytes are equal
        goto    blnkram     ;bytes equal
        movf    instr,w     ;get copy of instruction
        sublw   0x01        ;compare with 0x01
        btfsc   status,z    ;z flag set if bytes are equal
        goto    send16      ;bytes equal
        movf    instr,w     ;get copy of instruction
        sublw   0x02        ;compare with 0x02
        btfsc   status,z    ;z flag set if bytes are equal
        goto    sndtst      ;bytes equal
        movf    instr,w     ;get copy of instruction
        sublw   0x03        ;compare with 0x03
        btfsc   status,z    ;z flag set if bytes are equal
        goto    chr_ram     ;bytes equal
```

```
        movf    instr,w     ;get copy of instruction
        sublw   0x04        ;compare with 0x04
        btfsc   status,z    ;z flag set if bytes are equal
        goto    convhex     ;bytes equal
        goto    enterm      ;wait for next transmission
;------------------------------------------------------------
blnkram call    blanks      ;fill display ram with blanks
        goto    enterm      ;back to main
;------------------------------------------------------------
send16  call    disp16      ;send display RAM contents to LCD
        goto    enterm      ;back to main
;------------------------------------------------------------
sndtst  call    test        ;load display RAM with msg "TEST"
        call    disp16      ;send display RAM contents to LCD
        goto    enterm      ;back to main
;------------------------------------------------------------
chr_ram movf    addr,w      ;get copy of display RAM address
        movwf   fsr         ;store in file select register
        movf    char,w      ;get copy of character to be display
        movwf   indf        ;to RAM address pointed to by FSR
        goto    enterm      ;back to main
;------------------------------------------------------------
convhex movf    char,w      ;get copy of hex byte to be converted
        call    disphex     ;convert hex byte for display
        call    disp16      ;send display RAM contents to LCD
        goto    enterm      ;back to main
;------------------------------------------------------------
fill1s  movlw   0x31
        movwf   sa
        movwf   sb
        movwf   sc
        movwf   sd
        return
;------------------------------------------------------------
disphex movwf   hexbyte     ;store copy of hex byte
        call    blanks      ;fill display RAM with blanks
        call    sephex      ;separate hex byte into 2 ASCII digits
        movf    ms_dig,w    ;get MS digit
        movwf   0x20        ;to display RAM
        movf    ls_dig,w    ;get LS digit
        movwf   0x21        ;to display RAM
        swapf   hexbyte,w   ;get copy of hex byte, swap MS/LS
        andlw   0x0f        ;mask HI nibble
        call    hexbits     ;call hex to bits
        movf    sa,w        ;get first bit
        movwf   0x23        ;to display RAM
        movf    sb,w        ;get second bit
        movwf   0x24        ;to display RAM
        movf    sc,w        ;etc.
        movwf   0x25
        movf    sd,w
        movwf   0x26
        movf    hexbyte,w   ;get copy of hex byte
        andlw   0x0f        ;mask HI nibble
```

```
        call    hexbits         ;call hex to bits
        movf    sa,w            ;get first bit
        movwf   0x28            ;to display RAM
        movf    sb,w            ;get second bit
        movwf   0x29            ;to display RAM
        movf    sc,w            ;etc.
        movwf   0x2a
        movf    sd,w
        movwf   0x2b
        return
;-----------------------------------------------------------
sephex  movf    hexbyte,w       ;get copy of hex byte
        andlw   0x0f            ;mask hi nibble
        call    hex2asc         ;hex to ASCII conversion
        movwf   ls_dig          ;store
        swapf   hexbyte,w       ;get copy of hex byte, swap MS/LS
        andlw   0x0f            ;mask hi nibble
        call    hex2asc         ;hex to ASCII conversion
        movwf   ms_dig          ;store
        return
;-----------------------------------------------------------
hex2asc movwf   hold            ;store copy of hex digit
        sublw   0x09            ;subtract w from 1 less than 0x0a
        btfss   status,c        ;carry flag set if w < 0x0a
        goto    add37
        goto    add30
add37   movf    hold,w          ;get hex digit
        addlw   0x37
        return                  ;return with ascii in w
add30   movf    hold,w          ;get hex digit
        addlw   0x30
        return                  ;return with ascii in w
;-----------------------------------------------------------
hexbits movwf   hold            ;save copy of hex digit
        movlw   0x30            ;fill with ascii 0's
        movwf   sa
        movwf   sb
        movwf   sc
        movwf   sd
        movf    hold,w          ;get hex digit, use as offset
        call    table           ;get 2nd offset for subroutine table
        call    makbits         ;to appropriate create bits sub
        return
;-----------------------------------------------------------
blanks  movlw   0x10            ;count=16
        movwf   count1
        movlw   0x20            ;first display RAM address
        movwf   fsr             ;indexed addressing
        movlw   0x20            ;ascii blank
store   movwf   indf            ;store in display RAM location
;                                   pointed to by file select register
        decfsz  count1,f        ;16?
        goto    incfsr          ;no
        return                  ;yes, done
```

```
incfsr  incf    fsr,f         ;increment file select register
        goto    store
;-------------------------------------------------------------
hello   movlw   'H'
        movwf   0x20
        movlw   'E'
        movwf   0x21
        movlw   'L'
        movwf   0x22
        movwf   0x23
        movlw   'O'
        movwf   0x24
        return
;-------------------------------------------------------------
test    movlw   'T'
        movwf   0x20
        movwf   0x23
        movlw   'E'
        movwf   0x21
        movlw   'S'
        movwf   0x22
        movlw   ' '
        movwf   0x24
        return
;-------------------------------------------------------------
initlcd bcf     porta,1       ;E line low
        bcf     porta,2       ;RS line low, set up for control
        call    del_125       ;delay 125 microseconds
        movlw   0x38          ;8-bit, 5X7
        movwf   portb         ;0011 1000
        call    pulse         ;pulse and delay
        movlw   0x0c          ;display on, cursor off
        movwf   portb         ;0000 1100
        call    pulse
        movlw   0x06          ;increment mode, no display shift
        movwf   portb         ;0000 0110
        call    pulse
        call    del_5         ;delay 5 milliseconds - required
;                                 before sending data
        return
;-------------------------------------------------------------
disp16  bcf     porta,1       ;E line low
        bcf     porta,2       ;RS line low, set up for control
        call    del_125       ;delay 125 microseconds
        movlw   0x80          ;control word = address first half
        movwf   portb
        call    pulse         ;pulse and delay
        bsf     porta,2       ;RS=1, set up for data
        call    del_125       ;delay 125 microseconds
        movlw   0x20          ;initialize file select register
        movwf   fsr
getchar movf    0x00,w        ;get character from display RAM
;                                 location pointed to by file select
;                                 register
```

```
        movwf   portb
        call    pulse           ;send data to display
        movlw   0x27            ;8th character sent?
        subwf   fsr,w           ;subtract w from fsr
        btfsc   status,z        ;test z flag
        goto    half            ;set up for last 8 characters
        movlw   0x2f            ;test number
        subwf   fsr,w
        btfsc   status,z        ;test z flag
        return                  ;16 characters sent to lcd
        incf    fsr,f           ;move to next character location
        goto    getchar
half    bcf     porta,2         ;RS=0, set up for control
        call    del_125         ;delay 125 microseconds
        movlw   0xc0            ;control word = address second half
        movwf   portb
        call    pulse           ;pulse and delay
        bsf     porta,2         ;RS=1, set up for data
        incf    fsr,f           ;increment file select register to
;                                   select next character
        call    del_125         ;delay 125 microseconds
        goto    getchar
;-------------------------------------------------------------
del_125 movlw   0x2a            ;approx 42x3 cycles (decimal)
        movwf   count1          ;load counter
repeat  decfsz  count1,f        ;decrement counter
        goto    repeat          ;not 0
        return                  ;counter 0, ends delay
;-------------------------------------------------------------
del_5   movlw   0x29            ;decimal 40
        movwf   count2          ;to counter
delay   call    del_125         ;delay 125 microseconds
        decfsz  count2,f        ;do it 40 times = 5 milliseconds
        goto    delay
        return                  ;counter 0, ends delay
;-------------------------------------------------------------
pulse   bsf     porta,1         ;pulse E line
        nop                     ;delay
        bcf     porta,1
        call    del_125         ;delay 125 microseconds
        return
;-------------------------------------------------------------
ser_in  bcf     intcon,5        ;disable tmr0 interrupts
        bcf     intcon,7        ;disable global interrupts
        clrf    tmr0            ;clear timer/counter
        clrwdt                  ;clear wdt prep prescaler assign
        bsf     status,rp0      ;to page 1
        movlw   b'11011000'     ;set up timer/counter
        movwf   optreg
        bcf     status,rp0      ;back to page 0
        movlw   0x08            ;init shift counter
        movwf   count
sbit    btfsc   porta,0         ;look for start bit
        goto    sbit            ;mark
```

```
        movlw   0x80        ;start bit received, half bit time
        movwf   tmr0        ;load and start timer/counter
        bcf     intcon,2    ;clear tmr0 overflow flag
time1   btfss   intcon,2    ;timer overflow?
        goto    time1       ;no
        btfsc   porta,0     ;start bit still low?
        goto    sbit        ;false start, go back
        clrf    tmr0        ;yes, half bit time - start timer/ctr
        bcf     intcon,2    ;clear tmr0 overflow flag
time2   btfss   intcon,2    ;timer overflow?
        goto    time2       ;no
        bcf     intcon,2    ;yes, clear tmr0 overflow flag
        movf    porta,w     ;read port A
        movwf   temp        ;store
        rrf     temp,f      ;rotate bit 0 into carry flag
        rlf     rcvreg,f    ;rotate carry into rcvreg bit 0
        decfsz  count,f     ;shifted 8?
        goto    time2       ;no
time3   btfss   intcon,2    ;timer overflow?
        goto    time3       ;no
        return              ;yes, byte received
;---------------------------------------------------------------
        end
;---------------------------------------------------------------
;at blast time, select:
;       memory unprotected
;       watchdog timer disabled (default is enabled)
;       standard crystal (using 4 MHz osc for test)
;       power-up timer on
;===============================================================
```

APPENDIX E
KEYPAD

USING THE KEYPAD AND PIC/LCD WITH THE '63 ON A BOARD

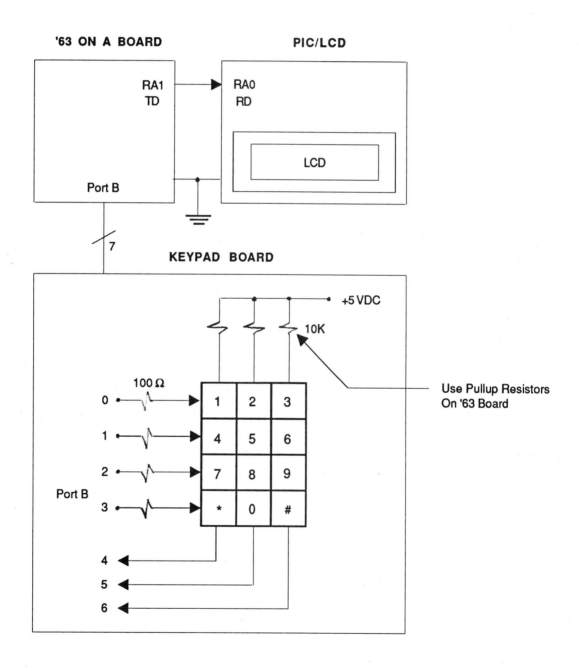

The keypad shown has 12 switches arranged in a 4 row by 3 column matrix. Pressing a key closes a switch which electrically connects one row to one column.

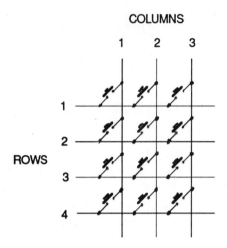

Each keypad switch in the matrix is connected to the microcontroller as shown:

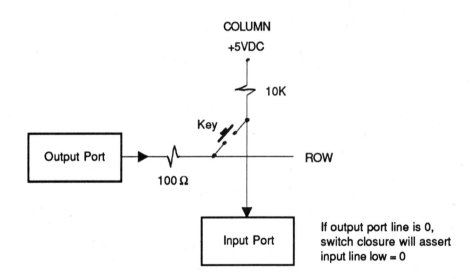

The 5-digit decimal to 16-bit binary entry program in the Designing And Building Your Own Test Equipment chapter can be used to test your keypad if you are using it the first time.

Details on scanning keypads are available in PIC'n Up The Pace.

APPENDIX F
SOURCES

Following is a list of sources for PIC16 parts, information and tools.

Digi-Key Corporation   Parts/Programmers
701 Brooks Ave. South
Thief River Falls, MN 56701-0677   USA
(800)344-4539
http://www.digikey.com

DonTronics   SimmStick *(tm)* Protyping
P.O. Box 595 Tullamarine 3043 Australia   Boards for PIC16
Int+ 613 9338-6286
Int+ 613 9338-2935 FAX
http://www.dontronics.com

JDR Microdevices   Parts/Programmers
1850 South 10th Street
San Jose, CA 95112-4108   USA
(800)538-5000

JAMECO   Parts/Programmers
1355 Shoreway Road
Belmont, CA 94002-4100   USA
(800)831-4242
http://www.jameco.com

Marlin P. Jones   Programmers
P.O. Box 12685
Lake Park FL 33403-0685   USA
(800)652-6733

Microchip Technology Inc.   Manufacturer of PIC16
2355 West Chandler Blvd.
Chandler, AZ 85224-6199   USA
(602) 786-7200
http://www.microchip.com

microEngineering Labs, Inc.   Programmers, software
Box 7532   and prototyping PCB's
Colorado Springs, CO 80933   USA
(719) 520-5323
http://www.melabs.com